CAMBRIDGE STUDIES IN AMERICAN LITERATURE AND CULTURE

The Poetry of Marianne Moore
A Study in Voice and Value

Cambridge Studies in American Literature and Culture

Editor:
Albert Gelpi, Stanford University

Advisory Board

Nina Baym, *University of Illinois, Champaign-Urbana*
Sacvan Bercovitch, *Harvard University*
Richard Bridgman, *University of California, Berkeley*
David Levin, *University of Virginia*
Joel Porte, *Harvard University*
Mike Weaver, *Oxford University*

Books in the Series

Robert Zaller: *The Cliffs of Solitude*
Peter Conn: *The Divided Mind*
Patricia Caldwell: *The Puritan Conversion Narrative*
Stephen Fredman: *Poet's Prose*
Charles Altieri: *Self and Sensibility in Contemporary American Poetry*
Mitchell R. Breitwieser: *Cotton Mather and Benjamin Franklin*
John McWilliams: *Hawthorne, Melville, and the American Character*
Barton St. Armand: *Emily Dickinson and Her Culture*
Elizabeth McKinsey: *Niagara Falls*
Albert J. von Frank: *The Sacred Game*
Marjorie Perloff: *The Dance of the Intellect*
Albert Gelpi: *Wallace Stevens*
Ann Kibbey: *The Interpretation of Material Shapes in Puritanism*
Sacvan Bercovitch and Myra Jehlen: *Ideology and Classic American
    Literature*
Karen Rowe: *Saint and Singer*
Lawrence Buell: *New England Literary Culture*
David Wyatt: *The Fall into Eden*
Paul Giles: *Hart Crane*
Richard Grey: *Writing the South*
Steven Axelrod and Helen Deese: *Robert Lowell*
Jerome Loving: *Emily Dickinson*
Brenda Murphy: *American Realism and American Drama, 1880–1940*
George Dekker: *The American Historical Romance*
Lynn Keller: *Remaking it New*
Warren Motley: *The American Abraham*
Brooke Thomas: *Cross Examinations of Law and Literature*
Lothar Honnighausen: *William Faulkner*

The Poetry of
Marianne Moore

A Study in Voice and Value

MARGARET HOLLEY
Bryn Mawr College

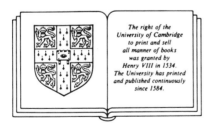

The right of the
University of Cambridge
to print and sell
all manner of books
was granted by
Henry VIII in 1534.
The University has printed
and published continuously
since 1584.

CAMBRIDGE UNIVERSITY PRESS
Cambridge
New York   New Rochelle   Melbourne   Sydney

Published by the Press Syndicate of the University of Cambridge
The Pitt Building, Trumpington Street, Cambridge CB2 1RP
32 East 57th Street, New York, NY 10022, USA
10 Stamford Road, Oakleigh, Melbourne 3166, Australia

First published 1987

Printed in the United States of America

Library of Congress Cataloging-in-Publication Data
Holley, Margaret.
The poetry of Marianne Moore.
(Cambridge studies in American literature and
culture)
Bibliography: p.
Includes index.
1. Moore, Marianne, 1887–1972—Criticism and
interpretation. I. Title. II. Series.
PS3525.05616Z684   1987   811'.52   86–33394

British Library Cataloguing in Publication Data
Holley, Margaret
The poetry of Marianne Moore: a study
in voice and value.—(Cambridge studies
in American literature and culture).
1. Moore, Marianne, *1887–1972* —Criticism
and interpretation
I. Title
811'.52   PS3525.05616Z/

ISBN 0 521 33284 2

For My Father

Contents

Preface

Traditionally one of the main provinces of art has been the reflection of those values by which men and women try to live. From Homer to the Elizabethan theater to the great nineteenth-century novels, literary art has depicted the human condition in ways that search and sometimes celebrate particular notions of what is true, beautiful, and good. Marianne Moore's work bears a special relation to this province of values in art, because her poetry announces very early its readiness to appraise, to pass judgment, and then sustains for some time an inquiry into the grounds and nature of such judgments.

Value itself, whether conceived as a standard of worth, as an ultimate principle of choice, or as an image of desire, is both a timeworn and a critically urgent dimension. Each of two world wars within memory has left Western culture somewhat less sanguine about human nature and less confident about our future on the planet. Furthermore, in the intellectual world in recent years post-modern critics have challenged radically many of our most fundamental traditional assumptions about the nature of language, the relation of art to the rest of the world, the meaning of meaning, and the sense of such basic notions as the author, the text, the act of speech, and the nature of public discourse. My study of the development of Marianne Moore's poetic voice and relation to value is prompted by the question of what it could possibly mean to be a moralist in the midst of the twentieth century.

Moore knew and truly loved the old pieties, and she brought them into a century in which often the only absolutes seemed to be uncertainty and tyranny. I find that as a moralist she started out in the mode of subjective expressions of opinion in her brief judgmental lyrics of the pre-war and World War I years. During the twenties and thirties she turned gradually toward an increasingly objective embodiment of value through a nearly

ix

total eclipse of the personal voice in her poems, producing virtuoso pieces in which the rhetorical forces of fact and of value are virtually indistinguishable. The outbreak of World War II then effectively broke the silence of her poetic "I" and ushered in a third orientation, an advocacy of values that was not a return to her early subjective verdicts but a newly shared sense of social and historical urgency.

This movement from subjective judgment to objective embodiment to shared advocacy is part of a broad development in Moore's work from isolation, confrontation, and satire toward community, representation, and sympathy. The marked evolution in her poems from compression to expansion and, significantly, back to compression is accompanied by clear shifts from substantive to attributive metaphors and from observation as sight to observation as insight.

The solitary spirit of Moore's early work and the conviviality of her late work frame the remarkable, more balanced, and exquisite poetry that she produced in the decades when she was between the ages of 30 and 60. Her entire published poetic work appeared in print in eight natural groups, which my discussion follows: the Bryn Mawr poems printed by the college magazines between 1907 and 1913, the Carlisle poems that she sent out from her home in Pennsylvania from 1915 through 1917, the later "observations" that appeared between 1918 and 1925, the group that Moore once lightly described to T. S. Eliot as her "animiles" of 1932–36, the lyrics of the war years of the early 1940s, the poems of the fable years (1946–56) when she was also translating La Fontaine, the late poems of 1956 through 1966, and the final poems that appeared between 1966 and 1970.

Moore's career is the map of a modern consciousness painstakingly seeking the grounds of a spiritual hope that permeated her vision of the world. All of her chosen techniques have implications for this search— her strongly spatial imagination, her deployment of emblems and mottoes, her blend of overt and covert quotation, her syllabic verse growing out of model stanzas, and her partiality to rhyme and to closure. Over the decades the poetic voice moves from the periphery to the center of the moral dilemma, and it moves from a singular confidence to an earned communal speech. These dramas of poetic development are just now coming into view, as we learn to read the whole oeuvre as it unfolded. There is so much to be done to illumine the marvelous strangeness of Moore's art that even raising some of the right questions about it will be useful.

A complete list of the poems published by Moore during the period covered in each of my chapters is presented at the end of the text.

When quoting from her verses, I have used the version found in the 1981 edition of *The Complete Poems of Marianne Moore* and the first published version of any work not included in that collection, unless otherwise stated. Copies of Moore's published poems that are not included in her *Complete Poems*—and there are sixty-six of them, about one-third of her complete work—are all available through interlibrary loan channels and from the Moore Archive, The Rosenbach Museum and Library, 2010 Delancey Place, Philadelphia, PA 19103. The Bryn Mawr poems are also available from the archives and manuscript collection, Canaday Library, Bryn Mawr College, Bryn Mawr, PA 19010.

I would like to take this opportunity to express my gratitude to the people who have personally assisted and encouraged me during my work on Marianne Moore. Al Gelpi has been a helpful and heartening editor; his suggestions have enriched this study greatly. Patricia Willis, Literary Curator of the Rosenbach and Curator of the Moore Archive there, has been a most congenial, knowledgeable guide through Moore's papers, her life, and current work on her contemporaries. Manuscripts librarian at Bryn Mawr College, Leo Dolenski has also provided refreshing and most informative companionship along the scholarly road. To archivists Lucy Fisher West and Terry Taylor, oral historian Caroline Rittenhouse, assistant Eleanor Beatty, and other members of the staff of the Miriam Coffin Canaday Library of Bryn Mawr College I offer thanks for work done with gusto and precision. Likewise my appreciation to Carol Bernstein for advice on portions of the manuscript. My heartfelt gratitude goes to Peter Briggs for opportunities and encouragement very generously offered; to Eileen Moran for good comradeship and the example of her stamina; to Shelly Weiss, Wayne Scott, John and Sue Strite, and David Swetland for the sustenance of friendship; and most of all to Susan Dean and Laurence Stapleton for the exceptional care they have both bestowed on every stage of this project and again for the sustenance of friendship.

Finally, I would like to thank the Mrs. Giles Whiting Foundation for the fellowship which supported my writing of the major portion of this study.

Margaret Holley

1

Art as Exact Perception

Originality, it seems to me, always comes in disguise, as the inevitable precipitated by the courage to be natural.

Marianne Moore

The emergence of an original poetic voice is an uncommon cultural moment, and even traced in retrospect it brings both the brief pleasure of surprise and the more lasting gift of an enriched world. The emergence of Marianne Moore's distinctive voice happened within the first dozen and a half poems that she published, all of them in the two Bryn Mawr College magazines *Tipyn O'Bob* and its successor *The Lantern* between 1907 and 1913. Read as a group these eighteen short pieces reveal the gradual refinement of Moore's unique poetic idiom in contrast to the style of late Victorian verse.

The Bryn Mawr poems announce explicitly and implicitly the aesthetic program that will establish their author as a leading poet of the modernist era. In the process of extricating her own work from the prevailing *fin de siècle* poetic mode, Moore issues in her verse a series of epigrams on the relation of perception and emotion to art. She declares herself unequivocally for an empiricism, an allegiance to sense perception, which she will first expand with virtuosity, then question, and finally transcend during the six decades of her career.

When she came to Bryn Mawr, Marianne Moore was not a young woman one would have marked as a future modernist, so traditional was (and would remain) her spiritual orientation. A student who, unlike her classmates, refrained from work on the sabbath was an unlikely candidate for advancing an aesthetic revolution. And while Moore never allowed her personal church practice to enter her verse, an insistence on the fundamental value of courage and the meaningfulness of hope permeated her work throughout her life. Moore did not enter the modernist stream through its challenge to the old spiritual order—she joined and advanced it through a radically new prosody set in the service of a clarity of vision that is the central value of these very early poems.

Moore brought with her to Bryn Mawr an already formidably educated mind. The setting of her childhood was the parsonage home of her grandfather, the Rev. John R. Warner, Pastor of Kirkwood Presbyterian Church near St. Louis, Missouri. Her father, John Milton Moore, had succumbed to a mental breakdown before her birth in 1887, and she never saw him, but she found her grandfather "a most affectionate man,"[1] and her mother, Mary Warner Moore, raised Marianne and her older brother Warner in a close, loving circle of family and friends. Both Mrs. Moore and this circle of friends provided rich ground for a fertile and original mind.

Moore once reminisced about how her mother had her and Warner "commit the catechism to memory," much of which she still remembered in her late sixties.[2] Mrs. Moore also read *Paradise Lost* aloud to her children, in addition to instructing them in French and music and encouraging their love of books. When the Rev. Warner died suddenly of pneumonia in the winter of 1894, Mrs. Moore moved with her two children first briefly to cousins in Pittsburgh and then to Carlisle, Pennsylvania, where their closest friends were the family of Dr. George Norcross, Pastor of the Second Presbyterian Church.

Marianne later recognized Dr. and Mrs. Norcross and their four daughters as "a main influence in my life as a writer. . . . An unfanatical love of books, music, and 'art' made Blake, Rembrandt, Giotto, Holbein, D. G. Rossetti and Christina Rossetti, Turner, Browning, Ruskin, Anthony Trollope, George Meredith household companions of the family and their friends. (The Wicksteed Temple Dante, was presented to me by Mrs. Norcross on successive birthdays.)"[3] During Moore's youth the pieties of the Warner and Norcross parsonages blended rather smoothly with a lively cultural life and with family warmth. "We were constantly discussing authors," she went on. "When I entered Bryn Mawr, the College seemed to me in disappointing contrast—almost benighted."

Friends of that time remember Moore as striking in appearance and agreeable in disposition. Recalling Marianne as a child, librarian Fanny Borden described her to Elizabeth Bishop as "a strange and appealing little creature with bright red hair."[4] And a neighbor from Carlisle and classmate at Bryn Mawr, Peggy Kellogg-Smith, remembers her fondly: "Marianne Moore at thirteen was slim, tall and graceful with one thick beautiful red braid down to her skirt top. A gentle pleasing companion, humorous and friendly."[5]

She arrived on the Bryn Mawr campus in the fall of 1905, shy and desperately homesick at first, but well prepared, having been tutored for over a year by Mary Norcross for the fifteen challenging entrance exams. Moore was one of thirty-seven students in her class of one hundred and eleven freshmen to be admitted "without conditions," having passed all of the exams; nevertheless during her sophomore year the English Department found her prose lacking in the clarity required to major in that subject. So she majored instead in the composite field of history, economics, and politics; minored in biology; and began to truly thrive on the rich fare of friendships, Philadelphia cultural life, writing, and the remarkable presence of M. Carey Thomas, President of Bryn Mawr, whom she would later quote in her poem "Marriage."

"When I was in college," Moore said, "feminism was not taken for granted; it was a cause. It was ardently implemented and fortified by Miss Thomas. . . . She made things easy for us, and she made them hard for us. . . . I remember her pleased smile, one eyebrow a little higher than the other, at the faintest difficulty, and her disdain for anything superficially airy. . . . We felt it a serious deprivation to miss morning chapel exercises. . . . Dr. Barton would read from the Bible in firm, even tones, and Miss Thomas would comment on political, literary, or campus matters. Our zeal to be present, you may have surmised, was not devoutness. It was attributed to President Thomas's unpredictable originality."[6]

Carey Thomas's absolute confidence that women should rise to the same level of challenge and expectation as men permeated the atmosphere of Bryn Mawr, and Moore wrote to her friend and fellow writer Bryher in 1921, "my experience there gave me security in my determination to have what I want."[7] She did not achieve what she wanted easily at first, and in the winter of her sophomore year, having failed to make it onto the editorial board of *Tipyn O'Bob,* she wrote to her mother, "I don't know why I am so possessed to write. I know it is not because of what nice things people say and its not for the doing itself, for I *cannot* express myself."[8] She did not know day student Hilda Doolittle well enough then to share their interest in writing or to provide mutual solace in their difficult times.

Looking back over her college years, Moore came to appreciate the relative freedom in which she grew. "At Bryn Mawr," she continued in her letter to Bryher, "the students are allowed to develop with as little interference as is compatible with any kind of academic order and the more I see of other women's colleges, the more I feel that Bryn Mawr was peculiarly adapted to my special requirements." The high point came when she achieved good enough marks in English to allow her during the spring of her senior year to take Georgiana Goddard King's course in Imitative Writing, a study of the seventeenth-century prose stylists. That year was her turning point. Moore had an abiding love for the seventeenth-century writers; she scattered a few trial lines of "A Jelly-Fish" in among her notes on Burton and Dryden;[9] and while she had already in 1907 and 1908 published verses that were imitative of the general poetic modes of the day, her own distinctive voice comes through clearly for the first time in the five poems that appeared in the spring of 1909.

The dominant poetic mode from which Moore gradually departed in her Bryn Mawr poems is the mode that Ezra Pound later called "pseudo-Swinburnian."[10] This common style of verse for the first decade of the twentieth century was musically metrical in sound and romantic in its fascination with mysterious and magical loveliness, with what Pound called "dim lands of peace." For example, Moore's first published poem appears on a page of *Tipyn O'Bob* (Welsh for "a little bit of everybody") that also features Mary Frances Nearing's poem "Letter-Magic," a piece ending

> For in my hand—you did not know—
> A talisman would paint the world
> With moonbeams, and from buds upcurled,
> Make fairy gardens grow.[11]

Nearing was a good friend of Moore and, unlike her, was found qualified to major in English. Marianna, as she was known to her classmates, tried her hand at the popular pre-Raphaelite mode in "To My Cup-Bearer," published in the spring of her junior year.[12] This early portrait of a lady has an exotic medieval air: "Her eye is dark, her vestment rich, / Embroidered with a silver stitch." Years later, when Elizabeth Bishop asked her "what the poems she had written at Bryn Mawr were like, she said, '*Just* like Swinburne, Elizabeth.' "[13]

Moore seems also to have been attracted to another currently popular style of verse, the Kiplingesque seaman's chantey, which we hear echoed, then quoted, and then self-quoted in "The Sentimentalist":

> Sometimes in a rough beam sea,
> When the waves are running high,
> I gaze about for a sight of the land,
> Then sing, glancing up at the sky,
> " 'Here's to the girl I love,
> And I wish that she were nigh,
> If drinking beer would bring her here'
> I'd drink the ship's hold dry."

The three layers of text here forecast Moore's later more subtle layering of voices and texts, and a certain distance from her derivative material is already indicated by the satiric note of her title.

Moore did not linger long in such apprenticeship. For a while she continued to make use of a conventionally jaunty sound for the doggerel with which she spiced her playful family newsletters,[14] but the crisp voice and rhythm that emerge in "To a Screen-Maker" of 1909 are now recognizably Marianne Moore's:

I.

Not of silver nor of coral
But of weather-beaten laurel
Carve it out.

II.

Carve out here and there a face
And a dragon circling space
Coiled about.

III.

Represent a branching tree
Uniform like tapestry
And no sky.

IV.

And devise a rustic bower
And a pointed passion flower
Hanging high.

The imagery is still in the pre-Raphaelite style, and the measure is metrical, but encouragement in the newly economical, somewhat clipped rhythm appears to have come from Miss King and the seventeenth-century texts that were used in her writing class. In February of 1909 Moore jotted in her course notebook, "The indispensable thing is *restraint* wh [*sic*] gives on the one hand simplicity. . . . By the time you have simplic and restraint combined you have austerity—that is going to cut out most of our friends."[15] The five verses that appeared in 1909 are models of simplicity, and one of them, "A Red Flower," explicitly celebrates the virtue of restraint.

We see an even more radical departure from the Swinburnian mode after Moore left Bryn Mawr. *The Lantern* for spring 1910 published fellow student Caroline Reeves Foulke's "Lullaby," beginning "Baby is drifting thro' Sunset Land / In a rainbow-craft of dreams" and ending

—Little Dream-Ship, with your white sails furled,
    Rest in your haven deep;
A moonlit silence is flooding the world
    And the baby is fast asleep.

This is followed immediately by Moore's

TUNICA PALLIO PROPRIOR

My coat is nearer than my cloak;
Inside
My coat is an integument of pride.

Repeatedly in *The Lantern* the sweet music of what W. H. Auden called "poetry-in-general" leads up to the "arresting and interesting" verse statements of the young Moore.[16]

One of these statements that stands out with particular force in contrast to the preceding music of moonbeams and fairy gardens is Moore's assertion in "Qui S'Excuse, S'Accuse" that

Art is exact perception;
If the outcome is deception
Then I think the fault must lie
Partly with the critic's eye,
And no man who's done his part
Need apologize for art.

It is through this explicitly stated program of "art as exact perception" that Moore swerves most sharply away from the Swinburnian lullabies and the "dim lands of peace." Two other verse statements buttress this project of poetry as clear perception: the two aphoristic titles "My Senses Do Not Deceive Me" and "Things Are What They Seem" announce an epistemology for the observations to come. The common theme of these three poems is reliance on direct perception. By the end of her 1924 collection *Observations,* Moore will have relied on direct perception long enough to begin her critique of its dangers and limitations. But for the duration of the verses printed at Bryn Mawr and those composed in Carlisle, the empirical ideal of "exact perception" serves to extricate her art from the legacy of dreamy atmospheres left by the end of the nineteenth to the early twentieth century.

Two elements in particular of Moore's characteristic style of perception are already clearly present in her Bryn Mawr poems—her interest in emblems and, underlying that, the fundamentally spatial orientation of her imagination. Moore's poetic sense of the still life, of the "still" as in a frame of film, a photograph, was always stronger and richer than her narrative impulse, and this spatial emphasis will permeate virtually all of her verse to come. What her friend Peggy Kellogg-Smith called the "arresting" quality of her college poems is created at least in part by their fixing of attention upon a spatial configuration, such as a carved laurel screen, in which form is emphasized over movement. A motive for this preference may be found in Moore's senior-year publication "A Red Flower":

Emotion,
Cast upon the pot,
Will make it
Overflow, or not,
According
As you can refrain
From fingering
The leaves again.

Stillness is perceived as a corollary of intense feeling and of forbearance from fussing over that feeling. Likewise, in "To a Screen-Maker" the "dragon circling space," the "branching tree / Uniform like tapestry," and the "rustic bower" with its "passion flower / Hanging high" are still shapes carved in wood and now in words: they are the art of deliberately arranged, enduring forms.

When Coleridge said that all men are either Platonists or Aristotelians, he was making the same order of general distinction as the one Raphael made in his "School of Athens" when he painted Plato pointing upward at the eternal and Aristotle pointing downward at the earthly. Such a broad generalization is useful even while it invites qualifications. On the same order of generality we may distinguish for analytical purposes two general types of poems: one is the poem that narrates an experience, immersing itself in the flux of time, and the other is the poem that focuses on a scene, on spatial arrangements or durable entities. The pure prototypes of these are the story and the still life, the plot and the photograph.

These two poetries are the yin and yang of one another and will often be intermingled in one work. The spatial dimension of experience is not the opposite of the temporal dimension but rather its complement. The spatial axis runs, let us say, at right angles to the temporal axis, intersecting it at every so-called point in time. Historically, however, certain artistic styles may reflect a preference for one axis over the other, the primary axis being determined by the dominant values of the culture. In a romantic and post-romantic age, the touchstones of nature and progress will urge one to value the temporal energy of organic development, whereas the medieval artist and classicist work from an atemporal ideal that would rescue significant form from the restlessness of the world.[17]

Thus certain poems tend to see things in motion, to present them as events, as ongoing happenings, while other poems tend to contemplate the momentary scene, to present things as products rather than as processes. The artist may emphasize either the becoming or the being of something, its subjective or objective aspect. At the subjective pole of awareness, experience is an ever-unfinished event unfolding within some human consciousness; the objective pole of awareness must be construed as composed of at least recognizably stable entities, however fictive, in order for any comprehension, again however fictive, to result. Marianne Moore worked more consistently and exclusively than most poets along the spatial axis of her subjects. The strongly spatial tendency of her imagination is basic to her work and responsible for much of its unique flavor, since this "predilection" influences the poetic voice, its rhythms, diction, and tones as much as it guides her selection of materials, focus, and textual arrangements. The spatial axis, in its highlighting of significant form over movement, is the perceptual counterpart of Moore's later reaffirmations of formal closure, rhyme, and determinate meaning, her return from inquiry to advocacy of certain values.

Later in life Moore recalled some of the media that nourished her imagination during her childhood:

> For anyone with "a passion for actuality," the camera often seems preferable to any other mechanism; or so I felt in 1896, enthralled by Lyman Travelogues at the Opera House in Carlisle, Pennsylvania. As sequel to lantern slides, cosmoscope, and stereopticon, Brooklyn Institute movies were an Aladdin's revel.[18]

The stereopticon is Marcel Proust's magic lantern, an early slide projector that brought to the child in a small-town Opera House the sights of a larger world, captured in image after still image. Many of Moore's poems are like a series of lantern slides cumulatively disclosing an invisible subject. One might well say of her work that "No one can more ably turn frozen surfaces into tractable worlds, 'appropriated by reflection, permeated by feelings.' "[19]

The contrast between the spatial and temporal types of poem may be exemplified by two works on the same subject, one written by D. H. Lawrence and the other by Marianne Moore. These are poets who share a love for "birds, beasts and flowers" and who write about many of the same subjects in this area, but whose temperaments and manifest messages are so different as to be nearly diametrically opposed. Lawrence's poem "Elephant" in *Birds, Beasts and Flowers*[20] and Moore's "Elephants" in *Nevertheless* both explore emblems and mottoes, both describe a ceremonial procession, and both display this animal as suggestive of certain human attitudes and possibilities. But Lawrence's poem narrates an ongoing experience and Moore's presents a series of scenes and shapes, and the difference is indicative of the overall difference in their visions.

Lawrence's immediately narrative approach takes us into an ongoing movement through time: "You go down shade to the river . . . / And you cross the ferry . . . / Elephants after elephants curl their trunks . . . / As they approach and salaam, under the dripping fire of the torches." We experience along with him a firelit "Pera-hera," the procession of elephants parading before the visiting Prince of Wales in the tropical night. Then we follow the elephants and natives home after the ceremony. The event is a confrontation: "tropical eyes dilated look up / . . . To that tired remnant of royalty up there / Whose motto is *Ich dien*." Lawrence makes the Prince's motto, "I serve," into part of the drama of this meeting, as he imagines that the elephants and the natives are disappointed in that "remnant of royalty," the "pale and dejected" Prince: "the night fell in frustration" because they had come "to bow before royalty . . . for it's good as a draught of cool water to bow very, very low to the royal." The poet wishes that he himself could have stood before them as a truly fine prince. After the ceremony the poetic voice imaginatively reinvents the scene, countering its failure with the depiction of a scene in which someone like himself orders the elephants to "Serve me, I am meet to be served. / Being royal of the gods."

Moore's presentation of the elephants, in contrast, begins with the stillness of "matched intensities," with the image of two trunks "Uplifted and waved till immobilized" into a "deadlock of dyke-enforced massiveness." She then presents a series of slides of elephants: "One, sleeping with the calm of youth," another with "his held-up foreleg," and a group of "these ministrants all gray or / gray with white on legs or trunk." She shows us repeated, symbolic types of behavior rather than a single event:

> With trunk tucked up compactly—the elephant's
> sign of defeat—he resisted, but is the child
>
> of reason now. His straight trunk seems to say: when
> what we hoped for came to nothing, we revived.

We are shown no motion of transition between these two poses, for the emblematic positions of the trunk are not subsumed in a plot but rather examined as a series of discrete and readable signs: "his held-up foreleg for use / as a stair . . . expounds the brotherhood of creatures to man." Even during the procession of the Buddha's Tooth, Moore focuses not so much on movement as on the pyramidal configuration of the bearers: "see / the white elephant carry the cushion that / carries the casket that carries the Tooth." And the poem ends on a note of complete composure: "asleep on an elephant, that is repose."

The reason for these differences in presentation, Lawrence's preference for moving narrative and Moore's for composed pictures, lies in the overall thrust of each body of work. Lawrence felt dissatisfied with the civilization of industrial England and longed for renewal by something like the elephants' "mystery of the dark mountain of blood." He projects his own yearning onto the elephants and follows the actual unsatisfactory procession with his imaginary, redeemed version. Movement and time, the mediums of restlessness and hope, are the life of his poem in both procedure and theme. To "capture the quick of the plasm" is both his means and his end.

In contrast to Lawrence's free-verse lines, Moore's rhymed quatrains are suited to a poem about equanimity. Their appearance of regularity and the constant return to an eleven-syllable line are a vehicle of composure for a poem that speaks admiringly of "calm . . . rest . . . serenity . . . reason . . . sweetness." Equanimity is "contrived" not only by the elephant but also by the poet in this "pilgrim's pattern" of signs and emblems. Just as Lawrence is filled with longing for an ideal, so Moore too admits that, compared with the ease-ful wisdom suggested by the elephants, "we are at much unease." The difference is one of primacy and emphasis. Lawrence writes primarily of a reality of dissatisfaction and longing, whereas Moore emphasizes an ideal of serenity and wisdom. And the verse form of her composition embodies, much as the poise of the elephant does, the intense stillness of a projected perfection. The real and the ideal are present in both poems, as they are in any vision, but each poem is a constellation formed noticeably nearer to one pole than to the other.

Moore's habitual preference for the spatial axis survives her various other developments, the stages through which her artistry grew. Thus we may follow a given motif—the dragon, for example, of which she was so fond—throughout her career and find it presented consistently with emblematic stillness. In "To a Screen-Maker" the suspended and composed energy of the laurel screen's "dragon circling space" is the first of a series of suggestively poised portraits of this dynamic and storied mythical beast. "In the Days of Prismatic Color" of 1919 embodies the "pestilence" of sophisticated complexity in Nestor's dragon from the *Greek Anthology,* emphasizing its absurd three-part sprawl and appendages:

> "Part of it was crawling, part of it
> was about to crawl, the rest
>   was torpid in its lair." In the short-legged, fit-
> ful advance, the gurgling and all the minutiae—we have the
>   classic
> multitude of feet. To what purpose!

From her source Moore selected this overview of the layout and habitual gestures of the beast rather than Nestor's dramatic narrative of how Cephisus kills himself by running into its jaws.

Even "The Plumet Basilisk" of 1933, one of Moore's most action-oriented poems, pauses to balance the habits of the lizard, the "living firework," with its architectural counterpart in Copenhagen, where the main door of the bourse

> is roofed by two pairs of dragons standing on
> their heads—twirled by the architect—so that the four
> green tails conspiring upright, symbolize four-fold security.

And finally in 1957, that immortalized cocktail-party remark, "O to Be a Dragon," confirms the emblematic role this creature has played in Moore's ongoing fascination with it:

> If I, like Solomon, . . .
> could have my wish—
>
> my wish . . . O to be a dragon,
> a symbol of the power of Heaven—of silkworm
> size or immense; at times invisible.
> Felicitous phenomenon!

The challenge of the verbal portrait or still life—the danger that plodding detail will dissipate its energy—must be met by swiftness of stroke. Here the movement not of the object but of the voice turning from grand Solomon to the humble silkworm invests the center between those poles with the same kind of energy-in-stillness as the "dragon circling space" maintains.

Moore's preference for the spatial over the temporal axis has not gone unnoticed. William Carlos Williams evoked it early when he wrote in 1925 that "this quality of the brittle, highly set-off porcelain garden exists and nowhere in modern work better than in Miss Moore."[21] In *Language and the Poet* Marie Borroff takes a syntactical approach to it: "Moore's grammatical preference for stative over dynamic bespeaks a deeper bias. Hers is an imagination that sees more meaning in fixity than in flux."[22] Borroff's illustrations of her point are those immobilized trunks in "Elephants" and the "water etched / with waves as formal as the scales / on a fish" in "The Steeple-Jack." And Bonnie Costello notes in her chapter on "Moore and the Visual Arts" that "Moore's was an emblematic imagination."[23] Costello's immediate context here is Moore's interest in traditional Chinese symbols, but she goes on to include in her broad conception of the emblematic a variety of plastic and pictorial forms—sculpture, tapestry, and painting.

As a special manifestation of the generally spatial bias, the emblematic imagination can itself take various forms. For example, Rosemary Freeman has documented the two quite distinct styles of the English emblem books of the Renaissance. These books all contain pictures accompanied by mottoes and/or verses spelling out the moral lessons intended by each illustration. The abstract idea is contained in both the image and the text, which serve each other equally. The fifteenth and early sixteenth century device or emblem was a conventional, almost coded image bearing a traditional moral message: "the words and the picture in it each formed self-contained statements of the author's conception and they were equally appropriate carved in jewels, blazoned on shields, embroidered on hangings or engraved in books."[24] In contrast to these stylized and often simply frontal designs, the emblems of the seventeenth century like those of Francis Quarles are more complex, realistically detailed, and individual in conception, for their themes are more "psychological," and hence they were seldom transferred to other media than the printed page.

Freeman emphasizes that neither of these styles of emblem "ever achieved the fulness and richness of emotional content of one of Blake's symbols," for the emblem writer, in making his "detailed equation of picture and meaning, . . . deals in fixities and definites, establishing parallel after parallel in a purely objective way."[25] She recognizes that George Herbert, whose work Moore admired and whose images are frequently emblematic, has transcended the usual limitations of that material to achieve "a richness of meaning and subtlety of tone which is the more distinctive for the simplicity of the means it uses."[26] Herbert has often achieved this richness, I think, by pitting the egoism and desires of the psychological, earthly self against the clarity and constancy of divine emblems of the earlier, more objective kind. For Herbert the emblematic exercise is a patterning of the otherwise unruly self, a redemptive shaping of the soul: the intimacy and energy of the earthly personality are subjected, poem by poem, to the rigor and perfection of the divine emblem.

Moore, too, was drawn to the earlier "preliterary" emblems, and while her work is undoctrinal in effect, she often uses the emblem and/or its motto as a determinate foil for the indeterminate dimensions of her subject. In many of her poems, the conventional emblem's clarity of message, what Freeman calls (after Coleridge) its "fixities and definites," is set as a figure against the background of a complex and ambiguous human condition. In "Elephants" the "pilgrim's pattern" of symbolic poses and "Sophocles the Bee, on whose / tombstone a hive was incised" are set in tension with that central, restless "As if, as if, it is all as ifs; we are at /

much unease." The four brass dragons of "The Plumet Basilisk" that "symbolize four-fold security" are placed next to the crowd of tuateras and other flighty, frilled lizards of the insecure, unpredictable earth outside of emblems.

Even in the early Bryn Mawr poems, Moore is able to capture this difference between the rather fixed sense of the emblem and the ambiguities of the images arranged beside it. In 1912 *The Lantern* printed "A Talisman":

I.

Upon a splintered mast
Torn from the ship, and cast
Near her hull,

II.

A stumbling shepherd found,
Embedded in the ground,
A seagull

III.

Of lapis lazuli;
A scarab of the sea,
With wings spread,

IV.

Curling its coral feet,
Parting its beak to greet,
Men long dead.

The three elements of this poetic scene—the scarab, the wreck, and the shepherd—juxtapose the simpler, fixed emblem with larger, contrasting uncertainties. First, the emblem is the "scarab of the sea," the carving of the seagull which bears a certain definite sense underlying the magic power of the stone. The bird is presumably to be understood as the seamen's emblem of swift passage and safe return to land. Second, the image of the splintered mast and hull where the scarab is found carries a less definite and richer import: somehow or other the talisman has failed; the emblem of safe return now lies amid wreckage. Here the poem both relies on and undoes the sense of its title, but one must understand the talismanic emblem's intended message in order to feel the irony of its discovery here. And third, the reader of the poem is presented the wider image of the shepherd stumbling on the talisman in the wreck, offering the contrast between his pastured life and the seafarers' perilous journeys. Each inner circle of meaning is necessary to the larger one that encloses it. Likewise, each layer of determinate meaning leads outward toward a less determinate but broader sense.

This poem's rhyme and regular stanzas are outside of the free-verse program of the Imagists, and the last clause, "to greet, / Men long dead," is probably too explanatory for a purely Imagistic piece. Nevertheless, it is a good illustration of Pound's conception of the "Image" as "an intellectual and emotional complex in an instant of time."[27] "A Talisman," like its fraternal twin "To a Screen-Maker," frames its emblem with an image without subscribing to the Imagistic program. Moore's strategy of juxtaposing determinate and indeterminate modes of meaning will play a central role in her more extended poetic inquiries of the twenties, thirties, and forties.

Moore's sources of determinate meanings include the verbal as well as the visual dimensions of experience. The emblem as bearer of a certain definite sense is a counterpart of one of the most pervasive and provocative elements of her verse, namely her art of quotation. If the emblem is a kind of quoted image, the quotation is a visual reproduction of a found text. From her very first published poems to her last, Moore made her own distinctive use of acknowledged, and sometimes unacknowledged, quotations from the voices and texts of her immediate world. Her first published poem, "Under a Patched Sail" of 1907, opens with a quoted song of unknown origin. The song is demarcated visibly in writing, but to the ear it blends seamlessly with the style and voice of the unquoted persona of the last four lines:

> "Oh, we'll drink once more
> When the wind's off shore,"
> We'll drink from the good old jar,
> And then to port,
> For the time grows short.
> Come lad—to the days that are!

The opening layer of quoted text is delivered uncritically by the speaker, and it is not until "The Sentimentalist" of a year later that the poet indicates in that title, as we have seen, a definite measure of remove from her speaker.

By the spring of 1912 Moore closes her series of seamen's verses with a poem in which another author's lines about Captain Kidd are not respoken but literally observed as a thing. "Leaves of a Magazine" describes a "dim verse" as a piece of objectified text, a "ragged block of shade" on the page,

> with blurs and puckers where
> Admiring hands have often brought to bear
> Their pressure on the picture and the rhyme
> Of buccaneering in the olden time.

The words she is writing about have a certain presence and density as things, a shape on a page on which the reader has also left visible traces. And if the text is an object, an object can also become a text. "Councell to a Bachelor," beginning

> If thou bee younge
> Then marie not yett.
> If thou bee olde,
> Then no wyfe gett,

consists entirely of the motto that Moore found painted on an Elizabethan trencher or small wooden plate in Oxford's Bodleian Library.[28] She appended a title and modified the fourth line slightly, but otherwise she reproduced the verse verbatim, signing its double authorship, "Elizabethan trencher, Marianne Moore." Neither of the "authors" in this case would be conceived of as an original creator but rather as a medium of transmission, an occasion or setting for the text of a virtually selfless "councellor." As we shall see again later, quotation paradoxically both emphasizes and disregards the sense of a source, and thus of an "owner," of texts.

In between the two poles of a whole poem as observed object and of object as poem lies Moore's more usual practice of incorporating into her own lines fragments from other sources—recorded remarks, maxims, mottoes, aphorisms, and all forms of quotation that pass segments of language intact from one context into another. For the title and first line of her early poem on pride she chose the saying "Tunica pallio proprior [sic], My coat is nearer than my cloak," from Plautus' *Trinummus* (5.2.30). Her description of art as "exact perception" carries as its title the sixteenth century French maxim "Qui S'Excuse, S'Accuse." And the final line of that poem is a loose translation of its title maxim: "And no man who's done his part / Need apologize for art." Thus for the most part the early poetic voice appears to adopt the found text as central to the poem's manifest message. We shall eventually see how Moore becomes skillful at setting such quoted texts in deliberate tension with other elements of the verse in which they appear.

For the present we may merely note the way in which this early work displays and manipulates the intertextual dimension of poetry, the various ways in which the text is related to the prior and concurrent texts of its culture. Moore, like other modernists, brought a certain literal intertextuality into the foreground of poetry by recognizably quoting and paraphrasing other sources. On the one hand, this procedure has an effect of preserving the past by setting the new work into the context of its forbears; on the other hand, it has the effect of dismantling prior whole texts and of separating a fragment from its original context, exchanging its old field of meaning for a new one. Quotation thus gives the poem a double relation to the tradition from which the fragment was lifted. The conservative tendency of preservation is set in tension with the progressive tendency of dismantling and renewal.

If either of these tendencies comes to predominate in Moore's practice of quotation, we shall see that it is the progressive one. She does not quote for echoes, as Eliot does; like Williams she prefers to take as her written sources the ephemeral and non-poetic media of newspapers, magazines, and non-fiction accounts; unlike Pound she often takes her quoted material very far from its original field, sometimes losing that field entirely even in her own memory; and unlike all three other poets, she revises her quoted fragments freely, severing even further their relation with the parent text. In this way, as in her arresting rhythms and assertions, Moore from the beginning sets her own poetry at odds with poetry-in-general. We shall see her return in her mature work to a new level of interplay between the traditionally "poetic" and her very particular poetry.

Already in the Bryn Mawr poems of 1907–13, the marriage of opposites characteristic of enduring art is being prepared. Art as exact perception is her starting point, but the indeterminate is its silent partner. The spatial quality of her imagination has a certain conservative effect that balances the progressive tendency of her use of other texts, but so far she is only accomplishing one thing at a time. There is still a certain breach between the imagistic and the assertive modes. Some poems of these years produce visual configurations like the laurel screen, the scarab, the page of a magazine, while other poems deliver statements on the related subjects of pride, illusion, art, and appearances. A few pieces—"A Red Flower," "Progress," "Things Are What They Seem"—manage to combine these imagistic and assertive modes in a way that points toward the creations of her maturity, the poems that make her, in Randall Jarrell's words, "*the* poet of the particular" and "in our time, *the* poet of general moral statement."[29]

In February of 1915, Marianne wrote to her brother Warner, "I did a very craven thing today. Helen Taft wrote me for some poems for the

Lantern and I sorted out ten or fifteen and then subtracted all the better ones, (2 of the better ones) in the hope that I could sell them."[30] It was a turning point. 1915 brought her first professional publications and her personal introduction to the New York avant-garde literary world. It is the poems appearing in print from 1915 through 1917 that reveal what Moore was writing during those anonymous years at 343 North Hanover Street in Carlisle.

2

Diligence, Magic

The seven years between her graduation in 1909 and her move in 1916 to Chatham, New Jersey, demanded patience and perseverance of Moore. She felt ready to embark on her profession as a writer, but on two fronts—daily work and publication—she had to move more slowly than she would have wished. She arrived home from college with idealistic hopes of beginning her career by writing book reviews, but her brother Warner eventually pointed out to her the practical and financial reality that their mother had supported the family for fourteen years and, as he put it, "I think we should do something to help out."[1]

Marianne enrolled without delay in the business course at Carlisle Commercial College; on completion of that she took a clerical position at Melvil Dewey's Lake Placid Club, and in 1911—following a summer visit to England and Paris with her mother—she began teaching at the U.S. Industrial Indian School in Carlisle, where she became the head of the Commercial Department. Moore recalled the distraction of that job with perhaps better grace than she may have felt at the time, as she "bicycled every day to the school and taught rapid calculation and handwriting." "It was good for me," she said in retrospect. "I needed it. I was spoiled."

The days filled with classes in commercial law, stenography, and bookkeeping did not daunt her as a poet, but as her verse grew in both volume and distinctiveness, Moore faced an initially disheartening struggle to see her work into print. One of the consequences of her originality was the failure of numerous editors to appreciate her voice and technique. "A poem which I wrote in August, 1914," she remembered, "I had sufficient confidence in to submit to twenty-six magazines before it was accepted a year later."[2] Her tenacity began paying off in 1915. Like Frost, Moore found acceptance first in England, when Richard Aldington published two of her poems in *The Egoist* for April 1915, another in May, two in August, and two in October—by which time Harriet Monroe of *Poetry* and Alfred Kreymborg of *Others* had published another nine of her poems between them.

For a few more years, even as her published work was helping to shape modernism, Moore herself would remain a visitor and correspondent of her fellow artists. In response to the poems she submitted to *The Egoist,* Aldington's wife Hilda Doolittle wrote to her in care of Bryn Mawr College to ask whether she was indeed the classmate whom she remembered in a green May Day gown.[3] H. D. and her friend Bryher would eventually bring to light Moore's first book, *Poems,* in 1921. Kreymborg, too, took her up by inviting, indeed urging, her to come to New York so they could meet, and in December of 1915 Marianne set out with Laura Benét and another friend on the week-long trip that she described to Warner as the "Sojourn in the Whale."[4] She took back with her to Carlisle the memories of Kreymborg and his wife, of Stieglitz's astonishing studio "291" with its Picassos, Picabias, and landscapes by Marsden Hartley, and of meetings with J. B. Kerfoot (the literary editor of *Life*) and with Guido Bruno of *Bruno's Weekly*. She brought home also the conviction that someday New York would be her preferred home.

One of her earliest allies, William Carlos Williams, wrote to Moore in early 1916 to request a poem for the issue of *Others* which Kreymborg had asked him to edit. Moore sent along "Critics and Connoisseurs," which delighted him, but it would be several years before he and Moore could meet in person. Williams's abiding love for her seems to have been ready to bloom right from the start, and he was fascinated by Kreymborg's report of her beautiful red hair and by the seemingly paradoxical idea of her living in a parsonage and writing poems there in a thoroughly contemporary spirit.[5]

Indeed, her talent incubated and came into its first full strength outside of New York's avant-garde circles. We tend to think in retrospect of Marianne Moore as a New York poet and to forget that she was turning thirty-two and had already published nearly a third of the poems in the canon when she moved to Greenwich Village in 1918. Nevertheless, Moore's unmistakable originality as a writer during her twenties and thirties (the pre- and post-World War I years)—her clear-edged images, distinctive prose rhythms, and the critical intelligence of her poetic voice—went a long way toward liberating English-language verse from the spell of its post-romantic conventions. By temperament she was allied more with the imagist than with the symbolist strains of the broad modernist trend, although she did open her new Reading Diary of 1916 with a quotation labelled "Baudelaire."[6] Moore is perhaps best thought of as a modernist in style rather than in spirit, for she never shared the deep sense of social and spiritual dislocation, of alienation and anarchy, that eventually pressed some of her contemporaries into radically open-ended revolt against the old orders.

Since virtually all of Moore's work seen in print before the move to New York was composed in Carlisle, perhaps it is not misleading to call these pieces of 1915–17 the Carlisle poems. Their subject matter is not, for the most part, drawn directly from her hometown; on the contrary, much of it comes from far afield. And yet for her particular talent, the small town was an ironically ideal alembic, a place where culture arrived secondhand through media that could be fascinating in themselves: the printed word, the lantern-projected image, the sermon. And so she worked; she shared with her mother and friends *The Illustrated London News, The Boston Evening Transcript,* and *Literary Digest;* and she wrote a most distinctive group of poetic missives that gradually came into the hands of appreciative fellow poets.

Moore published more new single poems during each of these early years—far more in 1915 and 1916—than she ever would again. The group represents four or five years' worth of work which could not at first find its way into print, and so exact dates of composition for many of the verses are not to be discovered. Almost all of the Carlisle poems are quite brief, averaging about fourteen lines, and all but one are rhymed. It is as if the variety and multiplicity that will soon emerge in longer poems like "People's Surroundings," "Marriage," and "An Octopus" appear here in the form of a wealth of individual subjects, each one treated as concisely and formally as a cameo. A majority of these poems, nearly four-fifths of them, address their chosen subject as "you," and many pass judgment on the character or behavior of that subject, usually via metaphor and often also with the aid of quotation. These aspects of the early poems—brevity and rhyme, second-person voice, orientation toward judgment, spatial imagery, central metaphor, and quotation— merit attention in themselves and also because they prepare the way for the major work of Moore's maturity.

The brevity of the Carlisle poems is probably the first thing that strikes the reader's eye, and the pervasive rhyme strikes both eye and ear. In every stage of her career, Moore returned at some point to that "first grace of style," the snail-like compression of the short poem. We may note, for example, the similarity of the 1948 piece, "At Rest in the Blast," retitled "Like a Bulwark," to the early poems in its use of the second-person form, "You take the blame," and the end-stopped, accented rhyming of each of its ten lines. This brevity as a starting point is probably a simpler matter than brevity as a choice will be after decades of expansion.

Moore was also at the start and the finish an aficionado of rhyme. A significant shift in the sound of her poems occurs after her adoption of the hidden or light rhyme, of which T. S. Eliot would soon call her "the greatest living master."[7] On two occasions in print Moore has cited the young British poet Charles Hamilton Sorley, who had just died at the front in Germany, as a model for her efforts. "When I came on Charles Sorley's 'The Idea' (probably in *The Egoist,* London)—

> It was all my own;
> I have guarded it well from
> the winds that have blown
> too bitterly

—I recognized the unaccented syllable (the light rhyme) as meant for me."[8] In *The Accented Syllable* she again cited lines by Sorley—

> Little live, great pass.
> Jesus Christ and Barabbas
> Were found the same day

—in illustration of the principle that attracted her to the technique: "in the case of rhymed verse, a distinctive tone of voice is dependent on naturalistic effects, and naturalistic effects are so rare in rhyme as almost not to exist."[9] And so she set about to invent such effects.

The rhyme in Moore's first publications of this period is still rather heavy and accented by end-stopping, as in "To the Soul of Progress"—

> You use your mind
> Like a millstone to grind
>   Chaff.
> You polish it
> And with your warped wit
>   Laugh

—or as in "Diligence Is To Magic As Progress Is To Flight," where all ten lines rhyme on a single sound, "toes . . . goes . . . arose . . . chose . . . knows . . . crows" and so on. In contrast, the feminine rhymes of "George Moore" are made even less audible by being separated in the chiasmic form: "aspiration" is thirteen lines removed from "admiration." And in 1916 the truly unaccented rhyme appears in one of Moore's few narratively presented pieces, "Critics and Connoisseurs":

> There is a great amount of poetry in unconscious
>   fastidiousness. Certain Ming
>   products, imperial floor-coverings of coach-
>   wheel yellow, are well enough in their way but I have
>   seen something
>   that I like better . . .

The discursive tone and non–metrical rhythm discourage any expectation
of the rhyme of "Ming" with "something."

Several more extreme experiments in inaudibility followed. In December of 1916 she first tried out "the" as a rhyme-word in "The Just Man
And":

> His pie. "I would be
> Repossessed of all the
> Superlatives that I have squandered,
> That I might use them in praise of it."

In 1917 she rhymed a divided syllable in "Radical," the poem on the image of a carrot:

> The world is
> but a circumstance, a mis-
>   erable corn-patch for its feet.

Later Moore discarded the use of hyphens as "an arcane form of emphasis,"[10] and gradually she also abandoned her early practice of the rhyming
one-word line. In "Those Various Scalpels," the original pattern of
rhymed couplets, as in

> A
> Bundle of lances all alike, submerged beneath emeralds
>   from Persia,

was smoothed out to one line, "a bundle of lances. . . ." And during the
twenties she buried or dropped numerous rhymes in other poems, too, in
the course of revisions from stanzaic forms into freer verse.

Moore's frequent revisions, especially during the first half of her career, can suggest to us in retrospect the relative value of various poetic elements in her work. The poem " 'Sun!' " is her answer to the quoted couplet from John Skelton's "Upon a Dead Man's Head"—" 'No man may
him hyde / From Deth, holow-eyed.' " Moore's poem was first published in 1916, and it appeared in at least seven different versions before
she chose it half a century later to conclude her last single volume of poems, *Tell Me, Tell Me* of 1966. One clear tendency of her revisions is to-

ward brevity. The 1916 epigraph, "Hope and Fear—those internecine fighters—stop fighting and accost him," was abridged in 1917, omitted in 1924, reinstated in 1957, and then further abridged in 1961.[11] In its final form, "Hope and Fear accost him," it still retains its caption-like quality and points to the two poles that contend in the poem, but it does it in less than half the original number of words.

Moore also adjusted the wording of the third line substantially five times. In "But for you, twin spirits, that shall not suffice" she altered the second-person "for you" to "for us," dropped the "twin spirits," and changed "mortal truth" of 1917 to "inexorable truth" in 1957 and to "inconvenient truth" in 1961. The trouble she took with this one line suggests that it was the abstract formulations that she felt could be adjusted experimentally. The passages of vibrant visual imagery, on the other hand, the "fiery topaz" and hourglass of "Moorish gorgeousness," remain virtually unchanged over the years. The single exception is the much-altered first stanza of "Fear Is Hope" in *Observations,* where the topaz and prince are replaced by "An incandescence in the hand of an astrologer." The hiatus in the publication of the poem for thirty years after this change, its exclusion from *Selected* and *Collected Poems,* may be related to dissatisfaction with that image-altered version, for she abandoned it after its one appearance and returned to the 1917 text as her basis for the later versions. Like the compact structure and rhymed sound of the piece, the images had a certain rightness from the start, while the abstractions seemed, if not dispensable, at least subject to tinkering. The choice of this Carlisle poem to close her final volume indicates that the work of this period contains techniques and qualities that Moore will reaffirm in her later years.

Looking back on her Carlisle years, Moore remarked in an interview, "I recall feeling oversolitary occasionally (say in 1912)—in reflecting no 'influences'; in not being able to be called an 'Imagist.' "[12] But an immediate influence, a passing on of techniques and topics, is different from a sense of heritage, a sense of belonging to a certain order of endeavor and level of aspiration. And Moore's early work has its own way of affirming this sense of a heritage of English writing. Her use of the second-person "you" in many of these poems may be seen as having the extravertive effect of opening the poem out onto a larger world by placing the poetic voice on speaking terms with cultural figures of Britain and the continent. "To a Man Working His Way Through the Crowd" addresses theatrical designer Gordon Craig; "To the Peacock of France" speaks to Molière; and other figures are identified by titles: "To Disraeli on Conservatism," "To William Butler Yeats on Tagore," "To Browning," "To Bernard Shaw: A Prize Bird," "Blake," and "George Moore." The preponderance of British fig-

ures may be partly a result of her trip to England in May of 1911, but it may
also reflect the eastern seaboard's traditional sense of England and Europe
as cultural sources and models. A vivid sense of European heritage was
brought, for instance, to Bryn Mawr by M. Carey Thomas. Like Eliot and
Pound early in their careers, Moore looked eastward across the Atlantic
rather than westward into America for mentors. Her early form of direct
address creates an explicit link between the "masters" abroad and this unknown newcomer in small-town America.

But if the poems to well-known people seem designed to overcome a
sense of artistic isolation, some of the other poems of address of this period have an introvertive effect. Verses with anonymous subjects such as
"To an Intra-Mural Rat," "To a Steam Roller," "Pedantic Literalist," and
the polite piece of rage engagingly titled "To Be Liked By You Would Be
a Calamity" all form closed circles of communication in which the identity of the subject is known solely to the poet. Because the addressee remains curtained off in anonymity, there is an air of privacy about these
poems. Without the extra-literary subject to consider, the reader's attention is centered on the speaker's own thoughts and tone of voice. On the
one hand, there may be a motive of mercy in this privacy. Most of the
named individuals are praised, while most of the anonymous subjects are
condemned. On the other hand, for *Observations* Moore detached identifying names from several of the poems of praise: "To Disraeli on Conservatism" became "To a Strategist"; "To Browning" was retitled "Injudicious Gardening"; and "To Bernard Shaw: A Prize Bird" was shortened
to simply "To a Prize Bird." Thus the cultural figure appears to be not so
much the subject of the poem as an occasion for its real subject, which is
the human quality or behavior being judged in each case.

The third type of figure addressed in the work of these years will suggest the common denominator of the address poems. This is the non-
human object or creature—a lost head in "To the Soul of 'Progress,' " a
lizard in "The North Wind To a Dutiful Beast . . ." and in "To a Chameleon," a mummified ibis in "To Statecraft Embalmed," the goose, vulture, and loon of "Masks," the sun in " 'Sun!' " and the rose in "Roses
Only." Since the human and the non-human are often closely interrelated
in Moore's work, it is important here at the beginning to open the question of whether and in what ways her animal images point beyond themselves. The ibis and the rose appear to be enacting human situations,
whereas the non-human characteristics of the lizard, goose, vulture, and
loon are being affirmed in themselves and even in contrast to their human
counterparts.

The common denominator in all these address poems is the presence of
a personal voice, the intimacy of the second-person rather than the distance

of the third-person form. The apostrophic "you" entails a speaker, an implied "I," in a personal way that the more textual "it" does not. Moore is here writing the poet's youthful lyrics in an oblique and tacit form. The second person is the perfect choice for the lyric that expresses the feelings and judgments of the self without spotlighting that self directly or exclusively. Four-fifths of these poems use the you-address, and over half use "I" explicitly. This I/you axis predominating during these years is the form for personal encounter. It is the lyric voice of self-expression deflecting attention from itself to what it has to express about the other. Moore was never loath to use the "I" form explicitly—it appears in over half of all her poems. But she was wary of the self-absorption that is one of the dangers of the lyric mode. Some years later she wrote to a poet who had submitted his work to her, "in this series, the vividness of the verse is sacrificed to the vividness of the self that is writing the verse."[13] The you-address is the lyric mode of self-expression focused on the vividness of the verse and its issues of value judgment.

One further effect of this you-form worth noting here, for its contrast with later work, is its enclosure of an audience within the poem itself. During the Carlisle years Moore's main readership was her immediate family; she had not yet established the poetic audience she would have for *Selected* and *Collected Poems* or the wide popular audience that the awards and media exposure of the 1950s would bring. It seems natural that, in a strategy unique to this private stage of her career, the poet should make her chosen subject double as imaginary audience. Thus the reader of these poems enters an already complete dramatic situation and has the choice of identifying either with the speaking voice or with the "you" that is being addressed. The lyric using "I" or "you" makes a special syntactic demand on the reader to participate in its expression of feeling, and the "you" addressing a third party critically presents the reader with the dilemma of which side of the rhetoric, sender or receiver, to experience the poem from. The only way to avoid taking sides is to resist the pull of the poem's syntax and remain at one remove from both parties. Thus access to these verses is multiple and perhaps difficult, until one approaches them as lyrics and discovers the locus of feeling in the speaking voice. These are poems of self-revelation of a most candid and yet indirect sort, revealing, as judgments often do, more about the critic than about the criticized.

Of the thirty-four poems that appeared during 1915 and 1916, about half are judgmental pieces clearly praising or censuring their chosen subject. "You give me pleasure, fellow," the speaker says in "To a Friend in the Making." "You brilliant Jew," it commends Disraeli; and "you lack half wit," it declares in "To a Steam Roller." We may set aside for the moment those poems whose verdict is ambiguous or equivocal and concentrate on those in which approval or disdain is the singular manifest message. Engaging in their wit and incisive imagery, these lyrics nevertheless run a certain tonal risk of alienating readers who object to some of the implications of a judgmental rhetoric.

It may be useful here to call upon Elder Olson's distinction between mimetic and didactic poetry: "the one is concerned with beauty of form," he writes, "and the other with inculcation of doctrine."[14] In didactic work the devices of verse are set in the service of propounding a body of knowledge or championing a program of values. And while such a distinction as this is not always clear in practice, the judgmental lyric may seem to ally itself with the didactic mode by implying the existence of an objective or even absolute standard that authorizes the judgment.

This judgmental group of Moore's Carlisle poems, while it stands at the threshold of the modernist era, also grew out of a world that was soon to be altered radically in the few years of the "Great War." As Paul Fussell has observed, at the start of the war there was as yet

> no *Waste Land,* with its rats' alleys, dull canals, and dead men who have lost their bones: it would take four years of trench warfare to bring these to consciousness. There was no *Ulysses,* no *Mauberley,* no *Cantos,* no Kafka, no Proust, no Auden. . . . One read Hardy and Kipling and Conrad and frequented worlds of traditional moral action delineated in traditional moral language.[15]

It was, "compared with ours, a static world, where the values appeared stable and where the meanings of abstractions seemed permanent and reliable," a world, in short, in which judgment must have seemed more positive and desirable than it has ever seemed after the upheaval.

Modern critics who are more comfortable with caution and complexity than with confidence in the moral sphere may find that explicit authorial pronouncements carry less force than the implicit judgments that are inevitable even in mimesis. To the relativist reader, the explicit verdict of a first-person poetic voice can shrink the ethical dimension of a work to a limited subjectivity. The relativist perceives the author-judge as merely exposing a personal bias, especially in verses that treat the character of another person, as these of Moore do.

I call them "judgmental lyrics," because they seem to be strongly personal responses, expressions of their speaker's emotions and states of mind. They are judgments in the mode of discernment and delineation, exercises in perception as much as in pronouncement. Moore's own development will be to move away from explicit judgment and toward exploration of its grounds, toward inquiry into the less determinate aspects of value. But the typical verse that appeared in 1915–17 is still a subjective expression of moral feeling aroused by a specific encounter, a one-to-one confrontation having a strong flavor of immediate and actual, if unknown, circumstances.

However categorical the voice sounds in each poem, there is no single dogmatic program being carried through this group. In Bernard Shaw the deadliest sin is attractive: "Pride sits you well." However, it weighs dangerously on the figure of "In 'Designing a Cloak' ":

> Encumbered as he was with pride,
> But for that coat he might have died
>   So despicably
>
> That kindness might have seemed unkind.

Likewise, "we find no virtue" in the "dead grace" of the past in "To Statecraft Embalmed," and yet in the second of the two poems entitled "The Past Is the Present" (originally "So far as the future is concerned"), the poet embraces the past by saying, "I shall revert to you, Habakkuk." It is possible to discern a few similarities, especially among the virtues championed in these poems. The quality of unstudied naturalness in behavior turns up in the "candor" of a "Friend in the Making," in the "once spontaneous core" that has lamentably withered in the "Pedantic Literalist," in the poetry of "unconscious fastidiousness" admired in "Critics and Connoisseurs," and in the "nonchalance" that is found good "In This Age of Hard Trying." The colorful vibrancy that is commended in Disraeli as a "bright particular chameleon" is admired also in the jewel-bright spectrum of the literal chameleon and in the "broad tail" of Molière as "the Peacock of France." Even praise itself is perceived as a valued commodity, a "jewel" in the hands of "William Butler Yeats on Tagore" and a privilege to bestow in "The Just Man And." But apart from such general themes, which are evidence of the sensibility of a single author, an inventory of the virtues and vices in these poems confirms the impression of variety in both topic and response.

The hint of absolutes is dispelled, or undermined, by the specificity of each treatment: the abstract term is one part, rather than the center, of a complex portrait. One might argue that the judgment is as much the occasion for the portrait, the setting for an "exact perception," as vice versa. In such a piece as "To Bernard Shaw: A Prize Bird," for example, the complexity of the picture can have a satiric effect. The composite picture of a barnyard rooster with "Samson's pride and bleak / finality" is ridiculous enough to qualify the apparent praise. The wry opener, "You suit me well, for you can make me laugh," sets Shaw up equivocally as either the author or the butt of the humor. "No barnyard makes you look absurd" implies that perhaps Shaw is quite appropriately cast as a "colossal" fowl pecking beside the hayrick. The verse is a tantalizing entanglement of opposing suggestions.

The group of poems that Moore submitted to *Poetry* in 1915 was entitled "Tumblers, Pouters and Fantails." These names for domestic breeds of pigeons that somersault, puff out their crops, and sport fan-shaped tails suggest that the poet considered her own work, ironically or not, as a form of self-exhibition or display. And beside these more clearly judgmental lyrics there stands a group of deliberately equivocal verse communiqués that are the strongest argument of all against taking these early "moralities" in any dogmatic way.

In her 1916 poem "Diogenes" Moore affirms the positive doubleness of "contrarieties." These are asserted mainly by a series of rhetorical questions in the second stanza, where one of Moore's rare personae, Diogenes the ascetic, defends his own Puritan legitimacy in contrast with the more colorful Ashtaroth (Astarte), the ancient Syrian goddess of sexual love and fertility:

> Is Persian cloth
> One thread with Persian sloth?
>   Is gold dust bran?
> Though spotted Ashtaroth
>   Is not a Puritan,
> Must every gorgeous moth
> Be calico, and Thoth
>   Be thanked for it?

Returning to the theme that begins to seem like a preoccupation of this period, "Pride's open book / Of closed humilities," this poem argues that such contrarieties are to be recognized rather than resolved in favor of one side. The affirmation of differences in a poem like this one lays the groundwork for the plenitude and paradoxes of the observations that will follow the Carlisle period.

Perhaps the most important of the contrarieties, one which will remain a concern throughout Moore's career, is expressed in the New York moment, "Is Your Town Nineveh?"—the paradox of freedom within limitation. To her brother Moore had described her 1915 visit to the City as her "Sojourn in the Whale." So in chiding the rebellious modern Jonah, she may be speaking to herself as well as to another:

Why so desolate?
  And why multiply
    In phantasmagoria about fishes,
      What disgusts you? Could
        Not all personal upheaval in
          The name of freedom, be tabooed?

  Is it Nineveh
    And are you Jonah
      In the sweltering east wind of your wishes?

The semi-rhetorical questions lift the poem into modes of possibility and
challenge, even while they seem to urge an acceptance of the given situation. Actuality is affirmed in the language of possibility. The closing de-
clarative turns the focus from "you" back to "I," the speaker:

I myself, have stood
  There by the aquarium, looking
    At the Statue of Liberty.

It is a confrontation that ends by revealing the self in the midst of the other's condition. The sense of emotional struggle is answered by the emblematic pause, by a moment suspended between the statue standing for liberty and the closed-in aquarium, the fish that trapped (and preserved) the
prophet. A gloss on this poem might be Moore's later statement that "for
everyone, however favored, there is the consciousness of disparity between circumstance and inclination."[16] The contrarieties in the poem are
not only determinism and freedom but also turmoil and acceptance. The
fascinating negative emotions occupy three-fourths of the lines before the
positive point appears implicitly, that this bondage-and-freedom is the
shared human condition. It is a foretaste of "What Are Years?", and here
too the impulse of sympathy balances the impulse to chastise.

  "Is Your Town Nineveh?" also returns us to the issue of spatial
imagery being put to thematic use. The speaker represents herself as
caught standing between one emblem and another, between the finite enclosure of the aquarium and the Statue of Liberty. The stillness of the
pose expresses the balance of opposites that is to be affirmed since it cannot be escaped. Perhaps the aquarium is the nearer reality of the two, liberty being a somewhat more distant ideal, but the point still seems to be
the tension between them. Does spatial imagery always tend to serve an
ideal of equanimity as it did in "Elephants" and of acceptance as it seems
to here? To frame the question in a larger way, is the spatial imagination
essentially conservative in bent, and is it fair to associate it with the classical rather than the romantic temper?

These will not be simple questions to answer of a poet who perceives the carrot as a "radical . . . conserving everything." Nor is Moore's poetry single-minded enough to fit T. E. Hulme's distinction between romanticism, which sees man as "an infinite reservoir of possibilities," and classicism, which sees man as "an extraordinarily fixed and limited animal whose nature is absolutely constant."[17] Hulme considered romantic poetry to be the "moaning or whining" of emotions hovering about the infinite and metaphors of flight, while classicism replaces such tears and gloom with its "accurate description" and restraint. "The classical poet," Hulme says, "never forgets this finiteness, this limit of man. In classicism you are always faithful to the conception of a limit." In this light the speaker of "Nineveh" appears to be a classical persona, who recognizes the finite condition of man, confronting a disheartened romantic who is in anguish over the limitations. The emotions of this rebellious anti-Jonah are conveyed temporally as "phantasmagoria" or fluctuating phantasms, whose eerie ebb and flow mirror the state of inner upheaval. In contrast, the poised, spatial balance of the ending scene is a rejection of that upheaval, but also its complement and perhaps its goal.

Moore is already fulfilling many of the demands that Hulme would eventually make for "good classical verse": it should be "accurate, precise and definite description" purged of the "vagueness," exaggeration, and "unsatisfied emotion" of the romantics. In classicism, Hulme writes, "man is always man and never a god." His rather rigid dichotomy helps bring out the subtleties and mixed nature of an actual body of work. Moore's famous description at the end of "The Pangolin" of man as "the self, the being we call human, writing- / master to this world," seems to fit Hulme's specification of a classically "fixed and limited animal":

> Consistent with the
> formula—warm blood, no gills, two pairs of hands and a
>   few hairs—that
>   is a mammal; there he sits in his own habitat,
>   serge-clad, strong-shod. The prey of fear, he, always
>   curtailed, extinguished, thwarted by the dusk,
>   work partly done,

and yet it goes beyond that formula, when he

>   says to the alternating blaze,
>   "Again the sun!
>   anew each day; and new and new and new,
>   that comes into and steadies my soul."

Moore's very qualified classicism begins in the years of the First World War but will flower during the Second. This classicism lies not in a conception of man as limited but in her poems' faithfulness to the worth of finite things and to the heroism possible in the inevitably conditioned life.

The spatial mode, however, is not always positive in its implications. The romantic Coleridge wrote that "all objects (*as* objects) are essentially fixed and dead,"[18] and Moore sometimes uses the fixed object as a mode of negative judgment. The same contrast between a temporal and a spatial image as that in "Is Your Town Nineveh?" enacts the hardening of the heart of the "Pedantic Literalist" (1916 version):

> its
>> carved cordiality ran
>>> to and fro at first like an inlaid and royal
>>> immutable production;

but even this illusion of movement disappears, and soon a

>> little "palm-tree of turned wood"
>>> informs your once spontaneous core in its
>>> immutable reduction.

For *Observations* Moore altered that final "reduction" to "production," echoing the second stanza, a repetition that suggests absence of development and that contrasts with the imaginative opening list of metaphors. The literalist has made himself into an untouchable object, an artifact like the toy called Prince Rupert's drop, a glass bead which "appears attractive but flies apart when handled."[19]

The same kind of immobility characterizes the man "encumbered . . . with pride" of "In 'Designing a Cloak to Cloak his Designs,' . . ." Moore depicts him satirically as an insignia of himself:

> His foibles clustered underneath
> Him, dominated by a wreath
>> Of upright half notes.

And in the first of the poems entitled "The Past is the Present," the theme that "revived bitterness / Is unnecessary" is driven home with two wooden images of a finished and closed case:

>> Last weeks' circus
> Overflow frames an old grudge. Thus:
>> When you attempt to

> Force the doors and come
> At the cause of the shouts, you thumb
> A brass nailed echo.

The arrested images embodying arrested growth or deadness in all three of these poems serve obliquely the positive romantic values of organic flexibility, sensitivity, and development.

Moore's *tour de force* of satiric objectification of this period is "Those Various Scalpels," a poem which may be considered her "portrait of a lady" and which may be instructively compared with other poems of that kind. T. S. Eliot's "Portrait of a Lady," published in 1917, the same year in which Moore's poem appeared, is written almost wholly in the temporal mode. The speaker's dramatic monologue narrates the portrait indirectly as he, like Prufrock, comes and goes, ascends the stairs, takes the afternoon air, smiles, and drinks his tea.[20] Pound's "Portrait d'une Femme" of 1912 and Williams's "Portrait of a Lady" of 1934 both share Moore's predominantly spatial approach of arresting in order to metaphorically define their subject, but Williams, like Eliot, draws attention to a self-conscious speaker. Williams's lover-poet becomes so adoringly tangled up in his imagery that the comedy of his own befuddlement turns the portrait into a love lyric of considerable delicacy.[21] Pound's "Portrait" is most like Moore's in its direct address and rather exclusive focus on the lady herself through an extended metaphor and a lengthy catalogue of expressive images, and yet even here a strong sense of the passage of time in her life balances the endurance of what she essentially is.[22]

Moore's portrait is even more exclusively spatial than Pound's. It is accomplished by a procession of arresting and exotic metaphors, a catalogue whose opulence mirrors that of its anonymous subject. The poem creates a sense of metamorphosis by naming a physical feature, then describing it with a metaphor, then almost immediately transforming that metaphor with a contrasting image:

> your hair, the tails of two
> fighting-cocks head to head in stone—
> like sculptured scimitars repeating the curve of your
> ears in reverse order:
> your eyes, flowers of ice and snow
>
> sown by tearing winds on the cordage of disabled ships.

The opposing qualities of feathery rooster-tails and metallic scimitars, flowers and ice, are continued as the catalogue progresses: "your cheeks, those rosettes / of blood on the stone floors of the French châteaux, / . . . your dress, a magnificent square / cathedral tower . . . a / species of verti-

cal vineyard rustling." The long catalogue is as intense as it is ambiguous
in its pattern of antithetical images. The portrait both reduces and ex-
pands its subject drastically. On the one hand, the poem is a condemna-
tion by systematic reduction of an outlandish person to a pile of non-
human objects. On the other hand, it makes this individual embody a
whole chain of being. She is animal, vegetable, and mineral, wild and cultivated; she is a work of art. She is a whole world of disaster and blood-
shed and magnificence in which the extremes meet in the pairs of opposing metaphors: she combines the animal aggression of the fighting-cocks
with the stillness of sculptured stone, the fragile beauty of flowers with
the catastrophe of winter shipwreck, the upward aspiring cathedral tower
with the rootedness in earth of the vineyard. The portrait and the lady are
a microcosm, a panorama of possibilities.

The poem itself is a form of praise by imitation, for the poet has fashioned the verse with as "rich instruments" as the lady has used on herself.
Thus both of the final questions address the poet as much as the lady.
These personal and artistic forms, "are they weapons or scalpels?" and
"Why dissect destiny with instruments / more highly specialized than
components of destiny itself?" We will eventually see in what way
Moore's more fully developed poetic instrument of inquiry, of which
this poem is an example, will from now on tend to replace the earlier,
short weapon of the judgmental cameo.

Thus it will not do to identify the temporally cast image as such with
the romantic mode and the spatial with the classical, since the still image
can carry opposing connotations into different contexts. One of the most
vibrant and versatile of these stills is the image of the chameleon, to
which Moore returns three times in this early group of poems. First, in
The Lantern for spring of 1915 we find the "little lizard," a "Dutiful
Beast" with "conscientious feet" who is poised "Midway Between the
Dial and the Foot of a Garden Clock." In the same issue "To Disraeli on
Conservatism" portrays the controversial statesman somewhat allegori-
cally as a "bright particular chameleon" held in the hand of Prejudice.
And Moore was not able to leave this creature poetically until she had
done it fuller justice in "To a Chameleon," whose original 1916 title adds
a thematic dimension to the intriguing comparison:

> You Are Like the Realistic Product of an Idealistic
> Search for Gold at the Foot of the Rainbow
>
> Hid by the august foliage and fruit of the grape vine,
> Twine
>   Your anatomy
>   Round the pruned and polished stem,

Chameleon.
Fire laid upon
An emerald as long as
The Dark King's massy
One,
Could not snap the spectrum up for food as you have done.

The Dark King's massy emerald might be the jewel of King Sarandib described by Sinbad on his sixth voyage in the *Arabian Nights,* which
Moore quotes later in "The Student": "a great mace of gold whose head
is an emerald a span long and as thick as a man's thumb."[23] Or maybe
Moore had already read about Prester John of whom she writes in "His
Shield," the legendary Ethiopian elder-king who was reported in a
twelfth-century manuscript as "enjoying such glory and prosperity that
he uses no scepter but one of emerald."[24] Whatever its source, the poem
begins Moore's ongoing theme of natural simplicity contrasted with vast
wealth and artifice, a theme to be more fully worked out in "The Jerboa"
and "Camellia Sabina." In "To a Chameleon" the tension between the
classicist's grandeur of civilization and the romantic's wild nature is resolved in favor of the small creature hidden by foliage, its tail twined like
a tendril around a stem. Moore's is a significantly qualified classical verse.
    When the chameleon reappears much later in "Saint Nicholas" of 1958,
we again see the creature, as Eliot put it, "startling us into an unusual
awareness of visual patterns":[25]

a chameleon with tail
that curls like a watch spring; and vertical
on the body—including the face—pale
    tiger-stripes, about seven;
        (the melanin in the skin
        having been shaded from the sun by thin
            bars; the spinal dome
                beaded along the ridge
                    as if it were platinum)?

In this later poem the different parts of the chameleon are compared to
different things in a series of brief figures of speech. While the predominantly spatial character of Moore's imagery continues throughout her career, over the years her deployment of metaphor will undergo a significant development.

Elizabeth Bishop has made a provocative general statement on this subject of Moore's metaphor in a discussion of the line in "Elephants" reading "As if, as if, it is all as ifs; we are at / much unease":

> It is annoying to have to keep saying that things are like other things, even though there seems to be no help for it. But it may be noticed that although full of similes, and such brilliant ones that she should never feel the necessity of complaining, she uses metaphor rather sparingly and obliquely.[26]

This is an unusual interpretation of the "Elephants" passage, one which perhaps reveals more about Bishop, for Moore's line on the surface seems to express not an annoyance with metaphor but rather a regret that in fact we have only metaphor and cannot push the identity farther. The poem has just described the defenseless mahout sleeping on the body of his elephant "as sound as if / incised with hard wrinkles . . . invincibly tusked, made safe by magic hairs," in short, sleeping as soundly as if he were an elephant and possessed that creature's equanimity. But alas, he is not; that is only an "as if," a figure of speech, and we are left in our literal, human world "at much unease"—our own existential unease, presumably, rather than the poet's discomfort with technique. While it is true that Moore admired Poe and that he cautioned the poet to use metaphor only very carefully, "Elephants" alone contains about twenty metaphoric usages and three similes. Moore appears to have used metaphors with fair frequency: an inventory of her work turns up one about every five or six lines, not counting the similes. Where she is indeed more sparing than many poets is in the range of reverberation, the demarcation of each metaphor.

In Eliot's and Williams's portraits, the key to many of the images is what Moore once called "the essential aura of contributory vagueness,"[27] an evocative quality that depends on the metaphor being loosely enough applied to the woman that it also can permeate the scene and atmosphere of the poem. Moore's metaphor "your hair, the tails of two fighting-cocks" is rich in connotation but remains quite exact and local in its immediate visual effect. It is what Hulme would call "dry and hard," so precisely descriptive as to seem to verge on the literal. The watch-spring, tiger's stripes, and platinum of "Saint Nicholas" are the same kind of figure—local and visually descriptive. In contrast, the figures of speech in most of the early poems of the Carlisle years play an essentially different role.

The metaphors of these early poems function primarily as vehicles of judgment. In fact, the primary means of passing judgment here is through metaphors, which stand as analogues of behavior, a role which governs their source and effect in the poem. "To an Intra-Mural Rat," for example, presents its anonymous subject as a scurrying rodent remembered merely in a parenthesis of wit, a metaphor for this and other poems of this period. The subject of "To a Steam Roller" is both encapsuled and eclipsed by the image that sums up this crusher of subtleties. What we get is a hybrid, a person performing the actions of a machine:

> You crush all the particles down
> into close conformity, and then walk back and forth on
> them.

In logic, analogy is recognized as the weakest form of argument, whereas in rhetoric it can be one of the most dramatic, in poetry the most vivid. Hence these judgments by metaphor enjoy considerable license. The poem moves into the metaphor in its title "To a Steam Roller," then out of it with the human opening "The illustration is nothing to you," then back into the metaphor with "You crush all the particles down," partway out with "then walk back and forth," back into the figure with "Sparkling chips of rock are crushed down," and out again to "Were not 'impersonal judgment, etc.'" This oscillation between vehicle and tenor makes both those poles of the metaphor explicit, allowing the poem to proceed alternately via image and idea.

Unlike the later "Saint Nicholas," in which the aspects of the chameleon are described separately by a variety of local metaphors, one figure for each part, the earlier poems tend to follow the pattern of "To a Steam Roller" in exploring one metaphoric equation through its various aspects. Virtually all of the judgmental lyrics of this group follow this strategy of establishing a single metaphor or figurative complex at the center of the poem: the intra-mural rat; the Shavian rooster; Disraeli as a chameleon; Molière as a peacock; the "carved and inlaid" wood and little "palm-tree of turned wood" in "Pedantic Literalist"; and the weapon, sheath, and steel of "To Be Liked by You Would Be a Calamity."

Because this central metaphor is expressive of a type of behavior or sensibility, its origin is more of a conceptual than a sensual matter. The images of the early poems are more thought-oriented, whereas the multitude of metaphors of the poems of the thirties are visually oriented. The 1935 "Pigeons" with feathers of "needle-fine cat-whisker-fibred battleship / -gray lace" are visually served by their multiple attendant images, whereas the prize bird and peacock are themselves central metaphors expressing not so much the appearance as the character and temperament of their subjects, Shaw and Molière. All that we really see physically of the ibis who embodies ineffective statesmanship in "To Statecraft Embalmed" is its enactment of "dead grace" by stalking about the political arena "half limping and half-ladyfied." The painter Paul Klee once wrote that "art does not reproduce the visible but makes the invisible visible."[28] The emphasis in these early poems is on rendering the invisible. For Moore the evaluative act itself is a kind of seeing-as, whose selection of vehicle grows out of a value judgment rather than out of sense perception. Thus the ibis appears at the opening of the poem as a conceptual emblem:

> O
> bird, whose tents were "awnings of Egyptian
> yarn," shall Justice' faint zigzag inscription—
>   leaning like a dancer—
>   show
>   the pulse of its once vivid sovereignty?

Visually the bird only really appears to close the poem, "and with its bill / attack its own identity," in a passage that is more conceptually than descriptively vivid.

Furthermore, we find that in these early poems the majority of metaphors are substantive rather than attributive: they replace, or identify, one whole thing with another—Shaw with the rooster, outmoded statecraft with the ibis—instead of adding the metaphoric image as an attribute or quality to the literal object, like the "battleship-gray lace" of the pigeons' feathers. In "To the Soul of 'Progress' " the substance or soul of military progress is embodied as a severed head and torso, and the crows that flock to it are "black minute-men." Some of the intensity of such an early poem comes from the dreamlike aura in which something appears as something else. It is hard to know whether we have crows seen as soldiers or soldiers seen as crows. As they "seek their prize / Till the evening sky's / Red," is it blood suggestive of sunset or sunset suggestive of blood? The substantive metaphoric equation, unlike the attributive modifier, can unsettle our sense of differentiation between literal and figurative by foregrounding the vehicle so vividly that it upstages the entity it was designed to help present. Such a metaphor has the advantage in evaluation that it focuses attention on the vehicle-tenor complex itself and can leave the "victim" mercifully in the background. As Moore's poetic course veers away from judgment, we shall see the poems gradually dropping the central, substantive, conceptual metaphor in favor of an abundance and variety of local, attributive, visual figures.

A second vehicle of judgment in these Carlisle verses is Moore's practice of quotation, which she once described in a pair of spatial metaphors: "my writing is, if not a cabinet of fossils, a kind of collection of flies in amber."[29] This passage points clearly to the intimate relation between the spatially-determined image and the quoted text. Both extract for preservation one segment from the ongoing stream of experience—the one visual, the other verbal. On the one hand, there is a certain incommensurability between words and things, as Robert Pinsky has pointed out: "Language is absolutely abstract, a web of concepts and patterns; and if one believes experience to consist of unique, ungeneralizable moments, then the gap between language and experience is absolute."[30] On the other hand, language is not "absolutely" abstract; it has its concrete aspect, too, especially for the writer. Literature is not wholly an antithesis of life but also one of the dimensions of life, because all of experience, not just writing, is permeated by text and words, and these words are also objects and events with which we must deal. Moore was fascinated with the web and patterns of language, and this synchronic sense of the patterned tissue of language underlies her stanzaic and rhyming and visual patterns no less than it does her arresting way with words.

The conversation notebooks are a display of Moore's readiness to extract something from the everyday flow of words, remember it, write it down, and use it in a poem, completing the transformation from spontaneously uttered speech into literary text. At a 1919 gathering with the Zorachs in New York, she heard someone speak about early art and wrote down in her notebook, "This fineness of early civilization art. I have never seen such primeval color. It is color of the sort that existed when Adam was there alone and there was no smoke and nothing to modify it but the mist that went up."[31] That fall she published "In the Days of Prismatic Color" beginning,

> Not in the days of Adam and Eve but when Adam
>   was alone; when there was no smoke and color was
> fine, not with the fineness of
>   early civilization art but because
> of its originality with nothing to modify it but the
>
> mist that went up.

The poet's role here was to nurture a passage from speech into writing. The lines are an enactment of poetry growing out of prior voices and texts rather than being created absolutely or "out of nothing."

The poet as "bricoleur," to borrow a term from Lévi-Strauss, makes things out of "odds and ends left over" as opposed to the engineer who creates wholly anew.[32] The bricoleur builds "structured sets . . . by using the remains and debris of events," and Moore's work reveals poetry as a form of bricolage, a "continual reconstruction from the same materials," the words, phrases, rhythms, and tones that are on hand in the speech and writing available to us.[33] The romantic conception of the poet as creating an utterance originally out of his vision, soul, or unique sensibility must be tempered here by a conception of the poet as tinkering in textualities, recycling and transposing linguistic materials to make something useful to the present.

Half of the poems of the Carlisle period employ marked quotations, and the practice will grow to affect two-thirds of the poems of the twenties, thirties, and war years, and three-fourths of the poems of the fifties and sixties. There is no increase in the quantity of material quoted; the practice simply appears in an increasing number of her poems, suggesting that it grows to be a more and more reliable, even habitual strategy. None of the Carlisle poems follow the Bryn Mawr sea-chantey examples of modeling the rest of the verse or voice on the borrowed lines. However, many do develop the strategy we saw in "Tunica pallio proprior" and "Qui S'Excuse, S'Accuse" of incorporating an aphoristic saying in its entirety. A majority of the quotations of this time take this aphoristic form. A smaller but significant number of other poems begin the practice of incorporating excerpted phrases, fragments borrowed for their choice phraseologies and woven into the poem's own fabric of sentences. And a small number of quotations deliver conversational monologues by a speaker clearly other than the authorial voice. All three forms of quotation in the Carlisle verses—aphorism, phrase fragments, and monologue—contribute to subtle forms of interplay between voices, between voice and text, and between two or more juxtaposed textualities.

To begin with, Moore's quotation marks can be more judgmental than punctuation usually is. "My Apish Cousins," later entitled "The Monkeys," opens with a catalogue of "minor acquaintances"—the zebras, the elephants, the small cats, the parakeet—who are then contrasted with that singular "Gilgamesh among / the hairy carnivora." The minor acquaintances talked but had nothing memorable to say: "it is difficult to recall the . . . speech." But the memorable Gilgamesh delivers the last two stanzas' monologue on the aesthetic attitudes of an unspecified "they," whom he quotes without quoting,

> astringently remarking, "They have imposed on us with
> their pale
> half-fledged protestations, trembling about
> in inarticulate frenzy, saying
> it is not for us to understand art; finding it
> all so difficult . . . ."

Like the forgettable minor acquaintances, "they" who tremble in "inarticulate frenzy" do not warrant quotation marks for their speech within the speech of the Gilgamesh. Here the explicitly marked quotation suggests not due punctuation of words spoken but rather something durably worthy conveyed by them. Quotation is one of the poem's strategies for assigning relative value to its several types.

A similar but more frequent evaluative strategy is the juxtaposition of two quoted passages in one poem, pitting the vagaries of colloquial speech, for instance, against the authority of the printed word. An early version of "A Fool, A Foul Thing, A Distressful Lunatic," the 1916 poem "Masks" attacks those three derogatory metaphors of common speech:

> "Loon" . . . . "goose" . . . . and "vulture" . . . .
> Thus, from the kings of water and of air,
> Men pluck three catchwords for their empty lips.

Then in characteristic second-person form, the poem contests those usages by means of a more literary, quoted passage that belies the common preconception:

> "Egyptian vultures, clean as cherubim,
> All ivory and jet," sons of the burning sun,
> What creatures call you 'foul'?

The poem discredits the thoughtless words of "empty lips" by comparison with the more richly accurate metaphor, "clean as cherubim." Thus a number of these early poems are at least partly concerned with language use, what people have to say, the stories they tell, the words they throw away. Quotation as a judgmental strategy grows out of, or leads into, the theme of the value of words.

A similar juxtaposition of voice and text appears in a quoted monologue as opposed to a magazine aphorism in the 1916 "Sojourn in the Whale," a poem addressed to Ireland in the year of the Easter Uprising. Remembering her own Irish ancestry and her feeling that she had just experienced a "sojourn in the whale" in her trip to New York City, Moore may also be writing of herself when she addresses "You, Ireland— / you . . . have heard men say" the most scornful and discouraging things:

> "There is a feminine temperament in direct contrast to
>   ours,
>   which makes her do these things. Circumscribed by a
>   heritage of blindness and native
>   incompetence, she will become wise and will be forced
>   to give in.
>   Compelled by experience, she will turn back;
>
>   water seeks its own level."

At this depressing and smug prediction both Ireland and the poet "smile," citing a single line from *Literary Digest,* "Water in motion is far from level." The brevity of the aphorism undoes the pompous wordiness of what reactionary "men say" and opens the way for the poem's affirmative ending. And the concisely controlled retort "To Be Liked By You Would Be a Calamity" pushes the tension between voice and text a step farther. An aphoristic statement from Hardy's "A Pair of Blue Eyes," which Moore had recorded in her Reading Diary,[34] is contrasted with the poet's apparent retreat from a hostile person:

> "Attack is more piquant than concord," but when
> You tell me frankly that you would like to feel
> My flesh beneath your feet,
> I'm all abroad—I can but put my weapon up and
> > Bow you out.
> Gesticulation—it is half the language.
> Let unsheathed gesticulation be the steel
> Your courtesy must meet,
> Since in your hearing words are mute, which to my senses
> > Are a shout.

Hardy's text on attack is only apparently discarded in favor of the silent language of gesture. In fact, the poem itself represents the piquant attack, reasserting the effectiveness in this situation of literary text over social speech.

These examples should not, however, be taken to imply that Moore considered the literary text intrinsically superior to the speaking voice. Several other poems of this period resolve the tension between a quoted text and a quoted voice in favor of the personal voice. The second poem entitled "The Past Is the Present" (1915 version) counteracts the latest fashion in literature—"rhyme is outmoded"—with something said by the Reverend Kellogg in a Bible class at the Carlisle Presbyterian Church:

> This man said—I think that I repeat
> > His identical words:
> > > "Hebrew poetry is
> > Prose with a sort of heightened consciousness. 'Ec-
> > > > stasy affords
> > > The occasion and expediency determines the
> > > > > form.' "

We are not told whom or what the Reverend Kellogg is quoting, and in her revision for *The Complete Poems* Moore ends the quotation at "consciousness," letting the famous aphorism "Ecstasy affords the occasion . . ." stand unquoted in the poetic voice. But the quotation-within-a-quotation form of the original ending is an echo of the form of internal quotation of that 1915 version's titular epigraph:

> So far as the future is concerned,
> "Shall not one say, with the Russian philosopher,
> 'How is one to know what one doesn't know?' "

The double bank of quotation marks is an especially emphatic emblem of the poem's enclosure of past voices within its present text. This quotation of a voice undermines as much as it emphasizes the textual quality of the poem.

The 1916 appearance of " 'Sun!' " is something of a climax of this layering of quotations and affirmation of a voice. The reader is met with three layers of quoted opening statement—the exclamatory title, the caption-like epigraph, and the couplet quoted from Skelton—before the poetic voice itself is heard:

> "Sun!"
>
> Hope and Fear—those internecine fighters—
> stop fighting and accost him
>
> "No man may him hyde
> From Deth, holow-eyed,"
> But for you, twin spirits, that shall not suffice.

The epigraph mediates between the title as the voice of hope and light and the couplet as the text of fear and death. Here at the beginning of Moore's career and half a century later toward its end, the poem argues (or prays) for the voice of hope, "O Sun, you shall stay with us." The triple layer of found rather than newly written material out of which " 'Sun!' " grows emphasizes the characteristic effects of Moore's quotations as a general practice: they make her poems into texts explicitly reflective of other texts.

Moore's marked quotations display visibly what her unmarked borrowings enact invisibly and what all half-conscious or wholly unconscious borrowings conceal—the supra-personal dimension of the poem's origin, that general cultural matrix of speech and writing within which the language of the poem operates. By indicating a second and even a third "author" of its phrases, the quotation qualifies the conception of the poet as the personal source of the poem, demonstrating his dependence on the discourse and the textual possibilities of the larger cultural milieu. The creation of the work of art must be recognized as not only an individual act but also an activation of a whole impersonal network of textual conventions. The poem itself is both subject to and demonstrative of these conventions, and so it is both supportive and subversive of the social forces embodied in them. Thus the political thrust of such work is always theoretically double, that is, both reflective and critical. Moore has enacted this double thrust in an intriguing way by entitling a poem in her Reading Diary "Conservatism" and then retitling the same poem for publication as "Progress."[35] Whatever her personal allegiances—and they were not simple—her verses' politics are as complex as the implications of her spatial imagery and metaphors.

The Carlisle years, like the years at Bryn Mawr, brought some poems to print that Moore would consistently preserve and some that have all but disappeared from the hands of many of her readers. The swiftness of these second-person judgments by metaphor, these evaluative apostrophes, is virtually unique to this time of her life. We shall see how the Moores' move to Chatham, New Jersey, in 1916 and then to New York City in 1918 almost immediately produced significant changes in the poems' dimensions and sense of audience, their orientation toward value, and hence the relation in them between the literal subject and the figurative language. But repeating the Reverend Kellogg's "identical words," the transcription of a verbal landscape, will remain for Moore a task comparable to the exact and vivid delivery of sensuous observations. She will continue to treat both the verbal and the visual image with a classical sense of precision and balance and with a deepening awareness of the dilemmas inherent in the project of art as "exact perception."

3

The Romance of the Text

In August of 1916 Moore reported that "two chameleons entered the service of the Rev. J. W. Badger."[1] The closeness of this family group was, despite its inevitable tensions, a vital source of strength to all three members throughout their lives. One set of pet names for each other, drawn from Kenneth Grahame's 1908 classic *The Wind in the Willows*, reveals their different personalities and roles in the family: Warner was the paternal yet independent Badger; Marianne was the adventuresome Rat, scribbler of verses; and their mother was the home-loving Mole. It seemed natural, when Warner became pastor of Ogden Memorial Church in Chatham, New Jersey, for the two women to move with him to the parsonage. And in 1918, when he went to sea as a chaplain in the Navy, Mrs. Moore bowed to Marianne's desire to live in New York City instead of returning to Carlisle.

"The perfect thing," Moore later called life in New York in the early years. "I worked at the library diagonally across from the house. . . . It was a simple, unselfconscious part of town then."[2] The lure of the city was that it afforded "accessibility to experience," Henry James's phrase that Mole had copied from Dixon Scott's *Men of Letters* into a 1920 letter to Warner and that Marianne then appropriated for her poem "New York." "I like Santa Barbara," she later recalled, "Vancouver, British Columbia; have an incurable fondness for London. But of any cities I have seen, I like New York best." She loved its waterfront, its people, its cultural life, its bookshops—"Rizzoli's of international Old World grandeur, and the Gotham Book Mart's new world compactness . . . 'Wise Men Fish Here' the sign says, and they do"[3]—and for all these reasons she remained "convinced that it is the place where an artist thrives best."[4]

Once settled at 14 St. Luke's Place, Moore readily became part of the *Others* group of writers and artists that included Alfred Kreymborg, William Carlos Williams, Wallace Stevens, Mina Loy, Marsden Hartley, Lola Ridge, and Kenneth Burke. Kreymborg has immortalized the remarkable impression that she made on him and others as "an astonishing person with Titian hair, a brilliant complexion, and a mellifluous flow of polysyllables which held every man in awe. Marianne talked as she wrote and wrote as she talked, and the consummate ease of the performance either way reminded one of the rapids of a beautiful stream."[5]

During this time of friendly mingling Moore may well have appropriated, and then forgot that she had, her famous image of poetry as "imaginary gardens with real toads in them" from the passage in Williams's "Romance Moderne," that she would surely have read in the February 1919 issue of *Others*: "Childhood is a toad in the garden, a / happy toad. All toads are happy / and belong in gardens."[6] Williams would surely have felt complimented. In December of 1919 he wrote with customary appreciation to invite Moore to Sunday afternoon tea with "the rest of the crowd—in which you seem so out of place—so in place, like a red berry still hanging to the jaded rose bush."[7] "I was a little different from the others," she admitted.[8]

At a party given by Lola Ridge, Moore met Scofield Thayer, editor of *The Dial*. After her command-performance reading of her poem "England" at two o'clock in the morning, Thayer not only encouraged her to resubmit the rejected piece to him but also invited her to tea at the Dial offices at 152 West 13th Street to meet his co-publisher, James Sibley Watson. Moore reported that at this first encounter Dr. Watson said nothing at all and that she was impressed, so one suspects that his characteristic and fascinating quietness may have provided the inspiration for her poem "Silence." This meeting led in turn to an invitation to a Milhaud recital in February of 1923 in the Watsons' home, where Marianne met Sibley's wife Hildegarde Lasell Watson, who became one of her lifelong friends. The Watsons' group included Sibley's Harvard friend Estlin Cummings, for whom Moore came to care very much, and also the sculptor Gaston Lachaise, who produced portraits in bronze of Moore, Cummings, Thayer, and Sibley Watson.

Moore would not meet Pound or Eliot personally until the thirties, but she was in correspondence with both: Pound wrote her shortly after her appearance in *The Egoist,* and Eliot had written in April of 1921 to thank her for her *Dial* review of his work. During that same month she received a memorable letter from Bryher's new husband Robert McAlmon in England, who assured her that "people here do *get* you; don't think you over-cerebral; and do find music and rhythm in your poetry."[9] McAlmon went on to say that his friend Eliot "thinks you the person who has most definitely established an individual, unique, beautiful and musical rhythm, with intellectual content. He rates you more highly than anybody he has spoken of, and we have talked of [just] about everybody." This combination of stimulating New York friends, first-rate publication, and critical respect made the early 1920s an exciting and particularly expansive time for Moore as a poet.

While the star of her career was rising very rapidly indeed, Moore's private life was taking its own special shape. In July of 1918 Warner was married to Constance Eustis, a Wellesley graduate of 1911, and their four children arrived over the next eight years—Mary, Sarah, Marianne Craig, and John Warner. In 1921 Bryher and Robert McAlmon eloped, and Moore expressed to him her shock at what she perceived as a lack of appropriate romance in the arrangement. And her journals of this time reflect an interest in the subject of marriage well before her preliminary drafts of her poem about it. The fact that Moore never chose to marry, that she was not "matrimonially ambitious," as she put it,[10] seems to have been partly a matter of circumstance and partly a chosen protection of the environment in which her creative work was unquestionably flourishing.

Right from the outset both Chatham and Greenwich Village provided an accessibility to new and fascinating things that greatly enlarged the dimensions of the poems appearing from 1918 until 1925. I say "things" deliberately, for the verses of these years are indeed filled, even teeming at times, with things: objects, artifacts, types of people, sights, places—all the souvenirs and furnishings of a varied and populous public world. Even a first glance at these twenty-nine pieces confirms that it is in the vein of her recent "Critics and Connoisseurs" and "Those Various Scalpels" that Moore is now going to work. The more leisurely and discursive modes grow to contain and sometimes override the epigrammatic concision of the Carlisle apostrophes. "Melancthon" and "The Fish" of 1918, for instance, exhibit a multiplicity of images and insights that contrast sharply with the singular subject of "To a Chameleon." "People's Surroundings" assembles its crowds in one list after another. And "Marriage" and "An Octopus" approach the form of the long-poem by the manner in which the subject of each poem works in a broadly inclusive way. Thus, although it is not entirely sudden or complete, the widening of the poet's world is clearly discernible. The tightly focused intensity of the Carlisle poems gives way to the expansiveness of these larger works that by 1924 complete her *Observations*.

The second-person "you" of the Carlisle poems led us toward their covertly lyrical voice, and hence to the subjective ground of the judgments they pass. Likewise, in the poems that Moore wrote while she was in her thirties, the more frequent third-person voice and the larger, freer dimension are vehicles for a new poetic orientation toward value. These later "observations" are surely the ones that prompted Eliot to classify Moore's poetry as " 'descriptive' rather than 'lyrical' or 'dramatic.' "[11] We shall find her poetic voice here less concerned with judgment of a single individual and more concerned with establishing the general criteria for judgment by investigating whole groups and types of people. Hence two ways by which the words of the verse are raised into another register show corresponding developments. Metaphor, released from a centrally evaluative function, is now deployed in a more descriptive role and therefore with much greater variety. Quotations, too, appear with greater frequency and a new kind of latitude and occasionally with something like symphonic effect. Thus one largeness of this period reflects another: plenitude of worldly matter makes way for, and is ushered in by, greater liberality of tone and spirit in these poems of the 1920s, the *Dial* decade when, as Moore agreed, "things were opening out."[12]

We have seen that a significant formal development of the Carlisle years was the shift from audible to inaudible rhyme. The traditionally poetic effect of the heavier rhymes yielded to visible but unheard rhymes embedded in a more discursive style. Continuing this trend, the main prosodic development of Moore's observations of the twenties is their gradual turn to free verse. One might well call this a formal experiment rather than a development, for there is evidence that it was undertaken quite tentatively at first, and it had already been partially abandoned by the time *Selected Poems* appeared in 1935. Nevertheless, the great poems that Moore wrote in free verse during the twenties have had a lasting effect not only on our modern conception of the poem as such but also on her own subsequent practice. She never abandoned the form entirely after this "experiment," but in the thirties she turned with care and originality to pieces that combined the repeated stanza shape with the naturally phrased line.

Moore began the transition to free verse as a process of revision. Several of her poems of the twenties have been printed in both stanzaic and free verse forms: "Picking and Choosing," "England," "When I Buy Pictures," "A Grave," and "Peter." The stanzaic version of each of these five has been revised into free verse, although the stanzaic original in two instances ("When I Buy Pictures" and "A Grave") was published after the free revision by editors working from non-current manuscripts. Occasionally the syllabically-determined lines of the original stanza show like bones through the contours of the free verse. The especially clear example of such partial reworking is the opening of "England," whose first two unaltered 20- and 15-syllable lines confirm the gradual nature of the shift. "England" stanzaically opens,

> with its baby rivers and little towns, each with its abbey or
> > its cathedral;
> with voices—one voice perhaps, echoing through the
> > transept—the
> criterion of suitability and convenience; and Italy with its
> > equal
> shores—contriving an epicureanism from which the
> > grossness has been

The incomplete stanza has been revised, mostly from line three on, to the mixed form that we find in *Complete Poems*:

> with its baby rivers and little towns, each with its abbey or
> > cathedral,
> with voices—one voice perhaps, echoing through the
> > transept—the
> criterion of suitability and convenience: and Italy
> with its equal shores—contriving an epicureanism
> from which the grossness has been extracted.

The inaudible rhyme pattern has been buried ("cathedral" with "equal" is now an internal echo) and the grammatical unit completed. This poem also tells us that Moore has already begun the process of weeding out her inferior poems: "England" contains phraseology in its second and third stanzas—"the East with its . . . emotional shorthand"—that appeared in "An Ardent Platonist" of 1918, a signal that the earlier poem has already been discarded.

Perhaps the most illuminating transformation from stanzaic to free verse appears in Moore's revision of "A Grave." The original typescript of "A Graveyard in the Middle of the Sea" contains an opening stanza and two other lines which Moore never printed. That stanza describes a scene underneath the water and so was easily detached from the shore perspective of the rest of the poem. As the only grammatically independent stanza, however, this one is surely the now-ghostly pattern on which the remainder of the poem was modelled:

> The cypresses of experience dead, yet indestructible by
> > circumstance; shivering and stony in the
> > > water; not green
> But white, surrounding all that is loathsome:
> > > inanimate
> Scavengers guarding permanent garbage: watched over by
> > sharks which cruise between

Them—petrine like death yet not so petrine as
        patient; everything everywhere
Yet nothing, because nowhere; infinity defined
        at last, still infinity because there
Where nothing is.[13]

The lines of this version are so long that Moore resorted to putting her paper into the typewriter sideways and typing across the length of the page. The inevitable division of such lines in book form may have been a spur to her search for a less awkward form. We know from one of Ezra Pound's letters to her that Moore had sent him a stanzaic version of the poem without that opening stanza by 1918.[14] This version of "A Graveyard" may well be the manuscript he used for *Profile, An Anthology Collected in MCMXXXI* to give us this one-time syllabically stanzaic publication:

Man looking into the sea, taking the view from those who
        have as much
  right to it as you have to it yourself, it is human nature to stand in the middle of a thing but you cannot
  stand in the middle of this: the sea has nothing to give
        but a well exca-
  vated grave. The trees stand in a procession each with
        an emerald turkey-
    foot at the top, reserved as their contours, saying
        nothing; repression
  however, is not the most obvious

characteristic of the sea; the sea is a collector, quick to
  return a rapacious look. There are others beside you, who
have worn that look: people now at their best, whose
        clothes are a
  testimony to the fact, row across them, the blades of the
        oars moving to-
  gether like the feet of water spiders as if there were no
        such thing as death.
  The wrinkles move themselves into a phalanx,
        beautiful under net-
  works of foam and fade breathlessly, while the

sea rustles in and out of the seaweed. The birds swim
        through the air at
  top speed, emitting cat calls as heretofore—the tortoise
        shell

> scourges about the feet of the cliffs, in motion beneath
>   them; and the ocean under the pulsation of lighthouses
>   and noise of bell
>   buoys, advances as usual, looking as if it were not
>   that ocean
>   in which dropped things are bound to sink; in
>   which if they turn and twist, it is
>   neither with volition nor consciousness.[15]

The scheme of two rhymes occurring in the original opening stanza has been preserved here but partly internalized. The second pair of rhyme words ("turkey" with "the," "death" with "breath-," and "ocean" with "volition") is now virtually invisible, for the second word of each pair falls four syllables from the line-end. This is because the four-syllable lines based on the original "Where nothing is" have been incorporated into a more naturally phrased last line of each stanza. The truncated phrase exposing a rhyme has been traded here for a half-internal rhyme and a more natural visual flow. Moore reworked the poem again, setting it in free verse for *The Dial* of July 1921, and none of the bones show through:

> Man looking into the sea,
> taking the view from those who have as much right to it as
>   you have to it yourself,
>   it is human nature to stand in the middle of a thing,
>   but you cannot stand in the middle of this.

The rhymes in this version are now completely hidden, and the line breaks are governed by the syntactic units rather than by a stanzaic pattern.

As in the other four of the poems revised to free verse, virtually all of the original wording of "A Grave" remains intact in its free form. The effect of letting the phrasing have its way with the line is to remove a certain visual evidence of artifice and to increase the sense of naturalness in the poem's appearance as written on the page. The fact that Moore changed such an insignificant fraction of her wording throughout these transformations (two or three phrases in an average of thirty lines) attests to the already natural flow of her poem as speech and to the visual or written nature of her free verse form. "A Grave" looks quite different but sounds much the same in its two incarnations, for with the help of the light or inaudible rhyme, Moore had already achieved the "naturalistic effects" which she admired in 1916 in "The Accented Syllable."

Moore's free verse gives up the regular patterns of rhyme in favor of a rich texture of alliteration. This is clearly audible, for instance, in the internal chiming of the opening lines of her poem on Washington's Mt. Rainier:

An Octopus

of ice. Deceptively reserved and flat
it lies "in grandeur and in mass"
beneath a sea of shifting snow-dunes.

She could even revise such music into her "quotations." We can see, for instance, how one source for this poem, M. C. Carey's account of "The Octopus in the Channel Islands" in the *London Graphic,* has been copied into the Reading Diary as

It can pick a periwinkle out of a crack & yet
crush a larger prey w/ the grip of a small python,[16]

and heightened both in rhythm and in density of alliteration to the lines,

"Picking periwinkles from the cracks"
or killing prey with the concentric crushing rigor of the
python.

Moore sometimes interlaces the special virtues of prose and those of verse in such a way that noticeably rich clusters of alliteration are followed by passages in which the sound relaxes to a more everyday level before being reconcentrated into a new cluster. We can see that this concentration and relaxation of alliteration characterizes both the stanzaic and the free verse versions of "A Grave," regardless of how the words are set out on the page, even in prose form: "the tortoise-shell scourges about the feet of the cliffs, in motion beneath them; and the ocean under the pulsation of lighthouses and noise of bell-buoys, advances as usual." Perhaps one reason for Moore's eventual return to the syllabic or shaped stanza in the thirties was her sense of the "merely printed" effect of the free verse form in her hands. She understood that she could cross an ongoing audible rhythm with the visual patterns of verse without stilting her poetic voice into an artificially poetic manner.

"A Grave" is also one of only three poems of this period that use the second-person form in addressing a central figure. The other two are "You Say You Said" and "To a Snail," and these are the last verses to be cast in this mold for about forty years—until "Saint Nicholas" of 1958 revives the apostrophe form. Furthermore, the addressee in "A Grave"— the "man looking into the sea"—no longer figures in the second half of the poem, for he has been rendered peripheral and then insignificant by the sea itself. We could almost take the 1918 draft of this piece as marking Moore's turning away from using the poem to criticize an individual toward using it to present and explore a general phenomenon.

Other instances of the "you" form in these observations tend to be more of a third-person "you" that is virtually synonymous with "one." Such interchangeability is illustrated by the pronoun shift in the passage of "Marriage" presenting

> the spiked hand
> that has an affection for one
> and proves it to the bone,
> impatient to assure you
> that impatience is the mark of independence,
> not of bondage.

Sayings delivered in the spirit of a proverb also turn the second-person form to a third-person effect, as in "Silence," which quotes Edmund Burke's " 'Make my house your inn.' " In "People's Surroundings" another such proverbial "you" appears in the line "When you take my time, you take something I had meant to use." And the opening of "Poetry" exemplifies Moore's new practice of detaching her response from a singular individual. "I, too, dislike it" is probably an echo of Samuel Butler's "I don't greatly like poetry myself," as she copied it into her Reading Diary.[17] But unlike the earlier responses to Browning, Disraeli, and Shaw, this poem (in its longer version preserved in the Notes in *The Complete Poems*) bypasses the individual Butler and concerns itself instead with the general phenomenon:

> In the meantime, if you demand on the one hand,
> the raw material of poetry in
>   all its rawness and
>   that which is on the other hand
>   genuine, you are interested in poetry.

This ending demonstrates how the reader-addressed "you," because of its general focus, functions rhetorically as "one" or as "anyone who."

The voice that emerges in these later "observations" to replace the earlier apostrophe is the first-person "we." This form does away with the confrontational effect of the judgmental addresses and invests these new poems with a sense of communal experience, a shared world. This communal spirit is present in "Poetry," becoming part of its implicit definition: "the same thing may be said for all of us, that we / do not admire what / we cannot understand." We see it in "The Bricks Are Falling Down," whose opening asks, "In what sense shall we be able to / secure to ourselves peace"; in "Reinforcements," in which "the words of the Greeks / ring in our ears"; and in "The Monkey Puzzle's" aphorism, "We prove, we do not explain our birth." This assumption of communal experience eases the reader's earlier dilemma of how to identify with the you-addressed judgments, for now the reader is automatically included in the first-person plural.

This communal "we" is not quite as pervasive as the "you" was: the "you" form appears in nearly eighty percent of the Carlisle poems, whereas "we" is a voice for about half of the works of 1918–25. Nevertheless, the emergence of a communal voice at this time in Moore's career signals a new sense of audience. The Bryn Mawr and Carlisle pieces are often, as we noted, private poems. Many of them appear tailored to a limited and familiar readership—family, classmates, friends, and the subject addressed imaginatively—one of whom will recognize the individual or occasion alluded to. In contrast, the later "observations" may be thought of as "poets' poems," for Moore had by then gained a forum in the literary press. These pieces could begin to assume a broader readership of people interested in literature, the arts, and current thought in general. The concurrence of the "we" form with a poetry-oriented audience would continue well through the nineteen-thirties. The grammatical fact that this "we" is also a possible counterpart of "I," that it might be taken as a "royal We," means that these "observations" share to some extent the subjective ground of the shorter lyrics. But "we" is also a form for attachment of the speaking self to the larger community, and we shall see that a corresponding shift in Moore's chosen subject matter from private and singular to public and plural makes this sense of community predominate over the disguised singular.

In contrast to the individual subjects of so many Carlisle poems, the later "observations" focus on types and groups, like "Reinforcements," "Dock Rats," "The Labors of Hercules," and "Novices," and on collective subjects like the ingredients of "Poetry," of "New York," of "People's Surroundings," and the multifarious worlds of "The Fish" and "An Octopus." The plurality of her subjects is not surprising, given Moore's new "accessibility to experience" at this time. But plurality of subject brings with it a new set of possibilities for what a poem can undertake rhetorically and thematically. The role of the single particular changes—it becomes a part rather than a whole. The earlier David's harp in "That Harp You Play So Well," the throne of "To Statecraft Embalmed," and the staff and bag of "In This Age of Hard Trying" are all centrally evaluative metaphors in their poems. The "baby rivers and little towns" of "England," however, or the "artichoke in six varieties of blue" in "When I Buy Pictures" are non-metaphorical. They may be exemplary, but they are used in a relatively literal way. Now the literal presence (so to speak) of so many objects in the poem's sphere imports a problematical element of objectivity. Cumulatively the many objects seem to argue for their actual objective nature, for their existence outside of the poetic speaker's mind. They appear to inhabit the public dimension of "we" rather than the private world of an "I."

Thus the plural subject matter of these poems, in bringing its items out of metaphorical use and into more literal use, raises the problem of knowledge: if "art is exact perception" as Moore claimed in 1910, whose perception is it, and how reliable can perception be if it must always be someone's? How can a poem purport to speak of the public world except through some private perception, and yet how can such perception be other than subjectively conditioned? Moore's move away from the subjective rhetoric of the earlier poems does not evade the dilemma of subjectivity but rather serves to heighten it. The problem of objective knowledge only becomes critical when the poem begins to strive for such knowledge, even ironically. Moore's work of the twenties begins to question her initial aesthetic program by raising, as we shall see, the issue of whether perception can ever hope to be "exact." Perhaps the notion of objective knowledge is itself a contradiction in terms, insofar as knowledge is a subjective condition or act of awareness.

In "England," for instance, the immediate flavor of the local, the particular, the diverse, is contrasted with a general quality of excellence. What the speaker aims to get from "England / with its baby rivers . . . Italy / with its equal shores . . . Greece with its goat and its gourds . . . the East with its snails, its emotional / shorthand . . . the sublimated wisdom of China" is a certain shared, non-local quality, the climactic "it," the "flower and fruit of all that noted superiority" which "has never been confined to one locality." The omnipresence of this abstract "it" is in cognitive tension with the variety of its local manifestations. The distinctiveness of each heritage contributes to the point that excellence transcends differences. But it is difficult, if possible at all, to apprehend both the abstract quality and the concrete instance in all its peculiarity. Thus this poem, like others we shall examine of this period, concerns itself with "misapprehension," with appearances about which "no conclusions may be drawn."

One of the most significant effects of this plurality and of Moore's gradual move toward a more objective grounding of her poems is their shift from the mode of judgment to an examination of the criteria or standards on which judgments may be based. "In the Days of Prismatic Color," "Poetry," "Picking and Choosing," "Novices," and "To a Snail"—all aim at explanations and embodiments of the intangible qualities that are the grounds for judgment. We see such criteria in a definition in "The Monkey Puzzle": "This porcupine-quilled, complicated starkness— / this is beauty." We see them in the aphoristic retort in the early version of "The Labors of Hercules," "it is one thing to change one's mind, another to eradicate it," and in the general prescriptive forms of "When I Buy Pictures" stipulating that "It must not wish to disarm anything . . . / it must be 'lit with piercing glances into the life of things'; / it must acknowledge the spiritual forces which have made it." These criteria-poems often proceed by juxtaposing a variety of objects with a search for the abstract explanation of the virtues of these particular images.

Some of Moore's revisions show that, as we saw in " 'Sun!' ", she could change her mind about the abstraction more easily than about the image. For instance, the last four lines of "When I Buy Pictures," the list of "it must's," were significantly reworded three times from the version in *The Dial* to that in *Poems* of 1921 to that in *Selected Poems* of 1935. Moore revised another poem, "In the Days of Prismatic Color," in such a way as to keep the image of the dragon while radically altering its abstract application. In the original *Lantern* version, Nestor's dragon— " 'Part of it was crawling, part of it / was about to crawl, the rest / was torpid in its lair' "—appears to be an image for truth. A line in the last stanza makes this link, stating explicitly that "Truth, many legged and formidable also, / is stationary by choice." The later omission of that link and the addition of the less dignified "short-legged, fit- / ful advance, the gurgling and all the minutiae" seem now to make the dragon an image for the pestilence of complexity, of "sophistication . . . at the antipodes from the init- / ial great truths." The early typescripts of the poem reveal yet a third interpretation that combines the two just given, perceiving that in

> all the minutiae—a
> resemblance has some-
> how been maintained, to wisdom that is formidable
> only in the darkness. Truth is no Apollo.[18]

Moore's eventual solution to this problem of a wealth of interpretive possibilities for one image will be to adopt the problem as a strategy, that is, to find an approach that gives free rein to her interpretive associations. Thus in the thirties we shall see the poet turning from poems with a plurality of items, from which she tries to extract a unifying idea, to poems centered in a generic-singular subject, like the jerboa or the pangolin, from which a variety of ideas and interpretations may be freely drawn.

Meanwhile, the multitude of literal particulars encompassed by these poems of the twenties has raised the epistemological issue of its technique: objectivity. In fact, Moore's turn to a more objective presentation of things in the public world seems almost immediately to bring up the issue of its own difficulties and limits. "I like to see people's surroundings," Moore recorded in her Conversation Notebook in 1919, "they answer one's questions."[19] And in those confident words she began "People's Surroundings." For *Observations* in 1924, however, she added the qualifying line 33: "these are questions more than answers." Art as exact perception must admit also the unnoticed and the imperceptible; the surroundings of this poem include "the public secrets" and "the highway hid." The vast assembly of furnishings—"the steel, the oak, the glass, the Poor Richard publications . . . the peacocks, hand-forged gates, old Persian velvet . . . Chinese carved glass, old Waterford, lettered ladies"—has a certain opacity. These things are "non-committal"; they are "personal-impersonal." Toward the end of the poem we are assured that, "with X-ray-like inquisitive intensity upon it, the surfaces go back; / . . . we see the exterior and the fundamental structure." And yet the imagery offers us more and more surfaces, a closing catalogue of types and settings in ever-lengthening lists. "People's Surroundings" shares with "England" a concern for misapprehension. Surroundings can be questions that seem like answers, vivid and precise images of things that are "lost" and that "disappear," things that are dyed and changeable:

> the acacia-like lady shivering at the touch of a hand,
> lost in a small collision of the orchids—
> dyed quicksilver let fall,
> to disappear like an obedient chameleon in fifty shades of
> mauve and amethyst.

Thus motifs of skepticism and uncertainty are here challenging the program of art as exact perception. This tension between perception and skepticism is especially vivid in "Marriage," "An Octopus," and "Sea Unicorns and Land Unicorns" of 1923 and 1924, a group which Moore facetiously called the "serial" poems because their length made them seem to her suitable perhaps to serial publication.[20]

Moore's worksheets of the twenties show that these three remarkable poems were being worked on at the same time.[21] One worksheet moves from "An Octopus / of ice—a stranded iceberg" to "I breakfast at home / *Marriage*." Another moves from "Adam in his seemliness . . . trips over marriage" to a dress that is "embroidered all over slightly with snakes of Venice gold and silver and some O's," a line that is now part of "Sea Unicorns and Land Unicorns." And so it is not surprising to find that the three share an underlying concern with the difficulty of achieving positive, exact, or objective knowledge. The speaker of "Marriage" recognizes that

> Psychology which explains everything
> explains nothing,
> and we are still in doubt,

and she calls in La Fontaine to underscore the paradox:

> "Everything to do with love is mystery;
> it is more than a day's work
> to investigate this science."

Love is both a mystery and a science, unfathomable and yet subject to careful scrutiny. Exact perception does not guarantee exact knowledge, although it may yield a rather precise poem about the imprecisions of the world as we see it.

The problem of positive knowledge appears even more pervasively in "An Octopus." This inventory of the glacial Mt. Rainier is laced with confident perceptual motifs: "its clearly defined pseudo-podia . . . recognized by its plants . . . time to see . . . the perspective of the peaks . . . a nice appearance . . . conspicuously spotted little horses . . . It is self-evident." But these motifs are continuously challenged by an equally pervasive recognition of error and blindness: "Deceptively reserved and flat . . . misleadingly like lace . . . you have been deceived into thinking . . . concealed in the conclusion . . . happy seeing nothing . . . hard to discern." The role of the Greeks "enjoying mental difficulties" in the second half of the poem is to enact this paradox of impossible knowledge:

> The Greeks liked smoothness, distrusting what was back
> of what could not be clearly seen,
> resolving with benevolent conclusiveness,
> "complexities which still will be complexities
> as long as the world lasts."

Thus perceptual complexity is the tissue of this poem from its opening metaphoric illusion, "An Octopus / of ice," to its closing similes,

> its claw cut by the avalanche
> "with a sound like the crack of a rifle
> in a curtain of powdered snow launched like a waterfall."

Seeing things as they are includes also not seeing all of them and seeing them as they are not. Like the world's, the mountain's "relentless accuracy," its "capacity for fact," is far greater than our own human capacity to grasp it.

The most pointed of Moore's dramatizations of the problem of objective knowledge is "Sea Unicorns and Land Unicorns." This last of the "serial" poems to appear in *The Dial* in 1924 is an examination of the nature of our histories, the grounds of our knowledge. The poem parades the textual sources of presumed "facts" about the unicorns:

> these are those very animals
> described by the cartographers of 1539,
>
> . . . .
>
> Upon the printed page,
> also by word of mouth,
> we have a record of it all.

But interwoven with the recorded "facts" are a wealth of imaginative, artistic images: Spenser's "mighty monoceroses" in *The Faerie Queene,* embroideries of the animals embellished with "knotts and mulberries," the heraldic emblem of Britain's lion and Scotland's unicorn, and painted maps "improved 'all over slightly with snakes of Venice gold, / and silver, and some O's.' " In the midst of this double exposure of fact and fancy, the speaker puts on a wry, ironic solemnity about the unicorn: "So wary as to disappear for centuries and reappear, / yet never to be caught . . . this feat which, like Herodotus, / I have not seen except in pictures . . . this strange animal with its miraculous elusiveness." She manages to mock credulity without discrediting it, for the "record . . . on the printed page" at the poem's end turns out ironically to be another poem, that anonymous verse from *Punch* magazine, copied into the Reading Diary of 1923, that describes the capture of the creature:

> Through flower and thorn Sir Unicorn
> With pavon high drew nigh
> Till magic hap upon her lap
> His mild wild head doth lie.[22]

"Sea Unicorns and Land Unicorns" displays the imaginative embroideries of our geographies, the adulteration of our knowledge, our reports and records, all our texts, with aesthetic fancies. Moore is displaying our cognitive enterprise as enriched from the very beginning by active imagination, so that half of what we "know" of the world is our own designs and fantasies. The object, in other words, is both an object and a reflection of our changing, subjective minds, a blend that for Moore did not undermine but made that much more interesting and imperative the artistic task of "exact perception." The poems suggest that we cannot learn of the world without learning of ourselves in it. And the division between objective and subjective, between outer and inner, begins to break down in a way that is going to open up new possibilities in the poems to come.

The task of presenting things of the world in some more objective way than before also moves figurative language into a new role in the poem. The single, centrally evaluative metaphor of the Carlisle years gives way in these "observations" to a variety of local metaphors; that is, to metaphors applied in passing to some part or aspect of the poem's scene. In "Melancthon," for example, the central metaphor of the elephant as "Black earth preceded by a tendril" is seconded by a series of discrete, local figures: the river mud as the "patina of circumstance," the elephant skin as "this piece of black glass through which no light / can filter," and the human being as "that tree trunk without roots." This variety of self-sufficient metaphors occasions the considerable variety of the poem's insights on circumstance, pride, power, self-absorption, depth—all unified here by the self-reflective persona. In "Melancthon" we begin to see the kind of internal transit from point to point that will characterize so many of Moore's poems of the twenties and thirties: each poem's subject becomes an arena for a relatively free play of perception and intelligence, for the adventure of seeing how many elements are offered up by the subject. The archly delivered verdict is giving way to a more relaxed examination, as is formally suggested by "Melancthon's" repeated spilling of the short, rhymed couplets into the longer, unrhymed lines.

The local metaphors that begin to appear in these Chatham and early New York poems also play a less conceptual and increasingly sensuous role. We can still find some evaluatively conceived images in and among the more purely descriptive ones in such a poem as "Novices," in which a thread of judgment—judgment of a type rather than of an individual—runs through the satiric presentation. Here the conceptual figures are applied to the novices—the "dracontine cockatrices," the "supertadpoles of expression" whose "suavity surmounts the surf"—while an impressive array of sensuous figures for color, texture, sound, and movement is deployed for the genuinely passionate expression of which the tadpole-novices are incapable: language "split like a glass against a wall . . . white with concussion . . . 'like long slabs of green marble' . . . 'crashing itself out in one long hiss of spray.' " Conceptual images perform a similar satiric function in "The Labours of Hercules," as the poem chafes at "those self-wrought Midases of brains" with their "fourteen carat ignorance," the "meet-me-by-moonlight maudlin troubadour," and the "snake-charming controversialists." But the criteria poems of this period already give precision and force to some of their exemplary objects by using sensuously conceived images of form and texture: the "snipe-legged hieroglyphic" of "When I Buy Pictures," "Poetry's" "immovable critic twitching his skin like a horse that feels a flea," and the "lion's ferocious chrysanthemum head" in "The Monkey Puzzle."

Poems that appear to have been nourished by the new environments in which the poet now moved make metaphoric translations out of what seems to be sheer delight in color, texture, and moving form:

<blockquote>

The Fish

wade
through black jade.
    Of the crow-blue mussel-shells, one keeps
    adjusting the ash-heaps;
        opening and shutting itself like

an
injured fan.

</blockquote>

"New York" is "starred with tepees of ermine," its "gilt coach shaped like a perfume bottle." And "Peter," the cat belonging to neighbors in St. Luke's Place, is presented part by part in a series of visually striking and cumulatively comic double exposures, making him look like all sorts of creatures other than a cat. He has "katydid legs above each eye," "shadbones regularly set about the mouth," a "prune-shaped head / and alligator eyes," "an eel-like extension of trunk into tail," and he springs "with froglike accuracy." The criterion in this poem, the "virtue of naturalness," is virtually smuggled in—and somewhat qualified—under the cloak of this metaphoric mode of description.

Thus Moore's turn in her thirties toward exploration of groups and types, even when it supports a value interest and not pure description, often releases metaphor from its earlier conceptual origin and evaluative function. As the syntax and texture of her poems become even more thoroughly objective, we shall have occasion to ask whether interest in value ever does vanish, indeed whether it *can* vanish from such verses, even when they seem to be wholly preoccupied with the factual dimensions of their subjects. The factual dimension is one aspect of objectivity, insofar as facts transcend the individual consciousness that comes upon them. Facts belong, or so we assume, to the public sphere of shared experience, while values may be more or less subjective. The complete ironic reversal of this distinction will not come about in Moore's work until the poems of the thirties. But her turn now in the twenties away from judgment of persons and toward description of things is probably the most liberating move she could have made at this time, for its domino effect, in releasing the poems' central images from a metaphoric task, sharpens the poetic speaker's eye for actualities. Or perhaps it was the other way around, that the newly accessible experiences weaned the poetry from its early judgmental bent. At any rate, metaphor has been diverted into a new role, and the actualities now seem to come crowding, en masse, as if observation is truly the natural and happy task for this time.

Moore's gravitation toward more objective materials and presentations is perhaps most evident in the appearance of the catalogue as a central feature of the Chatham and early New York poems. The earlier verses "A Jelly-Fish" and "To a Chameleon" were focused on one subject, whereas "The Fish" is a plural title, and the fish are the first of many things being compiled, one after another, into a composite picture. About half of the poems of this period incorporate lists of objects, persons, behaviors, or quotations. This exercise in extended parataxis, that is, in placing items side by side, one after the other, rather than in the dominating and subordinating relations of hypotaxis, is a direct reflection of Moore's new orientation toward value. The avoidance of hierarchy as a structural principle bespeaks her new preference for a report rather than a verdict.

Even in the pieces that consist almost entirely of catalogue, Moore's new sense of the plenitude of the world is rarely allowed to expand her poems into Whitmanesque inclusiveness. Diversity as an image for universality appears in "People's Surroundings" and "An Octopus," but there and elsewhere the principle of selection is always visibly at work. Thus Moore's procedure is only apparently inductive, for inspection will reveal either a notion or a rhythm underlying the make-up of the list. We have seen the pattern of antithetical metaphors that informs "Those Various Scalpels"; and "The Fish," published in the following year, is a carefully arranged meeting of opposites. An early draft and marginal note on one of the Chatham worksheets for this poem suggests the kind of ideas that were guiding its composition.[23] Originally arranged without stanza breaks, with each alternate line rhyming its first and last syllable, the early version contains about midway through it the following lines of thought on

> The turquoise sea
> Of bodies.
> Sincerity of edge, in
> Such recesses of the mind, we
> Find flowers entwined
> With bodies there.

In the margin of this passage about the mind, Moore has then pencilled in a further stage of thought:

> and
> Find beauty intertwined
>   with tragedy.

In its final version the poem's catalogue begins with flowerlike objects of beauty—

> the stars,

> pink
> rice-grains, ink-
>   bespattered jelly-fish, crabs like green
>   lilies, and submarine
>   toadstools

—and closes with the "defiant edifice" of the cliff, the implacable and wounded stuff of tragedy with

> all the physical features of

> ac-
> cident—lack
>   of cornice, dynamite grooves, burns, and
>   hatchet strokes.

But the tentative lines have been omitted that would have turned these things into an allegory of the mind or of beauty and tragedy. The objects are observed speaking for themselves. The poem is the water, with its colored delicacies and their verbs of motion, that "drives a wedge / of iron through the iron edge / of the cliff"; and while we may allegorize the subject, the poet has refrained from doing so.

"The Fish" is also a good illustration of the enlivening challenge that the plenitude of this period presents to the spatial imagination. The motion of the mussel-shells, starfish, jelly-fish, and crabs in the first part of the poem is not so much a narration of action in time as it is a description of characteristic and repeated movement: "one keeps / adjusting the ash-heaps," keeps opening and shutting, moving and sliding. We are still being offered a scene rather than an event. Likewise in "Dock Rats," the ongoing scenic movement is carried by the present participle, that adjectival verb qualifying a noun: the river "twinkling like a chopped sea," "the tug . . . dipping and pushing," and "the sea, moving the bulk- / head with its horse strength." These adjectival verbs add a certain element of movement to the spatial mode of perception. In the four middle stanzas on the sights of shipping, the main verb is always the simply listing copula "is . . . is . . . There is . . . There is." And yet Moore's arresting catalogue of ships gains a sense of muscular activity from the adjectival verbs that fill it—the "battleship like the two- / thirds submerged section of an iceberg"; the "steam yacht, lying / like a new made arrow on the stream"; the "ferry-boat—a head assigned, one to each compartment, making / a row of chessmen set for play."

In the longer version of "Poetry," too, Moore catalogues the genuine materials of poetry in such a way as to subordinate verb to noun: "Hands that can grasp, eyes / that can dilate, hair that can rise / if it must." Here again she presents ongoing action in the adjectival form of the present participle:

> elephants pushing, a wild horse taking a roll, a tireless wolf
> under
>
> a tree, the immovable critic twitching . . ..

The famous definition of poetry as "imaginary gardens with real toads in them" is a metaphor for the spatial imagination. In fact, one may well read this poem as a necessary reworking of the poet's own idiosyncratic relation to the term "poetry." In later years Moore remembered her "instinctive hostility to the word": "I disliked the term 'poetry' for any but Chaucer's or Shakespeare's or Dante's."[24] We may perhaps add Milton to this list, knowing her early familiarity with *Paradise Lost,* which her mother read aloud to her as a young girl. Moore herself admitted toward the end of her life that she could no longer remember where she got those gardens and toads that she placed in quotation marks in the poem, but Laurence Stapleton's suggestion suits the context of thought as aptly as my earlier suggestion. She recalls that the prototypical poetic garden is Milton's Paradise in which Satan, embodying evil, sits "Squat like a Toad, close at the ear of Eve."[25] Hence, even if verse has not the narrative grandeur of the old masters, Moore implies, it may still be considered "poetry" if it offers a comparable blend of the imaginary and the real, of the aesthetic and the ethical.

Even in the two cases in which Moore does appear to be working with some grandeur of dimension, "People's Surroundings" and "An Octopus," the work does not shift out of the descriptive into the narrative mode. The catalogue is still the pervasive way of handling the sense of multiplicity and variety. In both poems, additive juxtaposition piles object upon object, punctuated by pauses that move very slowly over the motionless scene. In the midst of "People's Surroundings," for instance, we come to a kind of epitome of the spatial image:

Bluebeard's Tower above the coral reefs,
the magic mouse-trap closing on all points of the compass,
capping like petrified surf the furious azure of the bay,
where there is no dust, and life is like a lemon-leaf,
a green piece of tough translucent parchment.

The moving surf is arrested, "petrified" into a metaphor for the motionless tower in contrast with the "furious azure of the bay," and life in this
still scene is indeed like a lemon-leaf, a piece of parchment, a space on
which to write.

The final extended roll call in "People's Surroundings" has just the quality of naming everything under the sun that is appropriate to its source in
Raphael's Horary Astrology.[26] Moore has selected items from the Astrology's inventory of professions and places appropriate to each of the plan-
ets, and she has rearranged these items into a series of gradually lengthen-
ing lists in the form "this, this, and this," a list of lists whose rhythm and
sense of inclusiveness builds slowly:

captains of armies, cooks, carpenters,
cutlers, gamesters, surgeons and armorers,
lapidaries, silkmen, glovers, fiddlers and ballad-singers,
sextons of churches, dyers of black cloth, hostlers and
                                    chimney-sweeps,
queens, countesses, ladies, emperors, travelers and
                                    mariners,
dukes, princes and gentlemen,
in their respective places—
camps, forges and battlefields,
conventions, oratories and wardrobes,
dens, deserts, railway stations, asylums and places where
                                    engines are made,
shops, prisons, brickyards and altars of churches—
in magnificent places clean and decent,
castles, palaces, dining-halls, theaters and imperial audience-
                                    chambers.

The naming moves along on the border between delight in the worldly
things and delight in the names themselves and often their ring of the
past, recording a world in both space and time. This poem's whole me-
lange of things is not, however, explicitly contained within one all-
encompassing consciousness. In fact, these surroundings share much of
the deceptive mystery of the world of Mt. Rainier in "An Octopus": both
worlds resist the "inquisitive intensity" of the observer. Thus rather than

presenting things as contents of an ongoing Whitmanesque consciousness, both personal and cosmic, Moore's namings and inventories tend to
increase the opacity or object-ivity of their objects. Her frequent refusal
to subsume the material of the poems under a speaker's subjective experience is probably the fundamental source of the arresting, non-narrated effect of what I have called her "spatial imagination."

The sobriety of much of "An Octopus" is largely maintained by the
steady movement and concentration of the catalogue's procedure through
the world of the mountain from glacier to firs to the minerals, animals, and
vegetation, to the human implications of the place, and finally back to the
glacier itself. This unusual combination of the observer's close perceptual
concentration and the sprawling lists of observed things, of namings and
qualifications, notations and asides—this blend of exactitude and endlessness is a self-challenging text par excellence. Dropping right and left, from
the first line to the last, those warnings about deception, prejudice, conceal-
ment, the "unimaginable," and the unspeakable, the poem proceeds, apparently undaunted, along its path of inspecting and inquiring, proceeds with
its program of art as exact perception. Moore here acknowledges the limits
of the phenomenological enterprise on which she has embarked. As Helen
Gardner puts it, this is not a world in which "the only alternative to certainty is total ignorance."[27] The inspection of appearances proclaims faith
in the search for knowledge, faith in the possibility of a knowledge that
takes skepticism as a starting point rather than as a roadblock.

Thus the poem consents to be transcended by its subject, the mountain, for among the elements there to be observed are the limit of observation, things "concealed in the confusion," and the bounds of language in
the face of "a beauty / of which 'the visitor dare never fully speak at home
/ for fear of being stoned as an impostor.' " The poet of "An Octopus" is
not that speechless visitor—although Moore personally might have been
one when she climbed on Rainier in 1922—but the recorder of the presence of such a visitor. The voice is not that of the romantic bearing unspeakable visions down the mountain but that of the secretary who assures us that visions of ineffable beauty are part of the natural, wild life of
the peak. The vision is there, but it is encapsulated in a methodical voice
and procedure.

Observation undaunted by its own awareness of deception is a Greek
procedure, a classical response, as Moore suggests in her forty-line passage on the "golden grasshoppers of Greece." "Like happy souls in Hell,"
the Greeks made clarity in the midst of obscurity, "resolving with be-
nevolent conclusiveness, / 'complexities which will remain complexities
/ as long as the world lasts.' " That any such resolution must be only temporary and fabricated seems to make it more, rather than less, of an ac-

complishment. The one exclamatory line that breaks through the patient sobriety of inspection is "Neatness of finish! Neatness of finish!" Both neatness and finish are the admitted province of the artist, who would make something finite out of endless material. To the catalogue of this mountain world that goes on indefinitely Moore stages a dramatic finish with a final "curtain of powdered snow." And the poem has identified such resolution not with romantic defiance or cognitive despair but with the Greek classical age and its acceptance of paradox.

The companion strategy of the catalogue is quotation, which presents verbal items ostensibly as directly as the list presents visual items. This practice, too, carries conflicting or mutually challenging implications. As we have seen, Moore's quotations differ in a general way from Eliot's and Pound's in that hers each offer us some unique or special phraseology, often from non-poetic sources, and are thus distinctly free of echo or literary allusion. Still, many of her most striking borrowings—"An Octopus / of ice," for instance—are not acknowledged as quotations in the poem, while some lines that are punctuated as quotations—"fond of the spring fragrance and the winter colors"—seem almost ordinary. In her "cabinet of fossils" passage in the *Reader* Moore explains, " 'Why the many quotation marks?' I am asked. Pardon my saying more than once, When a thing has been said so well that it could not be said better, why paraphrase it?"[28] Note that she speaks of quotation *marks*. She might well have smiled to herself as she wrote it, for source study of the poems often reveals what look like inexact or loosely rendered quotations, a provocative anomaly in the work of a poet so devoted to precision. We are not meant to overlook the qualifying "I think" in the prelude to the rendering of the Reverend Kellogg, "and I think I repeat his exact words." In fact, his exact words are usually not the point of Moore's quotations at all. One thing that perusal of the printed sources for "An Octopus" demonstrates is that the poet was engaged in an extensive process of rewriting those sources. As often as not, we are dealing with quotation as a formal appearance rather than as a literal practice. Quotation in Moore's text looks like repetition but often is really revision; it looks like transcription but is, in fact, transformation.

The source most frequently quoted in "An Octopus" is the Department of the Interior's 1922 *Rules and Regulations, Mount Rainier National Park*, a fifty-two page pamphlet describing the mountain itself, its wildlife, and the park's facilities and regulations.[29] The pamphlet is of composite authorship, one section written by a park ranger, one by an assistant biologist with the Department of Agriculture, and so on, but it is worded throughout with a degree of feeling and imagination remarkable for a rule book. Moore's title metaphor appears to have been appropriated from a section-heading and phrase on page 9 of the pamphlet: "A GLA-CIAL OCTOPUS . . . a snow-covered summit with great arms of ice." What Moore's own underlined copy of the pamphlet shows us is that not only did she copy into her poem numerous phrases from the pamphlet's text, tables, notes, and even its bibliography, but also that she actually composed some portions of her poem in the margins of the pamphlet. Here we can see her revisions of her source taking place literally between its lines. On page 11, for example, the pamphlet's author describes a scenic automobile approach to the park. Moore has underscored several phrases in that text and worked them through three handwritten versions of her lines 101–3, one at the top of the page and two in the right margin. She took "threads" from the account of the Nisqually River in one paragraph and "back and forth" from another paragraph on the mountain road; in yet another paragraph she cut "eternal" from "snows" by crossing out that word and the plural form, and she added the image of the snail-shell, presumably from her own observation (it does not appear in the pamphlet). Thus like a bricoleur she has constructed out of odds and ends of description the following half-used, half-new passage:

> the road "climbing like the thread
> which forms the groove around a snail-shell,
> doubling back and forth until where snow begins, it ends."

Her "quotation" is a new formulation of a prior text, a hybrid of creation and duplication.

For her description of the bluejay in the original version of the poem (ending thirty-two lines cut from the poem in 1951), Moore took similar liberties with the *Rules and Regulations'* note on page 24 on the behavior of the steller jay:

> Fond of human society, or, rather, of the good pickings that go with it. . . . A secretive nester. Comports himself with much dignity and the appearance of respectability and worldly wisdom, but is something of a villain in spite of that.

She reversed the order of the two sentences, altered some word choices, and telescoped the syntax to form her own lines:

> "secretive, with a look of wisdom and distinction, but a
> 		villain,
> fond of human society or the crumbs that go with it."

Moore's quotation, then, is a mixture of echo and artistry. Her quotation marks identify the poet at that point ostensibly as a transcriber rather than as an originator. The utterance is delivered not as primary utterance but as a transcript and therefore as secondary, as a record of words already used in the past. This appearance of used text also implies that the unquoted text is therefore original, whereas we can see from sources that the mixture of new and derivative material is more subtle and pervasive than could be shown by punctuation.

The romantic role of the poet as a visionary, as an original seer and sayer, appears to be subordinated by quotation to the non-romantic role of the poet as scribe, stenographer, recorder—as gifted technician like the "fabulous artificer" Daedalus, who constructs wings out of feathers and wax. The poet must, in fact, be both a visionary and a technician, but one role will often dominate the other. Moore is this Daedalian kind of artist, a bricoleur building a new text out of the fragments of old ones. But we should not forget that the whole point of the wings is that they fly. If the quotation marks tend to mask the poet's own voice behind the appearance of a borrowed voice, the poetic bricolage or assembled construct still serves a vision or utterance. The text has been selected, transcribed, revised, and recast in the service of a visionary utterance for which the poet simply declines exclusive credit. The voices and texts of our culture are also responsible for seeing and saying these things: the namings originate in and belong to all of us. And the poet fashions our poetry into poem after poem.

Moore's poetic quotation is also a way of indicating the sense of a difference between the words of the poet and the words that come from "outside" the poem, even though that difference has been partially overcome by the unseen revisions. The quotation marks are a visible threshold, a boundary dividing poetic discourse from the ordinary discourse which it borrows. Quotation opens a window in the poem onto language from outside it, language now included but demarcated. The quotation marks signal a shift in register from one text or voice to another which is enclosed in it—a voice breaking into the writing, a text recalled by a speaker, a voice ventriloquizing another voice, or one text framing another. Each level or type of language is shown by the quotation marks to be partial, divisible, portable, and dependent on the other modes of language from which it is kept visibly distinct. Thus quotation both blends and divides the two realms of discourse: it incorporates "nonpoetic" language into the poem, while demarcating that language from the poet's own words. Quotation appropriates everyday discourse into art yet refuses to naturalize it entirely; it insists on both inclusion and separation. Poetic and practical language are thus made to collaborate openly in the production of the poem.

By means of this open collaboration the tacit intertextuality of the literary product is made visible. The way in which the poem inevitably involves itself with other texts that precede and surround it is acknowledged there on the page. Thus instead of remaining a concealed element, intertextuality becomes part of the specific and displayed content of the poem. The three "serial" poems of 1923 and 1924 probably represent the epitome of this collaborative effect in Moore's verse, for their range of sources is as broad and varied as we will find it. "An Octopus" weighs the singular mountain in all its elusive grandeur not only against our fragmentary perceptions of it but also against the polyphony of our descriptions— the words of the workers of the Department of the Interior, Sir William Bell of the British Institute of Patentees, Francis Ward and M. C. Carey of the *Illustrated London News,* W. P. Pycraft, John Muir, John Ruskin, Clifton Johnson, W. D. Wilcox, Cardinal Newman, Richard Baxter, W. D. Hyde, and probably more than one anonymous voice—all the marshalled resources of a culture. Each instance of a "poetry" such as this represents a nucleus, a concentration of multiple lines in the network of public discourse, a bricolage which brings together various voices and texts in one poetic construct and thus makes many voices out of one and one voice out of many. The romance of the text, of textuality, its pursuit of a vision through many voices, is synthesized and realized within the enclosures of one writer's craft.

In September of 1924, when she was completing "Sea Unicorns and Land Unicorns" and still working on "An Octopus," Moore was also arranging with Scofield Thayer and The Dial Press for the publication of *Observations*. In response to Thayer's inquiry about the sources she was quoting in these poems,[30] she arranged to include "Notes" identifying the contributors to these and earlier poems, a practice she then continued throughout her career. In general theory, one may say that these notes have the same countervailing effects as the quotations do: they distinguish sources that are extrapoetic, emphasizing the otherness of the text that remains also outside the poem, while at the same time forming a bond between the poem and its contributory materials. The note suggests both the absence and the presence of these materials. It extends the poet's province of authority one step beyond the lines of the verse, and it extends the province of the verse itself, since we must carry its lines with us to the back pages' contextual quotations and references.

In Moore's major collections, the author's province is also extended a step beyond the notes by the inclusion of a "note on the notes." This is an initialed message in which M.M. or M.C.M. offers some remarks on the appended "provisos, detainments, and postscripts" or, in the case of *Selected Poems,* covers an absence of specific notes on her mother's contributions "where there is an effect of thought or pith in these pages." The poet as a personality is of necessity more or less hidden or eclipsed by the poem; yet through the notes she comes into partial view in the adjunct role of reader and collector sharing with us some of the stages of discovery that led to the poem. And in the notes on the notes the poet speaks to us in a first-person "I" that stands outside the notes themselves, just as the notes stand outside the poems. Thus the refinements of apparatus lead us, in a simpler and more literal way than the poems do, toward the impression of a person within or behind the work.

Moore's addenda, then, share with Eliot's notes to "The Waste Land" the general effect of creating a sense of an authorial presence through the implication of a reading consciousness in which the poem coalesced. We may suppose that the "I" in their notes is the voice of a persona once removed from the "I" in their poems, since the note form distinguishes itself from the poem in the act of referring to a portion of it. But in Moore's case the distinction between the note and the poem is even greater than in Eliot's. As "The Waste Land" references are invariably printed directly after the end of the last section of verse, it is not too difficult to consider them as part of the complete piece, continuing in a different key the thread of commentary on the relation of contemporary culture to its past. In her own collections, Moore's notes are generally separated from the verse. The half dozen exceptions to this all occur in later poems and drop their own hints about that time of her career. The separate placement of the notes is the most obvious indication of the separate role they play from the verse. In fact, the functions of the notes and the verse are more distinct than one might think at first.

Turning to Moore's notes during or after reading a poem generally sheds very little light on what the poem is doing or even the particular context in which it moves. Occasionally they answer a question rather cryptically, as does the note " 'NOTHING WILL CURE THE SICK LION . . .' / (page 86) / Carlyle." Often the note simply identifies the source or author of a quotation, but this information can leave one nonplussed and oddly distanced from the passage in question. We read, for instance, toward the beginning of "Marriage,"

> I wonder what Adam and Eve
> think of it by this time,
> this fire-gilt steel
> alive with goldenness;
> how bright it shows—
> "of circular traditions and impostures,
> committing many spoils,"

> requiring all one's criminal ingenuity
> to avoid!

The note to this passage reads: "Lines 14–15: '*Of circular traditions* . . .' Francis Bacon." This, however, does not begin to solve the ambiguity of whether it is marriage or just its impostures and spoils that one would avoid. We may wonder whether the aura of Bacon's reputation, his cultural image, might add something to the passage, but the note does not help us to decide what or how that might be. The full statement from which the phrase was lifted would perhaps be more helpful, and in this case the Reading Diary does provide the illuminating passage. Moore copied into it a long excerpt from "The Dilemma of Marriage" on D. H. Lawrence by Alyse Gregory in *The New Republic* for July 4, 1923, and she inserted a personal note that leads into the Bacon passage:

> It is too late! Mr. Lawrence must adapt himself / I wax now somewhat ancient . . . 30 yrs is a great deal of sand in the hourglass. I confess that I have as vast contemplative ends as I have moderate civil
>
> ends,
> for
>
> Encycl. Brittanica Bacon 136   I have taken all knowledge to be my province and if I could purge it of 2 sorts of errors, whereof the one with frivolous disputation, confutations and verbosities, the other with blind experiments and circular traditions and impostures hath committed so many spoils, I hope I shall bring in industrious observations. . . .[31]

This association of marriage with Bacon's enemies of "observations" is probably as candid evidence as we have that Moore was concerned about the possible effect marriage could have on her work, which was then just reaching its maturity. This diary passage highlights the cognitive theme of the poem, its theme of understanding, and thus leads logically into the next observation that even "psychology which explains everything / explains nothing." There was much that an explanatory note could have done here, had its task been to awaken more resonance in those lines of the text. Clearly its purpose, or at least its effect, is something quite other than that.

Thus, while the fact and form of the notes collectively create the impression of an authorial reader, each of Moore's notes taken singly has the opposing effect of cryptic opacity. Like the Bacon note, the shorter ones are nearly abrupt. To line 3 of "Sea Unicorns and Land Unicorns" we are given simply " 'Mighty monoceroses,' etc. Spenser," and to "Line 66:

'Impossible to take alive.' Pliny." Such brief identifications really tell us only that the poet read in Spenser and Pliny. She also read in Henry James's *English Hours*, C. H. Rodgers's *Adventures in Bolivia*, Violet A. Wilson's *Queen Elizabeth's Maids of Honour*, and *Punch* magazine, but what she actually made of these sources is all there for us to see in the poem. And the longer notes can have the disconcerting effect of taking us just that much longer and further away from the context of the poem. It is easy to forget that "Line 32: Apropos Queen Elizabeth's dresses, 'cobwebs, and knotts and mulberries.' 'A petticoat embroidered all over slightly with snakes of Venice gold and silver and some O's . . .' " also applies to the image in lines 76–77 of an "old celestial map" in which a unicorn was etched. Individually such notes are often merely curios. The fabric woven by the whole list taken together, however, makes its collective point, and that is the cumulative impression of the many-sided literate culture of which both the poet and the poems are products. In short, the notes appended are not so much to poems as to a book, to "the poetry." They are occasioned solely by the quotation marks, and there is no real reason to append many of them except to recognize this complicity of texts. They are a reflection of the process by which the literary artifact is fabricated out of the materials of its culture—out of the debris, so to speak, the odds and ends of discourse that converge in the literate mind. The notes close each of Moore's books by opening it out onto its own beginnings. Read thus cumulatively and for their own sake, as a last chapter, the notes may be seen as offering an indirect portrait of the artist and of the work of art in its nascent stages. They are one of the first and most direct and vivid images we have of the self-conscious intertextuality of the literature of our century.

Observations received the Dial Award for 1924, following in the footsteps of the work of Sherwood Anderson and T. S. Eliot's "The Waste Land." And so it was as a writer of considerable stature in the poetic community that Moore accepted in 1925, at Thayer's and Watson's insistence, the acting editorship of *The Dial*. She consulted closely with them during her tenure—with Sibley during the later years as Scofield's health deteriorated—and the judgment of these three at various times made the magazine a remarkable compendium of much of the very finest new work in letters and the arts from both sides of the Atlantic. Moore admitted to occasionally taking an editorial hand to a submission (Hart Crane was nowhere near as quiet about her suggestions as Eliot was about Pound's), and there were limits of propriety beyond which she could not bring herself to go, but for the most part the best contemporary work flowed through her hands into the pages of the monthly issues.

Moore remembered her years at *The Dial* fondly. "The compacted pleasantness of those days at 152 West Thirteenth Street; of the three-story brick building with carpeted stairs, fireplace and white-mantlepiece rooms."[32] She recalled among the staff "a constant atmosphere of excited triumph; and from editor or publisher, inherent fireworks of parenthetic wit too good to print." She fielded work from various foreign correspondents, among them Thomas Mann in Germany, Ortega in Spain, and Gorky in Russia. The goal she had always in mind was the magazine's stated one of "encouraging a tolerance for fresh experiments and opening the way for a fresh understanding of them."

A number of reasons have been offered for the closing of *The Dial* in 1929, any one of which could have been sufficient—Thayer's poor health, Sibley Watson's distance from the enterprise, and the diversion of his interest to photography. Moore once attributed the decision to chivalry, "because I didn't have time for work of my own," but years later Dr. Watson confirmed the financial motive for closing.[33] Moore continued to produce memorable prose during the time of her editorship, but no poems appeared between "The Monkey Puzzle" of 1925 and "The Steeple-Jack" of 1932. She did indeed feel the burden of her poetic silence during these years, as she wrote to Lola Ridge, who edited *Broom,* in 1921: "I have been very nearly just what you thought me—at the end of any vigorous output. You haven't been an editor without knowing that routine work is not exhausting and does not prey upon one—that strategic problems are the greatest drain upon one's vital force."[34]

The twenty-nine poems of the Chatham and early New York years had brought her out of the Carlisle obscurity, when she had difficulty getting work published, into the spotlight of avant-garde American letters. The appearance of her verse in *The Dial,* in broadside, and in book form mirrored and also influenced the literary currents of the time. These poems engage, in both subject and format, some of the larger aesthetic issues that have come to the fore in modern and post-modern writing: intertextuality, the nature of authorship, the poetic in relation to the extra-poetic, and the problem of how and what we can know. Moore's poetic silence at this point in her career suggests the importance to her of *The Dial* undertaking as a public forum for the working out of these issues, trends, and practices.

Moore's move in the direction of objectivity of statement is accompanied by her growing recognition of the impossibility of complete objectivity as an ideal of knowledge. There is no such thing as a purely "objective point of view," since the two terms are mutually contradictory. We are always somewhere on the mountain, on the shore, looking at something with eyes and minds immersed in memories and associations that, in helping us to see and understand, also partially blind and condition us. "Society's not knowing is colossal," Moore says in "The Monkey Puzzle," and yet one can still be "damned by the public" like Henry James in "An Octopus." The poems, like Bacon, "have taken all knowledge to be [their] province," and yet our judgments cannot and do not wait on complete understanding. The project of Moore's poems of the nineteen-twenties seems to be to embrace and embody this paradoxical human condition. The verses' expanding dimensions, their experiment with free verse forms, their departure from the "you" address in favor of the communal "we," their removal of metaphor to an adjunct role, and their exhibition of a vastly enlarged field of literal images, voices, and contributory texts—all these developments conspire to open the poems up to more complex issues of knowledge and value. And these very problems of knowledge and value, confronted in practice rather than in theory, will be at the heart of Moore's remarkable work of the nineteen-thirties.

4

Poetic Fact, Poetic Value

After the final issue of *The Dial* in July of 1929, Moore was able to turn her attention to a problematic situation at home and to her move into the apartment at 260 Cumberland Street in Brooklyn where she would live until her last years. She describes some of the circumstances of the move in a letter to Lola Ridge in mid-September: "Mother was dangerously ill for nine weeks and her recovery, my brother and I knew, was retarded by conditions at St. Luke's Place. So when he got us away from town he found the apartment we are now in, where we can have the use of a sunny roof, and have in our rooms a circulation of air that we could not have at St. Luke's Place. Besides, we are relieved from noise made by neighbors."[1]

Hildegarde Watson has captured for us a sense of the sanctuary quiet in which Moore was able to turn once again, with saved and renewed vitality, to the writing of poems: "Her long, dim apartment was lined with books, beginning in the hallway, and there were books in heaps in bookcases and on the floor. A crystal chandelier caught the light coming through windows that framed the spires of a church; her own Presbyterian church was just beyond. Her bedroom faced a courtyard in which grew a single ailanthus tree. Sometimes, when I was there she would hand me a pair of opera glasses and I would see, like a sapphire among the emerald leaves, a bluejay perched in 'a tree that grows in Brooklyn.' I never knew a place of such remoteness and utter simplicity."[2]

Remoteness is only part of the picture, of course, for while the Moores welcomed a more peaceful refuge from the "social and professional duties" of Manhattan, Marianne found life in Brooklyn quite stimulating enough.[3] The Pratt Institute Free Library, for instance, was a frequent temptation. "The row of new accessions near the circulation desk went to one's head, new books appearing almost simultaneously with the advertising. . . . One winter I attended so many 'presentations in the lecture room or auditorium that I was pitied at home for not being able to sleep in the building—on certain days absent morning, afternoon, and evening." There she heard Thornton Wilder lecture on literature and George Russell on extrasensory phenomena, listened to Stravinsky perform his own work, and on one memorable evening was barely missed when a snake, brought by a lecturer from the Staten Island Zoo, shot off his display branch into the lap of a boy near her in the front row. "I like living here," she said some years later. "Brooklyn has given me pleasure, has helped to educate me; has afforded me, in fact, the kind of tame excitement on which I thrive." And on which, needless to say, her new poems thrived.

Mrs. Moore soon regained her health and remained, as she always had been, Marianne's sternest critic and one of her steadiest sources of inspiration. The relationship between Marianne Moore and her mother may well be the most remarkable and influential mother-daughter relationship in the history of literature. It is a kinship that sustained one of the seminal voices of modern poetry, and so we may rightly feel curious about Mrs. Moore's character and ideas and their effects on the work that her daughter produced.

Mary Warner was born on April 11, 1862, and was educated—not a privilege to be taken for granted by girls then—at the Mary Institute in St. Louis, Missouri. Her marriage to John Milton Moore turned to misfortune when his nervous collapse left her alone to bring up their small son and newborn daughter. She survived this by repairing with the children to her father's home and then by working for many years as a teacher at the Metzger Institute in Carlisle. A woman of varied talents and no small initiative, she had developed her musical ability assiduously; one of her watercolors was always displayed on Marianne's living room wall; and she wrote a brief memoir of her father, the Rev. John Warner, after his sudden death in 1894.

In 1918 when Warner left Chatham, home-loving Mole's first wish was to return to her friends in Carlisle, but she gave in to her daughter's longing for the artistic community and opportunities of New York. And she left more than friends behind. Moore once mentioned to Donald Hall "a Steinway on which my mother had practiced ten hours a day. We gave it to a young girl when we moved to New York."[4] Nevertheless, she was able to join the literary enterprise with considerable gusto—she had "a passion for books, finding gems amid the debris of booksellers,"[5] and she was always supportive of Marianne's literary ambitions, even when she was severe about individual poems. She had strong personal and literary tastes, the core of which might be understood as a disdain for the facile.

Two anecdotes will serve to sketch her style of counseling the modern poet in her own household and another who asked for advice. In an undated Conversation Notebook entry just prior to October 7, 1915, Marianne recorded her own remark, "Now with what poems I have published and my general wellbeing, I could publish a book any time." "I wouldn't," was Mole's reply.

> Rat: "Never?"
> M: "After you've changed your style."
> Rat: "Huh! Then you would omit all these things I prize so much?"
> Mole: "Yes, they're ephemeral."[6]

An exchange such as this may well account in part for Moore's reluctance thereafter to publish a collection of her verse until, and even after, H. D. and Bryher finally took the matter into their own hands by printing her *Poems* without her knowledge or consent at The Egoist Press in 1921.

On the eve of publication of one of his books, William Carlos Williams wrote to Moore for advice on whether to title his volume simply *Al Que Quiere* or to add a subtitle.[7] Moore's handwritten draft of her reply, with all its deletions, revisions, and shorthand, echoes a lively dialogue between her and her mother. "There is no doubt in my mind but that Al Que Quiere or the Pleasures of Democracy is the better title for the book," she begins. "Al Que Quiere is succinct and a beautiful title . . . but the length of the conglomerate title is more than compensated for by its rhythm and incisiveness. Yours sincerely." Then she launches into two postscripts detailing her mother's contrasting view of the matter. It is a passage that suggests the values that Mrs. Moore may well have been encouraging in her own daughter's work:

> Notwithstanding my own opinion I cannot refrain from giving you my mother's comments. She thinks Al Que Quiere the better title for its beauty attracts even where not a word of Spanish is understood and involuntary curiosity will lead people to go further and find what the book is about while the other title gives the superficial the impression of knowing all that it is about and a book wh is approached without curiosity has something to overcome at the outset. And some might think the second title a literal trans of the first, thus making the first title superfluous. P.S. My mother thinks that the people who would read yr book wld be more attracted by something elusive than by something bald.[8]

Mrs. Moore was as demanding of every audience, however personal, as she was of Williams's would-be readers. She was a deeply pious woman who did not stint at coaching Warner in the writing of his sermons or at admonishing Marianne's friends in the most explicitly Christian terms for their behavior. For example, she wrote Lola Ridge a very long, kind, but firmly exhortatory letter on the religious morality of accepting gifts of money.[9] It is little wonder that in her verse Marianne became a virtuoso of the ever-changing tones and terms of the moral voice.

Elizabeth Bishop has captured the memorable quality of Mrs. Moore's speech: "her sentences were Johnsonian in weight and balance. She spoke more slowly than I have ever heard anyone speak in my life."[10] Her aphoristic piety is clearly one of the foreground voices in her daughter's poems, and Moore recognized this by noting in her postscript to *Selected Poems* that "in my immediate family there is one 'who thinks in a particular way;' and I should add that where there is an effect of thought or pith in these pages, the thinking and often the actual phrases are hers." Laurence Stapleton has detailed the process by which "In Distrust of Merits" was virtually born out of the Conversation Notebook in which Marianne recorded her mother's attempts to come to terms with the problem of World War II.[11] When Marianne read aloud a very witty remark from the Faber catalogue, Mole's response was, "Oh, the mind is an enchanting thing!"[12] The daily presence of such artfully spoken prose must have gone a long way to heightening the poet's enchantment with the rhythmic resonance of mottoes and aphoristic sallies.

It is important to remember, however, that for all the credit Moore gave her mother as a silent collaborator in the literary enterprise, it was Mole's personal example and spirit that she valued above all. "She advantaged me more than by exciting texts, when she remarked under crushing disappointment, 'Sursum corda; I will rejoice evermore.' "[13] The energy of affirmation that permeates so many of the poems was occasionally quite literally drawn from her mother, as Moore attests in a letter of the forties: " 'Satisfaction is a lowly thing how pure a thing is joy.' (I got the idea from Mole.) Am worse than a rodent about appropriating,—as you know."[14] The effects of this intense but often productive relationship become even clearer in contrast with the work of the later years, when the poems were subjected to its crucible only in memory.

Moore's seven-year poetic silence was broken by the nineteen astonishing new pieces appearing over the years 1932 through 1936. Midway through this period, in the summer of 1934, Moore and T. S. Eliot were preparing via transatlantic mail for Faber's edition of her *Selected Poems*. Eliot suggested that the volume open with her most recent and challenging poems, the ten pieces from "The Steeple-Jack" through "Nine Nectarines and Other Porcelain," including "The Jerboa," "The Plumet Basilisk," "The Frigate Pelican," and "The Buffalo." Moore answered him, "Your congregation of animiles at the front is wiley in the extreme."[15] Her newly-coined collective term "animiles" means literally "pertaining to animals," but it is also loosely perhaps an echo of something like "Anglophile," the form of affinity. Since Moore used this term to cover her five animal and five non-animal subjects together, we might justfiably extend it to cover also the rest of her verses of these years, many of which focus on animals. Virtually all of her poems appearing in 1932–36 explore common forms and concerns, are bounded by another poetic silence from 1936 until 1940, and are visibly distinguishable from her earlier work of the twenties and from her later work of the forties.

One formal pattern that came and went during the thirties is the set or cluster of related poems. "The Steeple-Jack," "The Student," and "The Hero" came out together in *Poetry* and *Selected Poems* as "Part of a Novel, Part of a Poem, Part of a Play." "The Buffalo" and "Nine Nectarines and Other Porcelain" were first printed as "Imperious Ox, Imperial Dish." And four poems growing out of a trip to Virginia—"Virginia Brittania," "Smooth Gnarled Crape Myrtle," "Bird-Witted," and "Half Deity"—were collected in *The Pangolin and Other Verse* under the title "The Old Dominion." The expansion of the later "observations," the same imaginative move through plenitude toward larger wholes that culminated in the long "serial" poems, appears to be carried over here in the thirties' three clusters. These titles and groupings did not last; Moore soon dropped them when reprinting the poems, and she returned by 1940 to the basic unit of the single, lyric-length poem. Yet these transient clusters are suggestive of a larger conception or overall project linking the individual animiles.

Moore's ongoing project in her verse of this period, as at other times in her career, may have resulted from a deliberate effort, a set of conscious choices. Or it may be that a semi-conscious preoccupation, even an unconscious tendency, once more shaped the final products into as cohesive a group as the work of the two periods we have already looked at. I shall call it a project, then, in whatever degree of consciousness, as a way of emphasizing that poetry is an ongoing enterprise as well as an institution. Moore's project may be preliminarily described as an effort to push past our century's early positivist ideal of cognitive certainty and its attendant polarization of the factual and non-factual dimensions of our discourse. This project, or at least this effect, manifests itself in several new, pervasive characteristics in her poems of the thirties. We find here a significant and nearly total disappearance of the poetic speaker's self-referential "I," a return from free verse to stanzaic and rhyme patterns, a proliferation of local, complex, sensuously conceived metaphors, an even more frequent insistence on facts and information than in the later "observations," and a featuring of traditional emblems and mottoes as distinctive forms of spatial imagery and quotation. At the same time, these new poems continue to incorporate certain innovations of the preceding poems—their length and inclusiveness, their catalogues, quotations, notes, and their interest in forms of knowledge—in such a way as to confirm our impression that the animiles are an extension and refinement of the move toward objectivity. We shall see how the positivist distinction between the factual and the non-factual dissolves as Moore's poetry appropriates some of the prerogatives of science.

What lies behind the clustering of these thirties poems into stanzas and into sets is a shift in the role of the poet. The shift is most clearly signalled by the poetic speaker's studied avoidance of the self-referential "I." This pronoun occurs with its normal frequency during these years' verses, but in almost no case is it used directly by the poetic voice itself. Moore was always more careful than many poets about inserting a first-person self explicitly into the center of her verse. In the various stages of her career, anywhere from one-third to two-thirds of her poems use the pronoun "I." For example, it occurs in a third of the later "observations," in half of the animiles of the thirties, and in two-thirds of the poems of the early forties.[16] What is distinctive in the work of the period at hand is its adoption of a mediated first-person form, that is, of a quoted or internally set off form of nearly every instance of "I." Gone is the central speaker of "Melancthon" saying "I do these / things which I do, which please / no one but myself"; of "Poetry" declaring "I, too, dislike it"; and of "Marriage" musing "I wonder what Adam and Eve / think of it by this time." In the animiles there are only three instances of such an authorial "I." One is parenthetical, "as I have said," in "The Plumet Basilisk"; one is the aphoristic ending of "Half Deity," "His talk was as strange as my grandmother's muff"; and one occurs in "Old Tiger" in "you / see more than I see but even I / see too much." The I/eye pun here undercuts the simple self-reference, and as a composition of 1918, "Old Tiger" will also offer other contrasts to the poems of this period.[17]

Virtually every other instance of the first person singular occurring in these pieces is enclosed in some form of direct or indirect quotation. Some are explicitly attributed to another speaker locally identified in the poem. The title subject of "The Hero" is quoted in the last stanza,

> It is not what I eat that is
> my natural meat,
> the hero says,

just as Joseph and the frock-coated Negro have been quoted before him. "Walking-Sticks and Paper-Weights and Water Marks" presents a "bold, outspoken gentleman" who "says modestly, 'This is my taste, it might not be another man's.' " That poem ends with the song lines, " 'On the first day of Christmas / my true love he sent unto me. . . .' " And in "The Pangolin" it is a generic man, "the self, the being we call human" who

> says to the alternating blaze,
>   "Again the sun!
>   anew each day, and new and new and new,
>   that comes into and steadies my soul."

The effect of such quoted first-person singulars is to enclose the directly self-expressive voice within a limited portion of the poem rather than letting it be the voice of the whole poem. The lyrical self is preserved, yet it is removed from the center of the poem. The lyrical mode of utterance is kept and yet is presented as one more item among others, and the poem that frames them all can emerge as a whole out of the lyrical mode.

By encapsulating the lyrical voice into a reported line or two, these verses present subjective self-expression as an object, as an occurrence in the public world. In "Pigeons" the poet appraises one message carried by a bird: " 'So please write me and believe that I / am yours very truly;' fine words those." The combined ingenuousness and formulaic quality of the message is heightened as the "words" are displayed for inspection. The framing of the I as "I" is a framing of the subjective self as words. The effect of this enclosure is not to reduce the sense of self or cancel it, for it is still present, but to highlight its expressive forms. Like "So please write me" in "Pigeons," these quoted first-person passages often have a simplicity of diction and a personal, inner quality that is very different from the multisyllabic abstractions and technicalities which Moore also occasionally quotes. They are expressions of feeling, as in "Smooth Gnarled Crape Myrtle,"

> —this bird
> which says not sings, "without
>   loneliness I should be more
>   lonely, so I keep it,"—half in
> Japanese.

The words before and after the quotation marks qualifying how the passage is delivered make us pause and reflect on it; they make, as Shelley put it, "familiar objects be as if they were not familiar."[18]

By not enveloping the material of her poem explicitly in the consciousness of a speaker, Moore gains a sense of perspective on the subjectively cast material that it includes. This sense of perspective can become part of the "message" of a poem, as we can see in "The Frigate Pelican," which brings out the paradoxes in the relation of the poet, as artist and as person, to other people. The "unconfiding frigate-bird" is compared with the artist Handel who also "hides / in the height and majestic / display of his art." Both are ironically concealed in their display. The poet appears to have a special understanding of this bird who "looks down and observes" (always a weighted verb for Moore) the lowlier creatures "keeping house all their lives in the crack of a / crag with no view from the top." These are the "less limber animals" whose mottoes include "Make hay. Keep the shop. I have one sheep." But in the last quarter of the poem, the poet turns and separates herself from that portrait of the artist looking down on the rest of us from a height. The loner's motto is framed by quotation, " 'If I do well I am blessed / whether any bless me or not,' " and then immediately the poem uses the communal "we" to include its own speaker among the common earthbound mortals: "We watch the moon rise / on the Susquehanna," while in contrast the artist-loner "wastes the moon."

Thus "The Frigate Pelican" shows us Moore's concern with the nature of romanticism and the relation of her work to some romantic values. She overturns the popular conception of romanticism, one which led T. E. Hulme to identify it with "metaphors of flight" and yearning for the infinite,[19] with her own romanticism:

In his way
this most romantic bird flies
to a more mundane place, the mangrove
swamp to sleep. He wastes the moon.

The bird takes flight again but not until he has been distinguished grammatically from the poet. Moore recognizes the "exclusion" from which the artist observes earthly life. As the original text in *Selected Poems* puts it, "It is not retreat but exclusion from / which he looks down." But her poem also marks off the loner's "I" from the rest of the text and includes the poetic voice in the general "we" who are romantic in a lesser way, gazing upward at unearthly beauty rather than looking down on earth. This release of the poem as a whole from the lyrical mode of expression preserves the tension between exclusion and inclusion of the artist. It makes the poem explicitly a vehicle for our observation of the artist-loner rather than a vehicle for the artist-loner's self-expression, which of course it implicitly is. The poet writes paradoxically both as a poet and as a person.

The true lyrical voice in Moore's poetry will not reappear until the forties, fifties, and sixties. The force and consistency with which the speaker's personal "I" will return in 1941 suggests that its absence in the animiles is indeed deliberate, or is at least the outcome of some larger intention, the push toward a radical objectivity. This project involves the fundamental shift in the role of the poet from the speaking persona of the earlier poems to the new persona here of the personally speechless poet. The early poetic voice that responds personally by expressing the views and feelings of the self gives way here to the poet as an artificer who records, designs, and textualizes the materials of the culture in a poetic way. The sense of the poet as a speaking person changes to a sense of the writer as a craftsman. Just as the techniques of catalogue, quotation, and notes continue to create the effect of subjectivity overcome, so the suspension of the "I" in quotation marks and the increasingly elaborate stanzaic and rhyme patterns announce poetry as a project of construction and schemata. The poet comes across not, as Charles Olson puts it, as "the private-soul-at-any-public-wall,"[20] a voice of the Egotistical Sublime in modern dress, but rather as the silent draftsman, as the agent of the formalization of the literary product. This product is not created romantically out of one individual's privileged soul and insights but is an artifact for which the writer is in one sense just a vehicle. The product is made to be textually recognizable as verse, to exhibit on the page the graces and ingenuities of pattern in which other language-uses take much less interest. But non-textually, as spoken or heard art, these poems resist the customary sounds of poetry. In her patterns and themes of this time, Moore's heightened concern with artifice is bound ironically to an equally heightened concern with its opposite, nature.

In her work of the thirties Moore has revived the format of syllabic stanzas which she had begun to use in many of her earlier "observations." We can go back and watch the appearance of this format in poems like " 'Sun!' " and "Critics and Connoisseurs" of 1916, supplanting the metrical form of the earlier poems. And then in the long 22- and 32-syllable lines of "England" and "A Graveyard in the Middle of the Sea," we can see the patterned stanzas being rearranged into the irregular lines of free verse. Moore's reinstatement of the syllabically measured stanza, blended or contrasted with meter at will, is an assertion of pattern that preserves the natural rhythms of language in a more radical way than is usually realized in poetry.

Metrical regularity demands that language be composed by the poet in one of the audible systems of stresses which produce the lilt or formal rhythm of our traditional poetry. Even though English is a naturally accentual language, people do not normally speak or think in iambic pentameter or Alexandrines. As Paul Fussell points out,

> to present them speaking metrically is to transform them from creatures of nature into creatures of art. And when it is the poet's voice that we hear speaking metrically, the meter announces or implies his vatic role, just as meter tends to invest with a mysterious air of authority and permanence the words that assume its patterns.[21]

This vatic or prophetic voice, what Moore called "poetry as divine fire,"[22] is not absent from her work, but it is released extremely sparingly, and one will not find it in her usual rhythms. English poetry from Chaucer to Milton to the romantics has traditionally championed its humanistic and spiritual values through, or at least in collusion with, the music of an accentual medium. And hence we may come to feel with Hugh Kenner that "metric is a system of emphases, centered in human comfort, human hope."[23] The music and thus authority of the sustained iambic voice seem, like Matthew Arnold, to assure us that poetry's elevation and beauty will continue to meet our spiritual needs and aspirations even when religious doctrines fail to do so. Modern poets like Yeats and Eliot have at times richly exploited the auras of traditional meters and rhyme by approaching a spiritual vacuum with the sense of a prophetic voice. But anyone coming to Moore's work expecting to find the reassurances of traditional metric music will be disappointed, for the purpose of her prosody, as we shall see, is to accommodate a wholly different kind of rhythm.

What is visually clear in these poems of the thirties is the repeated unit of the indented stanza. These units are constructed on some of the same principles as the indented stanzas of, say, Donne, Herbert, Keats, and Tennyson. They are a mixture of long and short, end-stopped and enjambed lines, with indentations determined by rhyme and sometimes by line length and symmetry. They are not made, as Kenner suggests, merely with "the left margin indented according to complex rules which govern the setting of tabulator stops,"[24] nor are they even "conceived in a typewriter," as Moore's many handwritten worksheets attest. The symmetry of the repeatable unit has been a characteristic of our poetry for centuries, from *rime royal* to rhymed couplets to romantic odes, and Moore continued to write in visually duplicated stanza forms long after all the "fiddle" about her syllables drove her to repudiate that approach.

The non-syllabic stanzas of 1965's "The Mind, Intractable Thing" are quite similar in appearance to the syllabic stanzas of 1933's "Camellia

Sabina," and both poems bear visual similarities to Donne's "The Canonization" and to Tennyson's "Mariana." Symmetry on the printed page does not by itself reveal whether the verse is metrical or syllabic or just uniformly shaped. One needs to read the poem while listening for a regularity of stress, or one needs to say its words while counting their syllables. And while meter will make itself more or less felt to the ear of the general reader, a syllabic pattern will not. It is true that we may count the syllables in line after line and discover numerical patterns in Moore's work of these middle years; but this counting procedure is quite antagonistic to even the simplest reading for sense, as anyone is aware who has sat tapping out syllables on the fingertips. And so while metrical verse organizes its language into audible patterns, syllabic verse, by not imposing an audible pattern, accommodates the natural rhythms of spoken and written language. Moore's syllabic practice, in other words, is a way of declining the metrically-invoked vatic or prophetic role of the poetic speaker as a creature of art, a way of avoiding the auras of mystery and authority often surrounding the traditionally metric voice. The inaudible syllabic measure has the effect of returning her words to the domain of creatures of nature, of ordinary people speaking and writing in their usual and memorable ways. Thus Moore's unheard syllabic procedure joins her unaccented rhymes in providing sub-sensory patterns that remove the "tunes" from the verse and push the Wordsworthian project of ordinary language in poetry beyond diction and tone into rhythm. "Combine with charmed words certain rhythms," she wrote, "and the mind is helplessly haunted."[25]

In sum, three things are happening simultaneously in the stanzaic patterns Moore resumes in the thirties. The poem as a text printed on a page looks like a series of traditionally formed, indented stanzas; invisibly and inaudibly a syllabic plan and rhyme scheme are imposing unobtrusive order; and the poem as read or spoken by a voice moves with the "unpoetic" naturalness that has become one of Moore's unnerving and haunting trademarks. Indeed, the longer and more intricate the syllabic pattern becomes, the less discernible it is and the more it releases our reading of the poem into the voice's everyday rhythms. It is easy to note the rhymed, pentasyllabic match in the concise opening of "The Jerboa" (original version):

> A Roman hired an
> artist, a freedman
>   to make a cone.

But it is astonishing finally to discover that in "Pigeons" there actually is a strict pattern, a twenty-four line series of 8, 11, 6, 8, 4, 12, 7, 8, 9, 8, 8,

5, 9, 10, 8, 6, 6, 5, 7, 8, 8, 12, 6, and 9 syllables repeated five times over without deviation. When Moore takes pains to distinguish her own practice from the romantic conception of the oracular poet, she is not being coyly modest:

> one thinks of poetry as divine fire, a perquisite of the gods. When under the spell of admiration or gratitude, I have hazarded a line, it never occurred to me that anyone might think I imagined myself a poet.[26]

When she refers to "my observations, experiments in rhythm, or exercises in composition,"[27] she is redefining the task of the poet. One might say that it was Eliot's acceptance of the oracular possibilities for the poet that led him early to write of emptiness in the unreal city; that it was Moore's declining of the prophetic role that led her to write of plenitude in the actual streets and newspapers. Given the complementary nature of their positions, their mutual admiration is gratifying.

Thus in usually avoiding the meter that would make the poetic voice more "aesthetic," Moore has restricted the poet's artifice to the textual dimension of the work. The stanzaic text prepared for the eye crosses the discoursing voice heard by the ear: "pattern intersects utterance," as Hugh Kenner puts it.[28] This crossing or counterpoint of the textual design and the flow of the voice is particularly apparent in passages where it involves an unusual line break. Critics often delight in demonstrating the oddities created by what they see as Moore's apparent disregard of the line as a unit of sense or even of rhythm. Excerpts from "The Buffalo" like "have significance? The" or like "foot horn-spread—decreased" or like "hump; to red-" seem to be easy evidence of the "implacable arbitrariness" with which Kenner suggests that the syllabic schema has been imposed.[29] And he adds, "the lines obey no rhythmic system the ear can comprehend." This may be true of the isolated line, but we should also recognize that the syllabic schema itself for each poem originates as an outgrowth of the natural pattern of utterance in what I call the "model stanza." Moore explained this to Pound in 1919: "I have occasionally been at pains to make an arrangement of lines and rhymes that I liked repeat itself, but the form of the original stanza of anything I have written has been a matter of expediency, hit upon as being approximately suitable to the subject."[30] Forty years later she described the same procedure in an interview with Donald Hall: "I never 'plan' a stanza. Words cluster like chromosomes, determining the procedure. I may influence an arrangement or thin it, then try to have successive stanzas identical with the first."[31]

In the poems of the thirties, which have been less revised than many of those of the twenties, we can see the words of the opening or closing model stanza clustering fairly naturally into a configuration of syncopated sense and rhyme. The model stanza for "The Buffalo," for instance, shows Moore's fondness for the unaccented, immediate rhyme:

> The Indian buffalo,
> led by bare-legged herd-boys to a hay
> hut where they
>   stable it, need not fear comparison
>   with bison, with the twins,
>   indeed with any
>   of ox ancestry.

We can now see that the peculiar excerpt "hump; to red-" is part of a formal quotation or echo of the light rhyme quickly rung between long and short lines:

>   or zebu-
> shape, with white plush dewlap and warm-blooded
> hump; to red-
>   skinned Hereford. . . .

What Kenner calls the "grid of numerical rules"[32] is really a formal pattern extracted from the model stanza, a stanza in which the words arranged themselves "like chromosomes" in a grammatically natural and intriguing way and in a complete unit. This formal pattern, then, is not just a set of numbers, like "The Buffalo's" 6-10-3-10-6-5-5 syllable count; it is a palpable pattern of long and short lines and rhymes which set up a rhythm of their own, here a quick light rhyme ("ox's" with "yes") followed by a delayed, heavier one ("beast" with "decreased"):

> The modern
> ox does not look like the Augsburg ox's
> portrait. Yes,
>   the great extinct wild Aurochs was a beast
>   to paint, with stripe and six-
>   foot horn-spread—decreased
>   to Siamese-cat-
>
>   Brown Swiss size or zebu-
> shape, with white plush dewlap and warm-blooded
> hump; to red-
>   skinned Hereford or to piebald Holstein. Yet
>   some would say the sparse-haired
>   buffalo has met
>   human notions best.

The reader's eye and ear together can sense the pattern of the whole in which the odd isolated lines make formal sense.

The typical poem that Moore wrote during the thirties sometimes opens and always closes with a model stanza in the natural grammatical unit of a sentence. The body of the poem repeats the formal design of this model, maintaining it through grammatical sequences that are independent of the design until, as in a musical piece, the model is revealed or repeated by the last stanza as a form of closure. So really what happens, from the point of view of composition, is that the utterance creates a pattern as a unit; the voice of the poem then carries on its discourse through and in contrast to the pattern, in tension with it, until the utterance ends up again harmoniously identified with the pattern. The expediency or suitability of the model stanza's form to the material itself is clearer in some poems than in others. The jerboa's movements "by fifths and sevenths / in leaps of two lengths" are reflected in the 5- and 7-syllable lines, each pair with an immediate rhyme, opening and closing the stanza. "The Frigate Pelican," which was deprived of its closing model stanza when it was radically cut for *Collected Poems,* also shows in its 1934 version a virtually imitative relation of stanza form to content. The stanzaic pattern decreases from the longer 15-12-11-9-9 to the quicker 7-9-7-6 syllables per line, enacting the shift of emphasis from large heaviness to nearly disembodied lightness:

> The reticent lugubrious ragged immense minuet
>   descending to leeward, ascending to windward
>   again without flapping, in what seems to be
>   a way of resting, are now nearer,
> but as seemingly bodiless yet
>   as they were. Theirs are sombre
>   quills for so wide and lightboned a bird
>   as the frigate pelican
>   of the Caribbean.

It is a form "uniting levity with strength" just as the bird does.

But the pattern may be more subtly suggested by syntax and verbal rhythm alone. In either case, the rarity of end-stopped lines gives any one end-stop a special force amid the usual enjambments, and likewise, the identity of pattern with utterance in the model stanza becomes a moment of heightened rhetorical force after the long process of intersection and interweaving in the body of the poem. No wonder Moore became impatient with her syllable-counting critics, for the mathematics of it really is secondary to the observations it grows out of, contrasts with, and finally heightens. As Moore once remarked to Laurence Stapleton, "Everyone writes in syllables!"[33] But few writers have perceived the formal possibilities opened up by the approach.

Artifice in general plays quite a different role in these complex studies of the thirties than it did, say, in the critical epigrams of the Carlisle years. The compact forms and audible rhyme of those earlier poems lent a certain deft finish and authority to the personal opinion of the poetic speaker. Directness and visibility of technique underscored the point of view being expressed. But in the longer verses that test objectivity, the "art" of the poem is both more subtle and more elaborate. The identity, then counterpoint, then resolution of pattern and utterance is an interplay of the natural and the artificial. It is a formal interplay that affirms the distinction and compatibility of these two poles, nature and art. Moore was as fascinated by human artifacts and technologies as she was by animals and the natural world. And the relation between the natural and the cultivated or man-made becomes a central preoccupation during this period. "The Jerboa," for instance, shows how man's art has often simply imitated nature: the contrived pine-cone fountain "passed / for art." The poem also shows how nature ironically in turn seems to imitate our arts in the jerboa's "pillar body erect / on a three-cornered smooth-working Chippendale / claw." The two subtitled parts of this poem—the Egyptians' "Too Much" and the jerboa's "Abundance"—are presented less as opposites and more as complements to one another, two kinds of plenty. The link between the two parts is additive rather than exclusive: "one would not be he / who had nothing but plenty." Moore's fascination with man's reproductions of nature is consonant with her own artful reproduction of the jerboa, and her poem is thereby identified also with the realm of Egyptian invention, of the artifact that copies something natural. The poem observing those artifacts imitates them as well by being itself a crafted reproduction. The poem imitates art as well as nature and reveals these "contrarieties" as also complements of one another.

This same complementary relation between artifice and nature is brought out in "Camellia Sabina." Structurally, Moore appears to be contrasting the painstakingly cultivated, indoor camellia of the first four stanzas with the simple, outdoor Bolzano grapes, the "food of a wild mouse" in the last four stanzas. But the link is again inclusive: "A / food grape, however—'born / of nature and of art.' " And the Bolzano grape is more immediately contrasted with the Bordeaux wine that "accomplishes nothing and makes the soul heavy." Thus we have the quartet of the cultivated "Sabina born under glass," the Bordeaux plum, the "sixty-four million red wines," and the Bolzano food-grapes. The poem will not be tied down to an indictment of the cultivated glass-enclosed flower and wine versus a celebration of the mouse's (a nickname for her mother) food-grape in the green vineyard. The speaker says that the flower and the plum together make "a fine duet," just as the food-grape is "born of nature and of art."

This complementary relation of nature and art is perhaps most explicit, and enigmatically implicit, in "Nine Nectarines and Other Porcelain," a poem alternately about the nectarine itself and about the nine nectarines enamelled on a porcelain plate. The speaker commends her source for refusing the strict distinction between the cultivated and the wild origin of the fruit: "But was it wild? / Prudent de Candolle would not say." Both the nectarine and the best "china-making" come from China, as does our term "china" for porcelain dishes. The natural fruit and the artifact and our word for the artifact all have a common origin. It is because their race " 'understands / the spirit of the wilderness' " that they excel in this art: "It was a Chinese who / imagined this masterpiece." Thus all three of these poems raise the issue of nature and art not to drive a wedge but to uncover the complicity between them.

Moore's interest in this complicity is reflected not only in her blend of natural utterance and artful pattern but also in her imagery, in the distinctive way she now develops of yoking the literal with the figurative, the actual with the imagined. We have seen how the poems of the twenties broadened their focus to include a wide variety of actual, literal objects. The central, conceptual, evaluative metaphor was then replaced by a series of sensuously conceived and locally applied figures, whose function was to present rather than to judge. This trend continues in the animiles but with the significant appearance, indeed the profusion, of complex, hyphenated, adjectival metaphors. We see this form in "The Steeple-Jack's" "sugar-bowl shaped summer-house," in "The Plumet Basilisk's" "snuff-brown" lizard, "clamshell-tinted spray," and "porcupine-quilled palm-trees," in "Pigeons' "

> lead-colored ostrich-
> plumes a third of an inch long, and
> needle-fine cat-whisker-fibred battleship-
> gray lace

and in the

> two-colored sea-pie-patterned semi-swan-
> necked magpie-pigeon, gamecock-legged
> with long-clawed toes.

Moore has always used hyphenated forms, but in the thirties these multiple metaphors proliferate until, as in "Pigeons," they almost produce a distinctive rhythm of their own.

These hyphenated attributive figures tend to load the literal image with competing images, so that the noun is in visual tension or double exposure with its adjectives. This double exposure can be seen, for example, in Moore's use of a favorite figure, the porcupine's quills. "The Monkey Puzzle" embodies a "porcupine-quilled, complicated starkness," the figure concretizing an abstraction. "Peter" the cat has whiskers that "droop or rise in unison like porcupine-quills," here with the comparative form of the simile. And "The Plumet Basilisk's" directly metaphoric "porcupine-quilled palm-trees" places two objects into the visual frame as one, so that one of them is perceived *through* the other. As Max Black puts it, the metaphor acts as a "filter," in that it "suppresses some details, emphasizes others—in short, organizes our view."[34] This filtering has two effects. First, the literal object is overlaid by an imagined object that is meant to help reveal it; the actuality is screened, even partially censored, through an inventive vision, so that the thing is handed over to us in vivid but qualified form. The adjective interferes somewhat with the simple noun, for the metaphor vivifies by qualifying its object. Thus "art as exact perception" is not a simple process but a complex and mediated one—cultivated, art-ful. Second, the density of Moore's hyphenated qualifiers often has the feel of literary rather than of ordinary language. We can see this in the highly musical "hothouse" language of "Camellia Sabina":

> the screw-top
> for this graft-grown briar-black bloom
> on black-thorn pigeon's-blood,
> is, like Certosa, sealed with foil.

In "Nine Nectarines" the same kind of artful alliterative music is concentrated in the "sprinkled blush / of puce-American-beauty pink" and the "small cinnamon-brown common / camel-haired unicorn" enamelled on the plate.

Nearly all the poems of the thirties exhibit this hyphenated adjectival metaphor (it is conspicuously absent from the 1918 "Old Tiger"), for it is a written form released by the suspended personal voice, a literary embellishment called out by Moore's heightened interest in artifice. "Walking-Sticks and Paper-Weights and Water Marks," a title of complex objects, is a meditation on the meanings of those artifacts, whose adjectives seem to imitate the complicated transforming process of production:

> It must have been an able workman,
> humorous and self-possessed,
>   a liker of solidity,
>
> who gave this greenish Waterford
> glass weight with the summit curled down toward
>   itself as the
>   glass grew, the look of tempered sword-
> steel; of three-ore-d
>   fishscale-burnished antinomy-
>   lead-and-tin smoky water-drop type-metal
> smoothness emery-armored
>   against rust.

It is an effort simply to keep in mind just what object the seven or eight multiple metaphoric adjectives are modifying; they almost threaten to eclipse the paperweight itself.

Another meditation on art and artifice, "Smooth Gnarled Crape Myrtle," goes a step further than this to note that "art is unfortunate," for just as "an aspect may deceive," so art can actually encourage us to misinterpret nature in terms of our artificial conventions of perception—in this case, that two creatures together always make a pair. Here we can see how the poet has translated an observation into an "observation," a natural perception into a poetic one. In her Gray Linen Travel Notebook, a diary account of her visits to Virginia in 1935 and 1936, Moore recounts simply,

> July 31 1936   3 redbirds in the meadow. One flew to the ilex tree, then perched on the stem on a twig breast toward the trunk, then flew to a little crape myrtle and flitted about among the pink sprays.[35]

In describing how this natural scene imitates art, the language becomes literary, poetic:

> A brass-green bird with grass-
> green throat smooth as a nut springs from
>   twig to twig askew, copying the
> Chinese flower piece—business-like atom
>   in the stiff-leafed tree's blue-
>   pink dregs-of-wine pyramids.

It takes effort to extract a clear picture from the metaphoric density of such a passage, for the adjectives retain much of their substantive force as nouns. The mind's eye sees a bird amid the "grass," the "nut," and the "Chinese flower piece," three different objects, while the myrtle flowers share the visual frame with "dregs-of-wine" and "pyramids." The multiplicity of objects involved in the description produces at first several distracting images rather than one heightened one. In its density this metaphoric language tends to foreground itself and to call attention to the perceptual and linguistic filters through which the material of the poem is being processed. Such language, released from audible meter, nevertheless is made to bear a certain artifice in syntax that reflects this poem's consideration of where art comes from and what it can do.

The verbal artistry of these clusters of compound metaphoric adjectives joins the artistry of inaudible rhyme, quotation, and syllabic design in altering our sense of the poet's presence in the poem. The poet as self-expressive voice gives way to the poet as artful composer of other voices. These voices include both explicitly quoted and implicitly borrowed assertions made available by science, history, the media, and one's friends. Subjectivity does not at all disappear from these poems; it is present in its usual concentration, but it belongs to a third person, to all of us together as a cultural group. In "The Steeple-Jack," awareness and preference are delivered by reporting in the third person that "Dürer would have seen a reason for living / in a town like this" and by reporting of the college student Ambrose that, "liking an elegance / of which the source is not bravado, he knows by heart the antique / sugar-bowl shaped summerhouse." The voice of "everyone" or of a whole group is delivered sometimes by direct quotation, as in the original opening of "The Student":

> "In America everybody must have a degree," the French
> man
> says, "but the French do not think that all can have it; they
> don't
> say everyone must go to college."

Sometimes the pronoun "we" is used to carry the consensus of the group, so that the poem quotes the feelings and views of an unspecified majority. "The Student" continues, "We / may feel as he says we do." And sometimes the poem simply quotes in an impersonal form some general body of knowledge, a repository of "facts," beliefs, and conventions about "how things are" in the cultural milieu of learning:

> In each school there is a pair of fruit-trees like that twin
> tree
> in every other school: tree-of-knowledge—

> tree-of-life—each with a label like that of the other
> >   college:
>
>   *lux,* or *lux et veritas.*

The language in these first two stanzas of "The Student" is gathered from the public stream of discourse and arranged by the poet. It does not belong to the poet's self in particular, was not born out of that self. It is utterance heard, read, and selectively preserved by the silent artist.

Such a statement of attitude or value offered impartially as one item among others is one of Moore's characteristic forms. One might hypothesize that it is one of the roots of her love of quotation, which presents the word-group as an entity appropriated and displayed by the poem. We have seen this kind of collective authorship still blended with the poetic speaker's "I" in previous works, such as "Marriage," where already the balance is light on the speaker and heavy on all other voices. That poem is virtually a catalogue of quotations, by which subjective expressions are rendered as objective items:

> He says, "What monarch would not blush
> to have a wife
> with hair like a shaving-brush?"
> The fact of woman
> is "not the sound of the flute
> but very poison."
> She says, "Men are monopolists
> of 'stars, garters, buttons
> and other shining baubles'—"

And it closes with an attitude so unindividual that one can hardly find the subject of the sentence, conveyed by an inscription, a book, and a pose:

> " 'Liberty and union
> now and forever';
>
> the Book on the writing-table;
> the hand in the breast-pocket."

Moore has had to insist repeatedly that this poem is not an expression of her views or feelings on the subject of marriage. Actually it is a compendium of our own, of our culture's views and feelings; the audience is its author. "Marriage" assembles the expressions of our attitudes and hands them back to us as data; it treats our value statements as facts in themselves, happenings, findings.

In Moore's work of the thirties, with its suspension of the poetic speak-

er's "I," the expressions of attitude are set in a more predominantly factual framework than ever before. Most of these studies deliver a significant amount of factual information on the habits and characteristics of
creatures, procedures for cultivation and production, historical events,
symbolic conventions, terminologies, and fragments of knowledge. In
"The Jerboa" we read of how the Egyptians "put / baboons on the necks
of giraffes to pick / fruit." "Camellia Sabina" informs us that "In the
camellia-house there must be / no smoke from the stove." In "Pigeons"
we are shown the "*Didus ineptus;* man's remorse / enshrines it now, abun-
dant still / in sixteen-one," and in "Virginia Brittania" the "little hedge- /
sparrow that wakes up seven minutes sooner than the lark." And in "The
Pangolin" we learn that the creature goes

> stepping in the moonlight,
> on the moonlight peculiarly, that the outside
> edges of his hands may bear the weight and save the
> claws
> for digging.

As we saw in "Sea Unicorns and Land Unicorns," this "factual" stream
contains a strong current of conventional wisdom, legend, myth, and
symbol running side by side with scientific accounts. In "The Plumet
Basilisk" fact is juxtaposed with myth:

> the tuatera
> will tolerate a
> petrel in its den, and lays ten eggs
> or nine—the number laid by dragons since "a true dragon
> has nine sons."

Moore continues to reveal our knowledge of the world as a mottled fabric of information we agree on, which we call facts, and information we
do not agree on, which we call opinion, myth, or illusion. Including or
not including ourselves in the agreeing "we" is what determines our
sense of the truth value at hand. We construct our total picture of how
things are by assembling the general company of scientific and superstitious claims on a given subject. Thus the plumet basilisk is first perceived
through a metaphoric setting of fire and jewels as the poem opens:

> In blazing driftwood
> the green keeps showing at the same place;
> as, intermittently, the fire-opal shows blue and green.

The attributes and habits of the various lizards—"wings from the
waist . . . knows how to dive head-first . . . feeds on leaves and ber-

ries"—are continuously interwoven with legendary beliefs about the dragon as "the harmless god . . . dragons [that] symbolize four-fold security . . . the basilisk whose look will kill." And he finally disappears amid the same traditional dragon settings of fire and jewels:

> the innocent, rare, gold-
> defending dragon that as you look begins to be a
>   nervous sword on little feet, with three-fold
>   separate flame above the hilt, inhabiting
>
> fire eating into the air.

The cultural stream of data on the basilisk is a rich blend of fact and fancy, which Moore presents without any particular differentiation or partisanship.

Now we can begin to see how the traditional dichotomy of subjective as inner, within the self, versus objective as outer, outside the self, is being dissolved in Moore's mature poems. Subjectivity as the sensations, feelings, and beliefs of the private self is now perceived as one more objective item out there in the public world, while that public world outside the self turns out to be thoroughly permeated with the subjectivities of others' limited points of view, superstitions, and fabulous stories. What Moore has done in her poetic language of this time is virtually to cancel out one side of that dichotomy, the subjective side, by suspending the poet's personal voice, and to throw the whole weight of the poem onto the other, the objective side, by reporting from impersonal, publicly available sources of knowledge. Another poet might prove the same point by attempting complete immersion in the single poetic self, only to find that non-self will not be eluded. The experiment of standing linguistically on one side of the boundary (for Moore, outside rather than inside of subjective awareness) reveals the specious nature of the separation itself. Subjectivity and objectivity are revealed by this method as linguistic conventions, grammatical forms and convenient fictions of discourse, rather than as actual realms of a divided world. All words as names are heuristic fictions to some extent because of the qualitative difference between language and other actualities. And just as this distinction between verbal and non-verbal modes is useful analytically, so subjectivity and objectivity are polarities that can enrich our thinking without being taken as literal domains or metaphysical substances. Dualism is a refinement, not a contrary, of monism. Thus Moore's press toward objectivity ends up inevitably highlighting the subjective aspect of that so-called outer, impersonal dimension.

The corollary, and it may also be a cause, of the overall shift in the poet's role from voice to text-maker is that Moore has come just as radically around in her development as a moralist. From the subjective expressions of value in the Carlisle lyrics, she has arrived at a form for objective embodiment of value in the animiles of the thirties. In her conversion of subjective material into objective form, Moore has moved the moral dimension of the poem to a source beyond the old poetic speaker and relocated it in the stream of public data, the general body of thought. This development from subjective expression to objective embodiment of value releases the studies of the thirties from the relatively singular point of view of the earlier poems. The poetic voice is also released from personal pronouncement into the more complex process of inquiry, Bacon's project of "industrious observations." Just as the radically objective form has revealed the permeation of the so-called objective world with many subjectivities, Moore's poetic appropriation of the languages of science, history, and the informative media—the "factual" sources—dissolves the traditional dichotomy between factual and non-factual realms of meaning.

This dichotomy at its strictest is at least partly a product of our own past century. The positivist thinkers from Auguste Comte to A. J. Ayer have appointed themselves the philosophic defenders of science, and they have spent a century sharpening its distinction between factual or scientifically verifiable propositions and metaphysical, religious, emotional, and ethical utterances, which Ayer calls "literally senseless."[36] As early as 1922, Ludwig Wittgenstein reformulated an old dualism in his *Tractatus Logico-Philosophicus.* "The world is the totality of facts," he wrote. "In it there is no value—and if there were it would be of no value"; therefore, he concludes, "ethics are transcendental."[37] This nearly circular reasoning, that there can be no value in the world, because if it were in the world it would be a fact, since the world is the totality of facts, serves to maintain the distinction between the two realms—in the world versus beyond the world, immanent versus transcendent. Ironically it also may be taken to argue implicitly the indistinguishability of fact and value *in* the world. Value becomes immanent in the form of fact. Wittgenstein also already acknowledges in his 1922 text the distinction between awareness and language—what he terms "thinking" and "the expression of thoughts"[38]—a distinction that will lead him to repudiate much of the *Tractatus* and open up his 1953 *Philosophical Investigations* to the diverse functions of words in everyday life.

This relation between fact and value has exercised philosophers for two millennia, and, given this heritage, the general distinction will continue to be useful to us, as Ray Lepley suggests:

Few will deny that for the purpose of common-sense interpretation and clarification, it is often helpful to make a distinction between, say, physical facts, on the one hand, and human values,
on the other.[39]

The convenience of this distinction should not, however, be confused
with the kinds of metaphysical and epistemological dualisms it may seem
to suggest—in the world versus out of it, objective versus subjective, empirical versus mystical—however the boundary is drawn. The appropriation by modern poetry, signally by Moore, of the usages formerly reserved for the sciences and informative media demonstrates that, just as
any passionate exclamation can be recorded as one more datum, likewise
there is no such thing as completely value-free language. We may agree
with I. A. Richards's view that "in its use of words most poetry is the reverse of science," because science strives to limit the connotative play that
poetry strives to release.[40] But the words of science and poetry may be
the same ones under different usages. And Moore's project of constitut-
ing poetry in as objective and factual a way as possible serves to disclose
the resonance of value latent in all kinds of language.

We might try to imagine theoretically something like a language with
"degree zero rhetoric," as Ricoeur calls it,[41] language with absolutely no
figurative, borrowed, playful, or judgmental reverberations. We would
be driven ultimately to the languages of symbolic logic and mathematics,
which replace words with non-verbal signs, for in words, as Ricoeur continues, "neutral language does not exist."[42] And why not? In words there
is no value-free language because there is no value-free thinker, speaker,
writer, or reader. Just as the *langue* or formal linguistic system conditions
our possibilities for thought and utterance, so the *parole* or specific speech
and textual acts are acts of circumstanced individuals. No actual language
in use—language that is thought, spoken, written, or read—is devoid of
implication. This is because the impulse toward meaning is an impulse toward plenitude, a widening, inclusive comprehension that tends toward
wholeness, toward the paradox of a complete yet unframed picture. This
tendency toward a total view is evident in the words of scriptures, in the
system of Hegel, in psychologies of the unconscious, in literature of the
absurd, and it is just as evident in the antimetaphysical "isms" of our day,
in Roland Barthes's apposition of "the world (the book)" and in Jacques
Derrida's "there is no outside-the-text."[43] Meaning, retrieved from the
constriction of denotation and retrieved also from the endless free play of
the signifier, is a form of ongoing familiarization, of orientation, of align-
ing our phenomena by whatever *oriens* or rising sun is currently shedding
light. Endless free play of signifiers is just as debilitating to meaning as its

polar mate, overdetermination, is impoverishing. The human spectrum of understanding lies somewhere in between them, and while humanism is no more true than non-humanism, it remains nevertheless our starting and ending point for thought and action. Meaningful free play depends on conventions of usage as much as on inspired deviation. This meaningfulness of language in use dissolves the dualism of facts versus values by conveying the sense of one through the medium of the other. Most clearly in Marianne Moore's poetry of the twenties, thirties, and forties, we see how language in the form of a value statement can have the force of a factual datum and how language in the form of a factual statement can have the force of an assertion of value.

Furthermore, the dissolution of the positivist dichotomy between the factual and the non-factual resolves the dualistic dilemma of the separation of knowledge from judgment. If information and emotion are linguistically divorced, then there remains that gulf in language which a subjectivist ethics cannot cross. In that case there is no medium by which feeling or thought may each educate the other, and we are left with the old prospect of technologies without conscience, with a grand but impotent spirituality—the ghost in the machine. One of the fortunate consequences of post-structuralism's assertion of free play in the text is its reopening of the text's potential for a cross-semination of various currents of thought and feeling, a mingling of codes, and for an emergence of what we might call the unconscious of language, its effects beyond intention. And while the free play of the signifier may well be theoretically infinite, that postulate bears within it its own deconstruction, namely the words by which it is conveyed, that is, the limiting conventions of denotation and connotation through which we actually move toward our senses of significance, including the anti-sense of the void. It is these two dimensions of language—its conventional forms and its ever-untapped possibilities, the limited and the illimitable aspects of meaning—that are distinguished and intertwined in Moore's poetry of this time. The irony is that often, instead of limited factual usages framing deeply resonant value statements, we are shown the opposite, the surfaces of conventional value forms setting off the nearly endless resonance of even our most apparently casual factual observations.

A compact demonstration of this interplay between determinate and indeterminate elements of language is offered by "No Swan So Fine." This poem presents three forms of language: a quotation from a newspaper article, a description in the poet's "own words" of a central image, and a fragment of a maxim. The opening quotation, "No water so still as the / dead fountains of Versailles," is a statement in factual form. Its author, Percy Philip, wrote, "There is no water so still as the dead fountains of Versailles," in an article on the restoration of the palace and grounds.[44] Since Versailles was also the site of the controversial treaty closing World War I in 1919, his remark also suggests, intentionally or not, the deathly stillness of the treaty by which the hostilities were ended. The explicit theme of nature and artifice, that no water can be as motionless as man's dry fountains, carries the implicit political judgment, "there is a deathly stillness attending the promises of this place." Moore's choice of the form of quotation here renders this judgment in the form of an observation, a found datum, an exhibit A: "this is what is now being said about Versailles."

The second unit of the poem is another comparison of nature and an artifact, a comparison whose syntactic form echoes that of the first unit: "No (natural thing) so (quality) as (man-made thing)." Here the relative values of nature and artifice are reversed from those of the opening unit, for the speaker says that no swan in nature is as fine as the china one in this candelabrum on auction at Christie's. The artifact is positive now, not ominously "dead" but "fine" with the pattern of chintz, the "fawn-brown eyes," a royal gold collar, and the baroque setting of "polished sculptured flowers" in which the china swan is poised "at ease and tall." As the title and central description suggest, man is sometimes capable of making things that are finer than nature, or at least more lasting, a classical observation enclosing the more romantic opening. That opening judgment in factualized form is countered here by the value-laden presentation of the object, just as the ominous stillness of the dead fountains and treaty is challenged by the graceful stillness of the Dresden china figurine out of a more distant past.

This lively response to the gloom of a dead Versailles is sealed in the poem's third unit. The virtual quotation of the half-maxim, "The king is dead," echoes the opening dead fountains, but its explicit gloom is cancelled by the other half of the maxim's implicit faith in the future, "Long live the king!" One of the poem's strongest statements is this one that it omits, the absent but implied words on the brink of which it halts. If the spirit and function of the king outlive his individual decease, as the candelabrum and maxim suggest, perhaps we need not mourn the spirit of the treaty after all. Thus the face values of the poem's language are reversed: the images of the past convey possibilities for a future, and the expressions of despair end up conveying an assertion of hope. The negative term "dead" that opens and closes the poem is suspended in quoted and formulaic forms, made into a factual datum, whereas the more positive value terms "fine," "at ease and tall," are spoken by the poetic voice itself. Thus one could say that hope is the authoritative message and fear its subversive threat and that the poem comes alive in this tension, a 1932 world tension whose urgency informs this short depiction of an artifact up for auction.

A longer piece appearing four years later, "The Pangolin" of 1936, reflects not only the deepening of that tension but also a more overtly factual medium for the embodiment of value. This poem has two different three-part structures that cross and complement each other: the first is creature versus man, and the second is creature as man as creature. The clearer structure is the description of the pangolin, the digression on grace, and the description of man. The anatomies of creature and of man are deepened by the linking middle section, a catalogue in the classical rhetorical form of the *occupatio,* the negative enumeration of all that grace is not. The message of this pattern is something like "This is what the pangolin is, who has grace, versus what man is, who confuses grace with all that it is not."

The poem's second structure is signalled by the motif of opposites in balance, "sun and moon and day and night and man and beast" in the third stanza and its echo "beneath sun and moon" in the third-to-last stanza. The message of this structure is the bringing together of opposites, for the nocturnal pangolin is a counterpart of the diurnal "being we call human." The creature is repeatedly presented in terms of the artist and works of art. He is "the night miniature artist engineer . . . Leonardo da Vinci's replica." He possesses the "fragile grace of the Thomas- / of- Leighton Buzzard Westminster Abbey wrought-iron vine," and he is "compact like the furled fringed frill / on the hat-brim of Gargallo's hollow iron head of a / matador." Having likened the natural creature to art, the poem then inventories man in a zoological manner—"warm blood, no gills"—that challenges the dichotomy between the natural world and man's. The anatomies both emphasize that man is "another . . . animal" and "among animals, one. . . ." The implications of Moore's repeated conjunctions of nature and art now become clearer. If there really is a gulf between the human and the natural worlds, then the distinctively human elements in man are up against something alien and oblivious, and the artist is obliged to represent nature as either inhuman and intractable or else nearly transcendent. We are left to choose dualistically again, to champion either nature over artifice as in romanticism or art over wild nature as in classicism. Moore's inclusive motif—"Sun and moon . . . each with a splendor"—and her hybrid anatomies—"the night miniature artist engineer"—close the gap between nature and culture so that the language of the one may carry sense in the context of the other.

The political context of "The Pangolin" is announced immediately at the opening of the poem. Its second and third words, "Another *armored*

animal," refer to man in the midst of his mid-thirties build-up of armaments, what Moore had already described to Eliot in 1934 as "the present
international unease and smuggling of machine-guns"—the threat of another war.[45] This is Moore's first explicit poetic reference to armor, and
its specific historical context of 1936 has been overlooked by critics who
prefer to take the image of armor as a sign of the poet's own personal de-
fensiveness.[46] Perhaps it is unfortunate that "The Pangolin" rises so
quickly beyond its original historical context that the link between armor
and the literal armaments of the 1930s can be obscured. The historical and
political occasion of the poem, embedded in its opening words, awakens
the resonance of value in the factual accounts that follow. The reference
to arms build-up creates a context of human issues, in the same way that
during the nineteenth century Darwin's theories suddenly humanized the
language of zoology, helping to close the traditional gap between "man
and beast."

Thus in neither "No Swan So Fine" nor "The Pangolin" is the dimension of value located in the explicit value statements; rather it is implicit,
carried in the implications, the absent presences, of the factual statements. Certain determinate value phrases have the effect of awakening
the indeterminate dimensions of value in the informational phrases, so
that the explicit but ossified attitudes serve as a foil for the vibrant but
more problematic issues. It is true, as Bernard Engel writes, that Moore
"wishes to advocate a set of values . . . courage, independence, responsi-
bility, genuineness."[47] She defends all these honorable things that a traditional moralist is supposed to be in favor of. For instance, we read in
"The Pangolin" that,

> Among animals, *one* has a sense of humor.
> Humor saves a few steps, it saves years.

We would not argue with that. But it is also true that other elements of
the poem do, in a sense, argue with it; it is also true that Moore does not
wish to advocate certain values but to inquire into their nature and possibility. And such inquiry is subversive of advocacy to the extent that it
must doubt and search rather than clearly exhort. Inquiry must make uncertainty its premise, whereas advocacy needs at least the sense of sureness. There is in "The Pangolin" something both comical and grimly hu-
morless about man, the armored animal "in fighting, mechanicked" with
all his "extra" armor. Man's armor, furthermore, is not only tacked on,
artificial and external to his natural anatomy, but it is also apparently
"consistent with the formula," part of his natural behavioral anatomy: in
man the unnatural is natural. Man-made culture is also excrescence of nature. Man is like the pangolin and yet different; no overriding generaliza-

tion can stand alone, for the particulars both prompt and undo it. Such paradoxes, while they paralyze advocacy, are the heart of inquiry.

Moore's choice of a paratactic or additive style of composition serves the openness of her inquiries. Placing the elements of the poem side by side, one after the other with or without the connective "and," produces among the accumulating items an equality which encourages a free mutual effect of support and challenge. A hypotactic or grammatically hierarchical style of dominant and subordinate elements (this therefore that, for instance) is a medium for logical ordering and argumentation, the form for proof or demonstration. Moore's parataxis—her listing of facts, ideas, sayings, propositions of constantly shifting sorts—is an empirical procedure that stops short of induction. Its particulars are not being marshalled toward a general conclusion, for such conclusions are already adopted as particular items themselves. The inconclusive nature of this strategy serves to keep inquiry and uncertainty alive in the teeth of the poem's useful surface of categorical, single-minded statements. In "The Pangolin's" movement from the creature's habits to the confused meanings of grace, to the sailboat, back to the pangolin, and on to man, each of these items is logically equal with the others in syntax. The mystery lies in the unspecified relation between them. The sailboat, for example— the simple, quiet, incongruous image following the fallen forms of grace—could be considered the poem's central image as much as could any other item in the piece. It completes the stanza on grace, climaxing the central digression; its short sentence echoes the stanza's aphoristic opening "To explain grace requires a curious hand"; it stands as a single unembellished image amid complexities; it links grace with the pangolin and then with man. And this link is additive: "made for moving quietly also." So we may say with Engel that the pangolin "represents the perfection of courage and restraint Miss Moore values."[48] But the poem also presents paradoxically "man in all his vileness" as "man and beast / each with a splendor . . . each with an excellence!" Man is both the "prey of fear" and the author of hope who "says to the alternating blaze, / 'Again the sun!' " The inconclusive inclusiveness of the paratactic form and the "curious hand" of inquiry undermine any single-minded stand by asserting the tentative and relative nature of each claim. They also make the investigation of value in these poems of the thirties a far richer undertaking, with more nuances open to thought and feeling, than any of the early judgmental lyrics.

The richness rather than emptiness of these indeterminate dimensions of value is constellated by Moore's conscious and ironic use of those determinate repositories of value, the mottoes and emblems that formulate a culture's traditional or accepted ideals. From her earliest college poems, such as "Qui S'Excuse, S'Accuse" and "Tunica Pallio Proprior," we can see her interest in the maxim as a poetic starting point. And her incorporation of emblems in those poems was even more frequent: the dragon circling space, the talismanic scarab gull, the lantern, David's harp, yellow roses, the ibis, the sun. Two poems of 1923 use a motto to close off the text. In "Bowls" Moore wraps up her catalogue of "precisionist" resolutions with a rendering of Alciatus' "Bis dat, qui cito dat": "since he who gives quickly gives twice / in nothing so much as a letter." And "Marriage" comes to rest in its penultimate lines on an excerpt from an 1830 speech of Daniel Webster, words Moore could see inscribed on his statue in Central Park: " 'Liberty and union / now and forever.' " Moore's increasing interest in these formulaic forms is attested by their presence and central position in over half of the poems of the thirties. This is not a surprising development, for the motto is a special form of quotation, of language fixed and reproduced, just as the emblem is a special form of spatial imagery, culturally fixed and reproduced.

The function of the formulaic phrase or image is to provide a kind of cultural shorthand, to accomplish a determination and concentration of value in a recognizable surface without having to retrace on every occasion the experiential origin of the symbol or lesson. In "The Steeple-Jack" the danger sign and the star that "stands for hope" together exemplify the contraries that can be quickly called up by familiar forms. These emblems contribute to the sense of innocuous familiarity that is a main theme of the poem. The hardened surface of the formula is fixed, even dead in a sense; repeated recognition makes it a thing of the past, even though at times its fullness may be renewed. In an early version of "The Student," for instance, this ossified quality of the emblem is part of the opening argument. The identical trees of knowledge and of life in every school come "each with a label like that of the other college: / *lux*, or *lux et veritas, Christo et ecclesiae, sapiet / felici.*" The interchangeability of these "labels"—what the later version calls "the unanimity of college / mottoes"—stresses the token quality of the expressions. They all label the same kinds of things, are all of one mind, and the rest of the poem must investigate from the ground up the still elusive nature of learning.

The gist of any way of being may be conveyed by a motto, as "The Frigate Pelican" demonstrates. This poem contrasts the "less / limber animal's mottoes" of Protestant thrift—"Make hay; keep / the shop; I have one sheep"—with the Hindu motto of the artist bird—" 'If I do well I am blessed / whether any bless me or not, and if I do / ill I am cursed.' " The first mottoes are based on a promise of material and social reward. "Keep thy shop, and thy shop will keep thee" is quoted by Steele in *Spectator* No.

509, and "Now I have a sheep and cow, / everybody bids me good morrow" is from Benjamin Franklin's *Poor Richard*. Both these commercial mottoes are contradicted by the more inward Hindu saying, just as "Make hay while the sun shines" is countered by "Festina lente" or "Make haste slowly." The contrary mottoes relativize one another and together point to the uncertainty that livens and deepens the poem, the sense of sacrifice exacted in both ways of living. The mottoes undo each other's insular confidence and the singular messages of their own face values.

One of the poems of the "Old Dominion" cluster, "Smooth Gnarled Crape Myrtle," offers probably the most direct poetic commentary that Moore made on her own use of mottoes.

> It was artifice saw,
> on a patch-box pigeon-egg, room for
> fervent script, and wrote as with a bird's claw
> under the pair on the
> hyacinth-blue lid—"joined in
> friendship, crowned by love."
> An aspect may deceive; as the
> elephant's columbine-tubed trunk
> held waveringly out—
> an at will heavy thing—is
> delicate.
> Art is unfortunate.

The motto is an artifice that enables us to finalize "an aspect," a singular point of view. Insofar as art fixes and reproduces "an aspect," a particular phase or part, it is "unfortunate," for through that limited view it may "deceive." Art as exact perception may turn out to be art as misrepresentation, just as the step between a "blameless bachelor" and Congreve is the step of altered perception by an observer, a shift of appearances rather than of substance. Consequently the poem has both to present the unfortunate appearance and to make it fortunate by undoing the deception that this singular aspect is the whole truth. The motto, then, is a determinate unit against which the poem can work, not by disproving it or offering an alternate determinate claim, but by unsettling the determinacy itself as the poem's univocal ground. The poet's questioning and anxious response to the final emblem and motto of "Smooth Gnarled Crape Myrtle" does not try to replace them with any competing claim:

> And what of
> our clasped hands that swear, "By Peace
> Plenty; as
> by Wisdom Peace." Alas!

Peace in the poem's year, 1935—the time of Mussolini's invasion of Ethiopia—was a tenuous affair; yet one would not like to let go of hope by complete cynicism about the promise. Thus Moore's frame for the motto—"And what of . . . Alas!"—doubts without denying it by giving us both the emblematic pose and a questioning, troubled response to it. The motto appears as a relatively monophonic statement of value that sets in motion a polyphony of surrounding ambiguities and possibilities.

We are now in a better position to see the role of the explicit statements of value that Moore herself has composed for the poetic speaker—her "home-made" mottoes. The characteristically aphoristic form of many of her passages concerning moral ideas and principles has been a part of Moore's poetry and her prose from their earliest years. Her strategy of quotation already suggests a preference for the memorable excerpt over the general flow, for the concentrated gist over the gradual unfolding, a preference that is the verbal manifestation of her spatial rather than temporal imagination. The aphoristic is a quality that she admired in the work of Sir Francis Bacon, of which she wrote, "The aphorisms and allusions to antiquity have an effect of formula."[49] This "effect of formula" often seems quite deliberate in her own poetic aphorisms, as if the statements might claim from that form some previously understood validity to which the verse is merely referring, without any burden of demonstration. In "Walking-Sticks and Paper-Weights and Water Marks" of 1941 we find such an effect:

> Patience, with its superlatives,
> firmness and loyalty and faith, gives
>   intensive fruit.

The choice of those three appositives has a formulaic quality, as if we all know and agree that firmness, loyalty, and faith properly belong to the accepted equation for patience, like items in the list of deadly sins or cardinal virtues, parts of a catechism. A point that is simply stated without any gesture of defense has the same confident air about it as the motto does. It has the sureness of its singular perspective.

Indeed at moments one has to see on the page, because one cannot hear it, what portions are quoted motto and what are the poet's aphorisms, as for example in "Walking-Sticks" as it appeared in *What Are Years:*

> "Stones grow,"
> as volcano-
>   sides and quartz-mines prove. "Plants feel? Men
> think." "Airmail is quick." "Save rags, bones, metals."
>   Hopes

> are harvest when deeds follow
>   words postmarked "Dig for victory."

This poem about three things and things in threes is a study in the extraction of formulaic value statements from objects treated emblematically. The poetic voice's nostalgia for an old way is plain:

> Stepped glass has been made in Ireland;
> they still have blackthorn walking-sticks, and
>   flax and linen
> and paper-mills; and reprimand
> you if you stand
>   your stick on such and such a spot.
>   You must keep to the path "on account of the
> souls." And all can understand
>   how centralizing loyalty
>
> shapes matter as a die is hid
> while used.

The old way is the way in which "all can understand" a thing clearly, with implied unanimity. The motto extracts from an emblem, as an aphorism does from an image, a single one of its multitude of senses, limiting and directing thought that might otherwise be tempted into free play by the image. In delimiting the possible senses of things, the formulaic motto or aphoristic form offers an assurance that such determination of sense is both possible and desirable, an assurance that other areas of the poem may undermine. Thus no determination remains final. Later in "Walking-Sticks" we see that an image can open up a field of possibilities and ambiguities, while a formula can then fix and frame one of these possibilities and convert the indeterminate image into a determinate emblem. Three times in two stanzas, as numbered below, the symbolic possibilities of images are limited by a single definite interpretation, and the rhythm becomes an alternation between indeterminate image and determinate sense:

> Postmark behests are clearer than
> the water-marks beneath,—than ox, swan,
>   crane, or dolphin,
> than eastern, open, jewelled, Span-
> ish, Umbrian
>   crown,—as symbols of endurance. (1)
>   And making the envelope secure, the sealed
> wax reveals a pelican
>   studying affectionately

> the nest's three-in-one upturned tri-
> form face. "For those we love, live and die"   (2)
>   the motto reads.
> The pelican's community
> of throats, the high-
>   way's trivia or crow's-foot where
>   three roads meet, the fugue, the awl-leafed juniper's
> whorls of three, objectify
>   welded divisiveness.   (3)

In the third unit, for instance, the word "trivia" has wide-ranging reverberations: trifles, trinkets, games, bits and pieces, inessential things from
the Latin *via* as road and "that which comes from the streets"; and from
trivium, "where three roads meet," the crossroads, the intersection, the
center, the meeting-place, a three-way cross. All these possibilities are
sorted out and centered ʹin the concept of "welded divisiveness." The
poem interprets its own images, providing an equation that controls their
play in the reader's mind. The formulaic motto or aphorism points up indeterminacy by having to militate against it again and again. It would be
difficult to say how conscious Moore might have been of this rhythm of
repeated centering. At the least we could imagine that her recurrent turn
to formulaic effects, found and made ones, was occasioned by her awareness of the relative indeterminacy of the image and by a wish to bring out
the irony and mystery of its relation to our conventional habits of definite
statement.

We can now see some significant differences between a 1920s
poem of place like "An Octopus" and a 1930s poem of place like "Virginia
Brittania." Like the Mt. Rainier piece, "Virginia Brittania" is composed
from a mélange of guidebooks, histories, and personal observations from
the poet's travels. The free verse of the Rainier piece, however, has been
left behind in the Virginia poem for a syllabically-ordered stanza form,
whose indentations highlight an elegant pattern of near and distant, accented and unaccented rhymes. This pattern grows naturally out of the
opening and fourth model stanzas, intersects and plays continuo through
much of the material, and comes to rest in harmony with the utterance of
the closing stanza. The formality and deliberate artifice of the verse are echoes of its attention to certain formulaic elements—mottoes and emblems—
that Virginia inherits from its past: the inscribed epitaph of Robert Sherwood, "a great sinner lyeth here"; the Indian's "fur crown"; Captain John
Smith's coat-of-arms "with ostrich, Latin motto, / and small gold horse-
shoe"; the emblematic rattlesnake and the motto of

> our once dashingly
> undiffident first flag, "Don't tread on
> me"—tactless symbol of a new republic;

and the closing allusion to Wordsworth's "Ode, Intimations of Immortality," in what is for Moore a nearly unique poetic paraphrase.

These emblems and mottoes signal the presence of the past, yet they also have a curiously unfamiliar effect that impresses us with their pastness. Most readers are not already familiar with John Smith's motto or the story of the sting-ray; they do not know who Pamunkey was. These things are now part of written history like the "tobacco-crop records on church-walls." Moore intertwines moving images of the present with these still images of the historical past; the living move around and among the dead.

> A fritillary zigzags
> toward the chancel-shaded resting-place,

and the "terse Virginian," the mocking-bird, graces an old artifact,

> alighting noiseless, musing in the semi-sun,
> standing on tall thin legs as if he did not see,
> conspicuous, alone,
> on the stone-
> topped table with lead cupids grouped to form the pedestal.

Where "An Octopus" concerned itself largely with the interplay of perceptions and deceptions of a place, the Virginia poem poses the enigma of time-in-place. The past, whose traces we visit and read of, is also fragmentary evidence of loss, of dead stillness amid the moving simplicities of the present. In this poem, nature frames and highlights history in overtaking it. This is the context of Moore's resetting of Wordsworth's motifs. The Immortality Ode's "clouds that gather round the setting sun" seem called up by the scene that she recorded on August 15, 1935, in her Gray Linen Travel Notebook:

> Sunset going toward Churchland . . . The trees were as if on fire   the tops etched dark on the greenish sky . . . The striking thing was the form of the darker cloud sweeping and unified.[50]

Moore's verse rendering of this scene includes Wordsworth's key terms, "child," "intimations," and "glory":

> clouds, expanding above
> the town's assertiveness, dwarf it, dwarf arrogance
> that can misunderstand

> importance; and
> are to the child an intimation of what glory is.

Wordsworth's portrait of the growing child is here implicitly juxtaposed with Moore's portrait of a changing place, of Virginia as a new young world now growing older, as if to suggest that a whole people, too, can lose their original vision of things and yet recapture it at moments.

While "An Octopus" is an exploratory work, a poem of the discovery of a place and its enigmas, "Virginia Brittania" is an elegiac ode, a meditation on the cryptic fragments of the past set among the natural movements of the present. While "An Octopus" concerns itself with nature, with perception and the formulation of knowledge, "Virginia Brittania" involves itself with the relation of nature to the processes of human history. This involvement with history and the historical dimensions of the present, which we saw also in "No Swan So Fine" and "The Pangolin," is a renewed theme in Moore's work of the thirties. A similar concern with world events was evident in the World War I poems, like "To Statecraft Embalmed," and it is a concern that we shall see intensified in her work of the forties.

During the coming decade, Moore's factual materials and impersonal syntax will again be tempered by the felt presence of a personal voice, by a self-referential "I." It is tempting simply to accept the outbreak of World War II as the event that called the personal voice back into her poems of the forties; it is sufficient cause, although the equation of fervor with subjective form does not really hold in her work. An additional possibility is that Moore began to sense that she had pushed the objective form—the poem as ironic factual network—to the limit and perhaps past it. Two of her longest and most factual poems of 1935 and 1936—"Pigeons" and "Walking-Sticks and Paper-Weights and Water Marks"—remain uncollected after their first or second appearance; she omitted both of them from *Collected* and *Complete Poems*. Perhaps, as her development decade by decade from apostrophe to catalogue to factualities suggests, she simply grew on to the next challenge raised by the successes of the animiles of 1932–36. Having exposed the myth of the "pure fact," having explored the ways in which determinate statements may awaken indeterminate meanings, and having found her own way of making facts bespeak value, Moore will now restore what sounds like the poet's "own voice" to her poems of the forties in a very different form from the personal voice of the Carlisle years.

5

The Sense of a Voice

During the 1930s Moore made the acquaintance of Elizabeth Bishop, who became one of her loyal friends and a poet with whom Moore's work is sometimes compared and often contrasted. In her memoir "Efforts of Affection," Bishop has told the story of their meeting in front of the New York Public Library, Moore's Titian hair now "mixed with white to a faint rust pink."[1] Bishop little suspected that the real reason she was not invited into the Moores' home for the occasion is that during that week in March 1934 the Cumberland Street apartment was being "renovated to the point of annihilating us."[2] The friendship and correspondence that sprang up between the two women soon revealed the difference—for them a comfortable difference—in their poetic temperaments.

In 1940 Bishop shared with the Moores her draft of "Roosters," which occasioned a lively exchange on the propriety and implications of its use of the term "water-closet" in its fifth stanza. This provoked from Marianne a declaration as clear as any we have of her own overall aesthetic intentions and also a note of affectionate respect for the younger poet's independent spirit. On October 16 Moore wrote,

> Regarding the water-closet, Dylan Thomas, W. C. Williams, E. E. Cummings, and others, feel that they are avoiding a duty if they balk at anything like unprudishness, but I say to them, "I can't care about all things equally, I have a major effect to produce, and the heroisms of abstinence are as great as the heroisms of courage, and so are the rewards." I think it is to your credit, Elizabeth, that when I say you are not to say 'water-closet', you go on saying it a little.[3]

111

Bishop did let the poem go on saying it, in fact, on the grounds that it helped to establish the essentially base nature of the roosters in this wartime poem.

I have no doubt that when Moore spoke of having a "major effect to produce" she was referring to the overriding fact of the Second World War, the tragedies of which she addressed now in a very marked new mode of moral speech. She felt the war's challenge to be in every way a major one, and her poetic response in the forties reveals definitively the parameters within which, temperamentally and by design, she chose to work. In some notes for a lecture at Bryn Mawr, Moore once recorded the view that "poetry delivers us from our *bassesse*."[4] This "heroism of abstinence" for her involved a reluctance to emphasize in art those elements in which life tragically abounds but which we would not wish to proliferate—war, chaos, senselessness, the negative and low sides of life. The new voice and texture of Moore's work of the 1940s embody this aesthetic heroism more openly and more movingly, I would suggest, than any of her other work.

"Four Quartz Crystal Clocks" of 1940 and the other fifteen poems that came out during the years of World War II constitute a group whose general approach and preoccupations distinguish them from her poems of the thirties. This group begins in the summer of 1940 with *The Kenyon Review*'s publication of "Four Quartz Crystal Clocks," "A Glass-Ribbed Nest" (retitled "The Paper Nautilus"), and "What Are Years?" There followed in quick succession "Rigorists," "Light is Speech," "He 'Digesteth Harde Yron,' " and "Spenser's Ireland." In 1942 only "The Wood-Weasel" appeared, but 1943 and 1944 brought to the pages of *The Nation* "In Distrust of Merits," "The Mind Is an Enchanting Thing," "A Carriage from Sweden," and "Propriety," and to other journals "It is Late, I Can Wait" (retitled "Nevertheless"), "Elephants," "Keeping Their World Large," and "His Shield."

These sixteen poems were soon assembled in three different volumes, *What Are Years, Nevertheless,* and the "Collected Later" section of *Collected Poems,* where they were all mixed unchronologically with earlier and later work. Thus in reading through *The Complete Poems,* it is virtually impossible to perceive the development this small group accomplishes. A chronological reading, however, shows that these verses of the forties carry out what may be seen as Moore's decisive reorientation of her work in relation to modernism. The choices that she made in her poems of this time—her turn in form toward greater compression and in content toward contemporary history—account to a large extent for the character of her verse in decades following this one and also for her particular status in the company of modern poets. The adjustments that she makes now in the figurative language, in the voice, and in the moral idiom of these pieces create a new relationship between the speaker, the subject, and the reader of her verse. They affect the dimension of value in Moore's work in a dramatic and lasting way, allowing her to come full circle in her development as a moralist.

In her longer pieces ("Marriage," "An Octopus," "The Plumet Basilisk," "Virginia Brittania," and "Walking-Sticks") Moore gained the kind of poetic expansiveness—freely discursive development, inclusiveness, range—that might have led her into the open-endedness that made certain American long poems possible, notably *The Cantos* and *Paterson*. Instead, after the animiles of the thirties, Moore reasserted that "first grace of style," compression. Her work of the forties affirms not only poetic unity and closure but also concision. None of these pieces runs over eighty lines, which is half as long as "The Jerboa," and their average length of thirty-eight lines is half the average length (seventy-six lines) of the animiles. Furthermore, the hefty stanzas of "Virginia Brittania" and "The Pangolin" now give way to lighter 3-, 5-, 6-, and 7-line stanzas, which are often streamlined by visibly shorter line lengths. This is by no means a return to the radical brevity of the Carlisle years, the twelve-line sally of 1915–16. But once again compression becomes a salient characteristic of Moore's verse, as if the expansive catalogues of "Pigeons" and "Walking-Sticks" had gone a bit far and were being reined in for intensity.

Like Eliot of "Four Quartets," like Stevens and Crane, Marianne Moore opted for the sense of formal unity and closure rather than, like Pound and later Williams, for the open-ended form of the poem as an ongoing process. Unity and closure imply the viability of a finite poetic thing, a product, the constitution of "a text" within the stream of textualities. Thus Moore's is an art that repeatedly posits wholeness of form as a statement alongside the fragmentary and obliquely juxtaposed materials of its world. In 1940 when *The Kenyon Review* group appeared in print, the success of *Selected Poems* had already secured for Moore a poetic audience sensitive to the messages of form. The incisive compactness of those four pieces, after several years of silence, announces a renewed "rigorism," a classical severity of form that is echoed in the poems' subject matters of exactitude and the virtues of enclosure.

Moore's renewed compression went against the general current, however; it took place in a decade during which many modernist poets were expanding into major longer works. The 1940s saw the publication of Eliot's "Four Quartets," of Stevens's "Notes Toward a Supreme Fiction," of Pound's *Pisan Cantos,* and of the first three books of Williams's *Paterson.* This is the decade that fuels such statements as Stephen Fender's that "the characteristic work of these American poets is the long, plotless, open-ended poem."[5] Moore's return at this time from the clusters of the thirties to the short individual lyric as her characteristic form is a move against that expansive trend, perhaps a move chosen deliberately to maintain the kind of essential brevity and intensity recommended by Poe. Moore entitled a series of lectures given at Bryn Mawr in 1953 "The Poetic Principle Unscientifically Approximated," showing that she still had in mind "The Poetic Principle," the essay in which Poe argues the brief duration of poetry's truly poetic or "elevated" moments. The relative brevity of her later forms is a choice that has had its repercussions in critical circles that associate the status of "major" poet with a work of extended length. It might be tempting to sigh for whatever long poem, if any, might have occupied the eight years from 1946 through 1954 that Moore devoted to the translation of the fables of La Fontaine. But the signs of the early forties confirm that she is already working concertedly not toward but away from such expansion, and so her reputation must rest, like Herbert's and Dickinson's, largely on the collection of lyric-length pieces.

The second significant turn in Moore's verses of the forties that will be amplified in her later work is their more frequent and explicit attention to issues of contemporary history. A good half of these poems refer openly to the war situation, its practical and moral exigencies, in even clearer terms than such pre-war pieces as "No Swan So Fine" and "The Pangolin." For instance, in "Four Quartz Crystal Clocks" the themes of truth and accuracy are tied in with the situation of France just after her declaration of war in 1939: Jean Giraudoux, just named "Commissaire Général de l'Information," is quoted as he examines "ces instruments faits pour la verité qui sont la radio, la cinéma, la presse" in the face of the German threat. This political context tinges the issues of accuracy in language in the second half of the poem with the problem of what Giraudoux calls "camouflage" and what Orwell has called political "double-speak." Moore politicizes the poem and then depoliticizes the clocks, identifying them as nature's and technology's independent standard for accuracy and truth.

Likewise in "The Mind Is an Enchanting Thing," the reference to Herod's oath reminds us of Herod's campaign to slaughter all the children of Bethlehem in an effort to eradicate any newborn King of the Jews who might threaten his own power. The 1943 context of persecution of the Jews is linked with this historical counterpart by the motifs of "memory's ear" and "memory's eye." Other pieces address contemporary history even more directly: "Light is Speech" speaks specifically of the situation of France under the Nazi occupation; "In Distrust of Merits" and "Keeping Their World Large" are explicit war poems. "What Are

Years?" speaks of courage and defeat, "He 'Digesteth Harde Yron' " of justice, freedom, and heroism; "Nevertheless" speaks of victory, "Elephants" of fighting, defeat, the soldier and the philosopher, "A Carriage from Sweden" of "Denmark's sanctuaried Jews"; "His Shield" speaks of creatures "battle-dressed," and "Propriety" of resistance.

It is not surprising that World War II should call out Moore's poetic response, just as World War I had. This time it is a more sustained response, and it has the advantage of informing her more mature work. We have already seen in her quotations Moore's sense of her verse as a collaboration, as sounding a community of voices. This overt intertextuality, this realization of the relation of each text to the cultural stream that bears it, probably springs from the same source as her interest in public and contemporary issues. There is no doubt that this immersion in the public world also stems from her conviction of the advisability of restraining the personal self in her art. "The Pathetic Fallacy—Ego," she writes in a letter of 1968, " . . . have we not suffered from it day by day!"[6] And I have already quoted the letter in which she warns against "the vividness of the verse [being] sacrificed to the vividness of the self that is writing the verse."[7] The worlds of science and contemporary events are Moore's natural, temperamental choices, and the question raised by these choices is whether, alongside or amid these public subjects, she now attains anything like a sustained lyric voice.

The question of lyricism is raised in Moore's work of this time by the marked and lasting return of the poetic speaker's "I," in which the first-person voice emerges out of the objectivity of quotation. This change is accompanied by related adjustments in technique and rhetoric—by a distinct split in the deployment of metaphor and by a new rhetorical approach to value that reflects the poet's changing sense of self and audience. The lyric as a genre is usually identified with the sense of a single speaker, a self that is the imagined source or medium of the poem's intended message. That self is a kind of persona, a fictional character created by the discourse, and to the extent that a poem yields this sense of a person speaking to us, we may say that it enters the lyric mode. And while Moore rightly has a reputation for being extremely circumspect about the role of the self in her work, she will now make at least a sustained enough use of the lyric voice to allow us to perceive a persona with significant differences from that of the Carlisle poems. The fact that we shall be able to discern the contrasting "personality" of the "I" of the forties confirms that this voice is not simply a rhetorical convenience.

Probably the animiles of the thirties, especially the famous opening pieces of *Selected Poems,* constitute Moore's most venturous experiment. As poems they are *sui generis;* they are of considerable theoretical richness to the critical reader; and they are often purely pleasurable. The poems of the forties that we approach now, however, are more relaxed than the animiles in several ways: they have the sense of a human presence suggested by the new poetic voice; often they have a more familiar choice of subjects, simpler-looking stanza forms, and a somewhat less dense verbal texture. These qualities make the lyrics of the war years more comfortable to the general reader than the animiles were, less strange, perhaps less demanding, and probably on the whole more moving and memorable. Certainly they are among her most frequently anthologized and best-known poems. Perhaps they are simply more "poetic" in the traditional sense than the animiles, without sacrificing Moore's distinctive signature throughout their lines. If the verses of the twenties and thirties show Moore's virtuosity, these poems of the forties argue the lasting greatness of her talent and accomplishment. Their special kind of richness, however, could not have happened without the ultra-fine tuning of the radical formal "essays," the elegant rituals of the animiles, just as those would not have been possible without the expansion, plenitude, and freedoms that paved their way.

The adjustment that Moore makes in her figurative language of the forties is related in a revealing way to the different subject matters and tasks of one particular group of those verses. The general principle, as Rosemond Tuve points out, is that "the nature of the imagery and the intention of a poem are indissolubly connected."[8] In this case, the appearance of "What Are Years?" and "Light is Speech" signals Moore's resumption of the idea poem, the poem centered in a general or abstract idea rather than in a concrete animal or artifact. Many of the "observations" of the early twenties were pieces of this type: "In the Days of Prismatic Color," "Poetry," "Picking and Choosing," "When I Buy Pictures," and "Novices." But where the recurrent concern of that earlier group was with aesthetic qualities and standards, the preoccupation of the idea poems of the forties is with the moral issues raised by the world's war situation—with courage and mortality in "What Are Years?", with justice and free speech in "Light is Speech." The idea-centered verses are nearly all among those works related in some way to the issues of the war: "In Distrust of Merits," "Nevertheless," "The Mind Is an Enchanting Thing," and "Keeping Their World Large." "Propriety" is a transitional piece, for it features the war-charged term "resistance," but it also points ahead to a new aesthetic concern, the celebration of grace that we shall see in poems of the fifties.

Moore's idea-centered poems of the war years offer a contrast in figurative language to the poems of this same period that are, like the animiles, focused on an artifact or an animal, a concrete subject. The verses on the crystal clocks, paper nautilus, reindeer, ostriches, elephants, the Swedish carriage, and Presbyter John are continuations of the animiles, in that their focal subjects are actual things, literal realities, presented visually with the aid of those hyphenated, sensuous, metaphoric adjectives. The "Paper Nautilus" hides a "glass ram'shorn-cradled freight" and has "wasp-nest flaws" and "close- / laid Ionic chiton-folds." The ostrich who " 'Digesteth Harde Yron' " has a "comic duckling head" that moves with "compass-needle nervousness," a "leaden-skinned back," and (in the early version) "moth-silk / plumage." In "Elephants" the "hunting-horn-curled trunk" is "wistaria-like" and "mouse-gray," and it grips with "dyke-enforced massiveness." In "His Shield" Presbyter John wearing a salamander-skin is "asbestos-eyed asbestos-eared"; his humility is a garb safer than that of the "dinosaur- / skulled, quilled or salamander-wooled . . . / and javelin-dressed." The attributive metaphors assist directly the visual clarity of the pictured thing and then contribute indirectly to the theme or conceptual dimension of the poem.

In contrast, the idea-centered verses of this time tend to avoid the sensuous metaphoric complexes and to employ substantive metaphors that are part of the conceptual statements of the poems. In "What Are Years?" the nouns are unadorned, and the metaphor is a noun-based verb:

> The very bird,
> grown taller as he sings, steels
> his form straight up.

The title "Light is Speech," itself an inverted metaphor, exemplifies the simplicity and directness of these substantive figures compared with the witty complexity of the sensuous adjectives. The main metaphors in "Light is Speech" are the "dot of rock," "remorse's saving spark," and a "scientist of freedoms." In "In Distrust of Merits" a procession of very traditional metaphors—"hate's crown," man as "wolf to man," "dust of the earth," "heart of iron"—emphasizes the differences in technique and intention between this poem and more elegantly worded pieces like "Four Quartz Crystal Clocks," and "He 'Digesteth Harde Yron.' " The other explicit war poem, "Keeping Their World Large," speaks simply and plainly of "that forest of white crosses" and the bodies that have become "our shield." Finally, the three similarly slim idea poems—"Nevertheless," "The Mind Is an Enchanting Thing," and "Propriety"—all consist essentially of a catalogue of substantive metaphors concretizing the intangible subject of the meditation. The strength of unadorned metaphoric nouns that is the backbone of these poems is clear in a passage such as "the mind

                        is memory's eye;
            it's conscientious inconsistency.

        It tears off the veil; tears
                the temptation, the
        mist the heart wears,
                        from its eyes—if the heart
                        has a face; it takes apart
        dejection. It's fire in the dove-neck's

        iridescence . . ..

It may be that the arena of the idea tends to invite concretizing figures in the form of things, substantives, while the arena of the concrete animal or artifact tends to relegate figurative play to a modifying or attributive function.

    In general, this difference in imagery between the idea-centered and thing-centered poems helps to account for the wholly different texture of these two kinds of verses. Moore seems almost to have alternated between the two kinds of subject matter, as if each were a refreshing change from the other during these years. "Four Quartz Crystal Clocks," "Spenser's Ireland," and "His Shield" have the denser, more playful, and more complex verbal texture created by passages of atypical diction, syncopated alliteration, and a heavier freight of qualifiers. "His Shield" opens,

        The pin-swin or spine-swine
            (the edgehog miscalled hedgehog) with all his edges
                                                        out,
            echidna and echinoderm in distressed-
        pin-cushion thorn-fur coats, the spiny pig or porcupine,
                the rhino with horned snout—
        everything is battle-dressed.

In contrast, "What Are Years?", "Nevertheless," and "The Mind Is an Enchanting Thing" are examples of the slender and seemingly simple format packing the power of plain diction and direct statement. In "Nevertheless,"

        The weak overcomes its
            menace, the strong over-
            comes itself. What is there

        like fortitude! What sap
            went through that little thread
            to make the cherry red!

The poet of these lines has shaken off the whole tangle of idiosyncratic word choice and linguistic complexity in favor of something more spare. As yet Moore refuses to opt finally for one texture over the other, and thus both baroque virtuosity and the power of plain statement continue to highlight each other in her work, even within a single poem.

We are now better able to see the place of a nearly unique experiment in Moore's career, the blend of traditional and idiosyncratic elements in "In Distrust of Merits." The key to this poem lies in its apparent refusal of many of the strategies that have so far come to be associated with Moore's verse: the unusual, even bizarre vocabulary, the Jamesian stamina for convoluted or periodic sentences, the peculiar imagery, and the extraordinary elegance of form. In contrast, "In Distrust of Merits" reads like a compendium of the culture's most traditional, familiar proverbs and emblems on war, as if it were setting out to transcribe the images and phrases that link this war in the general mind to war as such. It is as if the war at hand were yet another outbreak of the same war that has been going on ever since we first thought of saying these things—Plautus writing "Homo homini lupus" or "Man's wolf to man," and the Biblical poetry of the "star of David, star of Bethlehem," of "hate's crown," "Blessed deeds," "dust of the earth," and "Job disheartened by false comfort." Each stanza moves through a rhymed quatrain to a decasyllabic couplet to another rhymed quatrain like stately organ music, a processional of familiar images that underline the timeless nature of this horror. Moore's characteristic syllabic pattern and inaudible rhyme are both muted by a flexible line, especially in the stanza's closing quatrain, and by the hymnic music of many quite audible internal and end-rhymes. The passage conveying what Moore described as the impelling occasion of this poem—a *Life* magazine photograph of a slain soldier[9]—contains a relentless series of short statements in which Moore finally releases the effects of traditional meter and rhyme: ·

> The world's an orphan's home. Shall
> we never have peace without sorrow?
> without the pleas of the dying for
> help that won't come? O
> quiet form upon the dust, I cannot
> look and yet I must.

The visible stanzaic pattern of this poem is intersected and even overriden by repetition and by the strong sound of the metrical couplet:

> Hate-hardened heart, O heart of iron,
>   iron is iron till it is rust.

This was an audacious experiment: it could well have collapsed into a compendium of clichés, if it had not been sustained by a strong new poetic voice that enters Moore's work definitively during these war years.

The poetic speaker's "I," so long suspended in the drive toward objectivity, returns to her lines of the forties in a very different form from the arch, judgmental confrontations of the early verse. On the one hand, "In Distrust of Merits" is a poem of definitive statement, what Moore called "testimony—to the fact that war is intolerable, and unjust."[10] This is its determinate element, out of which arises its strength of conviction. Many of the traditional images reinforce this conviction: the halo, man as "wolf to man," the world as "an orphan's home," the "heart of iron," Iscariot's crime. On the other hand, the indeterminate or problematic element of the poem lies in the poetic voice's repeated assertion of its own complicity in "what causes war"—"they're fighting that I / may yet recover from the disease, My / Self." Unlike the early judgmental "I," this self seems to understand fully its place at the center of the moral dilemma. "It cures me; or am I what / I can't believe in?" And every other appearance of the "I" in this poem constellates just such a double, contradictory statement that lodges the contraries of *what is* versus *what ought to be* squarely within the speaker's self: "I cannot / look and yet I must," she says, and

> I must
> fight till I have conquered in myself what
> causes war, but I would not believe it.

The public world's external predicament is repeatedly traced to the private individual's fallen inner states and attitudes—selfishness, mistrust, blindness, hate, neglect—and the individual's inability so far to overcome those sicknesses. The "I" is therefore identified with the morally equivocal or problematic dimension of the poem. In the midst of a clear conviction, a "testimony," the poetic self is now the locus of the moral dilemma.

This helps us to see the consequences, for a first-person poetic speaker, of Moore's investigation of radical objectivity in verse. By removing the source of value from the self (its locus in the early judgmental pieces) and relocating it in the objective or factual world, the poetry reconceives value as transcending the single self, as existing independently of the personal perspective. Objectivity of statement was gradually attained by progressing from passing judgments to studying the criteria for those judgments and then to embodying the ideals that provide those criteria. The result, or prerequisite, is that the poetic self becomes no longer an arbiter but an attendant observer and finally an unobtrusive artificer. When the "I" returns now, it can never be the confidently judging arbiter it once was, for the nature of things has come to be reflected, in the poems of the thirties, as a tension between the determinate and the indeterminate, neither of which can be cancelled. Both dimensions have been affirmed in the language of those poems, in their definitive mottoes and aphorisms and in the play of doubt and implication that unsettles them. If Moore may be said to have expressed a view of the human condition in her mature poems, it is probably this: the individual self, as it speaks up in these poems, can perceive and champion determinate values, even though it remains itself a vessel of indeterminacy.

The contradictory and problematic nature of the human creature already has provided the basic serio-comic note of "Marriage" and "The Pangolin." When the poetic speaker's "I" first returns to Moore's work in "Spenser's Ireland" of 1941, it acts as a closing foil to the poem's catalogue, or travelogue, of specific cultural sayings, facts, and artifacts. The poem's central motif of liberation "by supreme belief" is echoed ironically in the speaker's "captivity" in an ire-ish temper:

> The Irish say your trouble is their
> trouble and your
>   joy their joy? I wish
> I could believe it;
> I am troubled, I'm dissatisfied, I'm Irish.

A similar contrast comes to light in "Nevertheless" between the images of plants that have successfully overcome obstacles and the dilemma of the "I" in the conditional mode: "Victory won't come / to me unless I go / to it."

The nature of the poetic speaker's "I" in the poems of these war years contrasts with the "I" of the Carlisle verses and that of the "observations" of the twenties. In her 1915–17 work Moore nearly always (in 17 out of 19 cases) coupled the first-person usage with the second, the address to a "you," usually embedding both personae in a concrete situation. "I can but put my weapon up and / Bow you out" is the response in "To Be Liked by You Would Be a Calamity." "You suit me well, for you can make me laugh," she writes "To Bernard Shaw: A Prize Bird." In "To an Intra-Mural Rat" we find "You make me think of many men / Once met," and in "So far as the future is concerned,"

> I shall revert to you,
> Habakkuk, as on a recent occasion I was goaded
>   Into doing.

The encounter itself is usually only suggested or alluded to, thus remaining cryptic, while the focus is on the speaker's response to it. In the "observations" of 1918–25, this anecdotal "I" generally gives way to a more authorial "I," a voice that is not involved in an encounter with a second person but that expresses an attitude directly to the reader. Of "Poetry" it begins, "I, too, dislike it," and in "When I Buy Pictures" it explains, "I fix upon what would give me pleasure in my average moments." We might also call this the editorial "I" in the way it frames or facilitates a poem's thoughts. Of "Marriage" it muses, "I wonder what Adam and Eve / think of it by this time"; of the land unicorn in "Sea Unicorns" it speaks of a feat "which, like Herodotus, / I have not seen except in pictures"; and it frames the speech of "Silence" with "My father used to say. . . ." In these "observations" the "I" is already subsumed in quotation about a third of the time, a practice that then permeates nearly all of the animiles and leaves those poems with only a borrowed first-person voice.

When the sense of a central speaker returns in the forties, then, it is neither in a cryptically sketched encounter nor in an editorial perspective. In the war-conscious poems the "I" is involved in a general situation, an aspect of the human condition, to which its response is in some sense exemplary. We do not need to wonder what the occasion might have been that provoked its reaction, for both situation and response are clear and general. They have the simplicity of urgency, and the "I" recognizes that urgency. In " 'Keeping Their World Large' " there is

> That forest of white crosses!
> My eyes won't close to it.

The general concern of "A Carriage from Sweden" is aesthetic, "this country cart / that inner happiness made art," yet its turning point is a cluster of questions facing the speaker:

> A Dalén
> light-house, self-lit?—responsive and
> responsible. I understand.

It is not for this "I" to inform others editorially but for itself to achieve understanding of the import of the country cart and "our decay," the roots and meaning of art.

It is surely not coincidental that *Nevertheless,* the collection that is first permeated by this renewed "I" of the speaker, is also a volume that was published without any Notes. Even in *Collected Poems* and *The Complete Poems* only one note has been added—a source for "Elephants," a piece in which the "I" does not appear. Earlier I have suggested that the practice of appending notes has the effect of creating the sense of an authorial presence through the implication of a reading consciousness, that the poet comes into partial view in the notes in a way she does not in the poems. If this is so, it makes sense that the volume in which the first-person speaker, after considerable absence, returns centrally to a majority of the poems should dispense with additional apparatus and rest on its renewed sense of a personal voice involved in the struggle depicted in their lines.

Probably the most dramatic example of the self at the center of the moral situation is the single "I" of "His Shield." After the verbally unusual and densely alliterative opening stanza on how "everything is battle-dressed," the diction suddenly thins out to a concise declaration:

> Pig-fur won't do, I'll wrap
> myself in salamander-skin like Presbyter John.

This statement of intent is preceded by the description of rampant, natural battle-dress and is followed by the description of Presbyter John's singular "freedom"—his shield of humility. Placed midway between these two choices, the speaker opts clearly for the second, albeit in the future mode of promise or intent. There is no pretense that the speaker has actually attained the freedom of Presbyter John, the "inextinguishable salamander," any more than our rivers bleed rubies as his do. The poem conveys the choice of an ideal, to try to be "a lizard in the midst of flames" rather than "javelin-dressed."

The brevity of this particular first-person usage returns us to another characteristic of the self in Moore's work. Rarely does the poet use the "I" as a consciousness to contain and condition the entire contents of the poem, as the more purely lyric poet does. The "I" has its place and perspective next to lines that are part of the text of the poem but not necessarily part of the self's personal speech. The opening of "His Shield," for instance, with its complexity of articulation and impersonal form, has the virtues of written text rather than of uttered speech. By not enveloping the entire poem in its awareness, but remaining rather one element among others, Moore's "I" formally recognizes a world beyond its own consciousness, an environment that is genuinely "other" and that has its autonomous existence in the verse. Moore as the poet, as distinct from the poetic "I," has undertaken to imagine and depict a world that transcends, even as it affects, the first-person singular.

"His Shield" is furthermore an illustration of the primarily ethical rather than psychological role of the speaker in most of Moore's verse. The whole poem is a reminder of the personal values of humility and sacrifice in a world that is permeated with military rhetoric and exigencies. The fraternal twin to this poem, "Keeping Their World Large," grew out of some of the same worksheets;[11] it repeats the motif of "our shield" and reminds us of the wartime context of the Presbyter John piece. "Keeping Their World Large" emphasizes the shield as protective armor, whereas in "His Shield" it appears by context to be intended rather in the heraldic sense of an insignia. The presbyter's symbolic dress is not designed by an armorer; to the contrary,

> His shield
>   was his humility. In Carpasian
> linen coat, flanked by his household lion cubs and sable
>   retinue, he revealed
>   a formula safer than
>
> an armorer's.

The imperatives that close this poem are voiced, then, from an attitude of intention rather than achievement, and thus they may well be directed as much at the self as at the reader.

These outright imperatives—"be / dull. Don't be envied or / armed with a measuring rod"—now raise the issue of where Moore's verse is headed in its ongoing exploration of value. In the animiles she played traditional, determinate statements of value off against the indeterminate reverberations of images and "factual" statements and kept vibrant the tension between these two. This balance is still maintained in certain of the animal and artifact poems of the forties. In "Elephants" the unspecified human "as ifs" and "unease" are set at the center of a procession of emblematic lessons in invincibility, equanimity, wisdom, and repose. The balance is present in the contrast between the virtue of an objective, concrete thing and suggestions of human failure to match that virtue. The concrete ideal of the carriage in "A Carriage from Sweden" is set next to the abstract human frailty of "Washington and Gustavus / Adolphus, forgive our decay." But also in a good number of poems of these years, the turn from things to ideas as subjects and Moore's awareness of the war situation have shifted that balance and influenced the tone in a way worth examining.

Many of the animiles—"The Jerboa," "Camellia Sabina," "Smooth Gnarled Crape Myrtle," even "Four Quartz Crystal Clocks" of this period—exhibit openly the irony involved in the balance of determinate and indeterminate approaches to value. Advocacy of a value, in the form of a motto or an aphorism, is challenged and even belied by the openness of exploration and inquiry into the grounds of that value. Advocacy, grounded in certainty, and inquiry, grounded in uncertainty, can proceed from the same speaker only through irony's deliberate duplicity. Each attitude is partially, but never wholly, subverted by the other: the neat aphorism and the unsettling implication highlight as much as they undercut each other, and there is a certain elegance in their interplay.

Such undercutting irony, however, is absent in "What Are Years?" in which the strength of the lines is largely monophonic:

> What is our innocence,
> what is our guilt? All are
>   naked, none are safe. And whence
> is courage: the unanswered question,
> the resolute doubt.

Nothing is being undercut here; indeed questions are being answered. The answer to "What are years?" is the answer to "Whence is courage?" Years as mortality, imprisonment, captivity can be an ultimate source of courage, if one takes it, or refuses it, in the right way:

>   He
> sees deep and is glad, who
>   accedes to mortality
> and in his imprisonment rises
> upon himself as
> the sea in a chasm.

These determinate statements are aphoristic, formulaic in form: "satisfaction is a lowly / thing, how pure a thing is joy." Yet they are not being reported ironically as cultural items. The poetic voice sounds fully behind them, because one can find no clear rent in the fabric, no lines offering a stance from which the poem appears critical of this point of view. Distance and reserved wit have been displaced by this ardent voice. In "What Are Years?" the element of irony has been appropriated by the questioning-answering voice for its own purpose: the couplet ending each stanza contains a rhymed contradiction that rephrases the basic paradoxical message of the poem:

> encourages others
> and in its defeat, stirs
>
> .   .   .   .
>
> in its surrendering
> finds its continuing.
>
> .   .   .   .   .   .
>
> This is mortality,
> this is eternity.

In arguing that years are both everything and nothing, the poem does not eliminate the problematic element, the contradiction, but subordinates it within the central statement. The poetic speaker takes a more definite stand than Moore allowed before the war, but what is being stood for is nothing so thin as a found motto. We are no longer dealing with two incompatible, mutually undermining tasks of advocacy and inquiry, but with an attempt at a definition of value terms, a statement of conditions.

During the war years Moore moved gradually from this kind of general statement of moral conditions to a subjective assertion of them that will eventually bring her full circle as a moralist. "In Distrust of Merits" carries the personal imperatives "I cannot / look and yet I must" and "I must / fight till I have conquered in myself what / causes war." "Nevertheless" translates the import of the images of vegetable growth into personal terms: "Victory won't come / to me unless I go / to it." Even though the self is identified with recalcitrance and possible weakness, it recognizes the unconditional terms of the moral requirement it faces. And by 1944 Moore came out with the direct imperatives closing "His Shield." "Be dull" is partly playful advice in the context of the bristling "hedgehog battalion of steel," but the final "Don't be envied" is earnest enough. The balance is shifting gradually in the direction of an advocacy that will become more explicit in the verse of the fifties. Poetry of overt moral exhortation takes an enormous risk in any age, and Moore's experiment with imperatives and the directive mode will be limited to about six poems. But its commencement toward the end of the war years is a sign of her relaxation of the objectivity of statement that reigned so stringently during the thirties.

In order to explore the suggestion that Moore is shifting from an ironic poise toward definite assertions of value, or at least toward more wholehearted statement, we must ask not only what is being asserted in these verses, but also on what grounds we can assume such assertion. The embodiment of value in objects and the implication of value through statements of fact, as in Moore's poetry of the thirties, leaves value in an indeterminate linguistic form, leaves it unconscious or unintentional in form, however intentionally happy the adopted effect. What happens, then, when the poetic speaker brings an issue of value into determinate form, when the poet appears to convey a sense of value consciously or intentionally? The relatively focused nature of conscious thought, its singularity of intention, implies already a selection from among the large store of unconscious possibilities, a choice of one or two that serve as a structure of thought, an assumption that makes meaning possible. The personal poetic speaker, the sense of a voice created by "I" and "you," reintroduces into the poetry this factor of human awareness and speech. Human subjectivity is no longer a found item but an imagined source for certain passages in which the poem has "something" to say. Or conversely, the project of a poetry that "makes sense" in some determinate form requires a ground for that determinate sense, and that ground is human consciousness and intention. But which comes first, the speaker or the sense? Chronologically in Moore's work, taking a wholehearted stand came first. An affirmation of certain values appeared first in "What Are Years?" of 1940 and "Light is Speech" of 1941, to be followed by the appearance of the speaker's "I" in "Spenser's Ireland" ("I"-reland) and other poems of 1941 through 1944. As always in Moore, what is to be said takes precedence over the self or presence of the sayer.

A poetry of determinate statement takes the same chances as any form of determinate statement does—of being found partial or inappropriate or false. Even such apparently analytic propositions as definitions and tautologies are not guaranteed assent. Theoretically they can all be opposed, disproven, deconstructed, or simply discarded, but Western culture (unlike Eastern) has so far been little daunted by this vulnerability. Certain of Moore's poems are good examples of our traditional confidence in the possibility of making sense in language and in the advisability of making that sense as clear as possible. From a fascination with specific factual material in the thirties, she turns now to the general terms, to a task of definition and an attempt to say what some of these general terms mean. Perhaps the best example of this task of definition is the issue that is the dominant thematic concern of this group of poems—the issue of freedom. The nature and significance of freedom is certainly a special preoccupation of these years, for a clear half of the poems (eight out of sixteen) deal with it, six of them centrally.

The common denominator of the poems concerned with freedom is their sense of paradox, not in the poem as a whole but in the pivotal issue of freedom, which the rest of the poem frames rather wholeheartedly. Each piece argues against the commonly negative conception of "free" as meaning not bound, not restricted, not obligated. In rejecting an absence of obstacles, the poems repeatedly affirm the occasion of human bondage as the ironic ground for freedom positively conceived as a special kind of potency. The poet, like the "Paper Nautilus" and like "Hercules, bitten / by a crab, . . . was hindered to succeed." He of "What Are Years?" is like the "sea in a chasm" that

> struggling to be
> free and unable to be,
> in its surrendering
> finds its continuing.

In "Spenser's Ireland" you are "not free / until you've been made captive by / supreme belief." "Light is Speech" and "He 'Digesteth Harde

Yron' " are both affirmations, one of "free frank / impartial sunlight" and one of "the power of . . . the invisible," in a political context in which "no tree of freedom grows." And the definition that puts this thematic concern to rest comes in "His Shield": "the power of relinquishing what one would keep"—not the renunciation but the power, the capacity for it—"that is freedom." The reader may differ extra-poetically with the validity of this cumulative definition of freedom as a certain power of surrender, but the poems themselves do not intentionally offset or undercut it. They pursue it consistently and unequivocally. They seem prepared—and Moore's considerable oeuvre so far is preparation, if only in hindsight—to stand wholeheartedly behind their point of view.

Finally, the variety of these poems of the forties, their mixture of critical and wholehearted approaches to value, makes this a good moment for pausing to consider the role of Moore's most frequent concrete subject: the animals. She wrote approximately forty poems featuring animal subjects from "A Jelly-Fish" in 1909 to "Tippoo's Tiger" in 1967. And from the moment of "Critics and Connoisseurs" on—"I have seen this swan and / I have seen you; I have seen ambition"—there has been an intimate relation between the animal images and the human concerns of Moore's verses. But whether that relation is justly described as emblematic or symbolic or even metaphoric at all is worth consideration.

On the one hand, we can see that emblematic devices of all kinds were of special interest to Moore as a poet. The emblem is an image whose metaphoric import is particularly defined and stable. It is a figure so determinate that it can be handled intact as social and political currency, in the style of Scotland's emblematic unicorn incorporated opposite the lion in Great Britain's coat-of-arms. Its equations are fairly durable: the lion represents England, the unicorn represents Scotland, and their combination stands for their political unity. Clarity and stability of meaning are of the essence in such a device. But such stable and clearly defined meanings are also useful to the moralist with an interest in embodying and demonstrating doctrinal messages. Thus the Continental and English emblem books of the sixteenth and seventeenth centuries could proceed in a fairly methodical way to translate a *pictura* or image into an *inscriptio* or motto and then into a *subscriptio* or explanation.[12] The process is described by Rosemary Freeman as "detailed equation of picture and meaning . . . establishing parallel after parallel in a purely objective way,"[13] and it depends on a certain determinate and even fixed mode of meaning.

The symbol, on the other hand, shares the emblem's stability but not the relative singularity of import that makes the emblem accessible through equation. Where the emblem is the most determinate of metaphoric usages, the symbol is the least determinate, the least fathomable, and the fullest. Philip Wheelright argues this view in *Metaphor and Reality:*

> A symbol, in general, is a relatively stable and repeatable element of perceptual experience, standing for some larger meaning or set of meanings which cannot be given, or not fully given, in perceptual experience itself.[14]

The amplitude of the symbol rests on its being allowed to remain indeterminate. The tenor of the metaphor as symbol, and the grounds that link the vehicle and the tenor, must be comprehended as broadly as possible, whereas the tenor and grounds of the emblematic figure need to be narrowed and clarified. Whether an image is employed emblematically or symbolically depends, therefore, not only on the image or vehicle and its history but also on the degree of determinacy with which it is presented. A certain tension between the two modes may be created in verse, as we see in the work of George Herbert, who proceeds formally in an emblematic style but invests this disciplined process with a turbulence and depth that repeatedly resist, overflow, and—with as much difficulty as grace—finally accept a determinate path.

But where Herbert's emblem is usually at the center of the poem, Moore's emblem of the twenties, thirties, and forties is generally a local equation at some point in the overall progress of a poem. In "Sea Unicorns and Land Unicorns" the English "lion civilly rampant" and the Scottish "unicorn also, on its hind legs in reciprocity" are referred to in passing; their emblematic function is enumerated as but one of the various attributes of the creatures. In "The Plumet Basilisk" the four dragons on the roof of the Copenhagen bourse that "symbolize four-fold security" represent one emblematic sculpture amid a variety of more mysterious and elusive views of dragon-like lizards. "The Buffalo" opens on an equation, "Black in blazonry means / prudence; and niger unpropitious," but the poem soon veers away from such brief, clear significations toward a four-stanza portrait of the abilities and virtues of the white Indian buffalo serving the Buddha. The ostrich who " 'Digesteth Harde Yron' " is identified with an equation—at the beginning as "a symbol of justice" and at the end as a "rebel"—as if this emblematic convention provides the perfect setting and stylistic foil for the intervening stanzas' close-up views of his appearance and behavior.

The emblematic equation and the process of behavioral observation are antithetical approaches which Moore juxtaposes as a way of yoking together different dimensions of her subject, the idealized and the real. Moore's ostrich is an emblem only at certain points, and the actualities of the creature in the body of the poem are not subsumed by these equations but work in tension with them, anchoring the cultural meanings firmly to natural facts, undercutting a didactic effect by making the moral ideal part of a list of historical actualities. In stanza four, for instance, we see first the emblem and then the actuality, the emblem plainly stated, the actuality vivified by metaphors:

> Yes, this is he
> whose plume was anciently
> the plume of justice; he
>   whose comic duckling head on its
> great neck revolves with compass-needle nervousness
> when he stands guard,
>
>   in S-like foragings as he is
>   preening the down on his leaden-skinned back.

In contrast to this quick shift, the pattern in "Elephants" is a gradual progression from the creature's observed behaviors—"one, sleeping with the calm of youth"—to its ceremonial role and finally to its emblematic poses—"his held-up fore-leg . . . expounds the brotherhood / of creatures." Both of these poems, however, are distinguishable as work of the forties by their assertions of value, their statements of principle that are not being consciously qualified or undercut elsewhere in the poem. These assertions are offered in aphoristic form, but they have been adopted, not merely inspected, by the poetic voice. Unlike the 1935 ending of "Smooth Gnarled Crape Myrtle," the last line of "Elephants"—the saying "asleep on an elephant, that is repose"—is not followed by any unsettling "Alas!"

Looking toward the other end of the metaphoric spectrum, we must ask whether Moore's animals characteristically function as symbols. Can creatures as singular as hers go beyond what Philip Wheelright describes as the "unique flash of insight" of the metaphor used once?[15] The stability or repeatable element of the symbol is one source of its amplitude of meaning, since each successive recognition of the image can enlarge and deepen it. Looked at in this way, the symbol has much of the conservatism of the emblem: both count to some degree on familiarity, on preservation of meaning. By this light, Moore appears to have selected her animal subjects almost with an eye for their resistance to the symbolic function. Her usual choice of a distinctly unfamiliar species and her portrayal of its unique habits could not be better designed to strike the reader with a sense of odd actuality, the feeling of "Amazing but true!" Although two of her favorites are the already significant elephant and lion, there is a certain pathos in the strangeness, the peculiarity of her less familiar creatures—the jerboa, the plumet basilisk, the frigate pelican, the pangolin. We hardly know how to pronounce their names. The unusual nature of the animal coupled with specific details of its anatomy and habits effectively block the amplitude of reverberations that a symbol would gather from its relative familiarity and simplicity.

Moore's images do have something in common with the conceit as a startling and ingeniously drawn parallel. And yet it is just that notion of the parallel that doesn't hold up, for the observational details that the poems offer are not elaborately translated into human terms, as the elements of the conceit usually are. In the early version of "He 'Digesteth Harde Yron,' " the information that the ostrich was "never known to hide his / head in sand, yet lagging / when he must, and dragging / an as-if-wounded wing" seems offered as a corrective to our prejudices, with the implication that perhaps we have underestimated the creature as much as we have betrayed its emblematic ideal. The virtue of the creature for its own sake is important to the sense of the lines. While undoubtedly the animal subjects do address human issues with metaphoric force in local ways, in flashes of insight, they also consistently resist purely figurative status. They remain literal images, which a gathering of attributive metaphors serves to make more precisely vivid, like the ostrich whose "comic duckling head on its / great neck revolves with compass-needle nervousness." The attributive metaphors that sensuously vivify the opening behavioral observations of "Elephants" disappear in the last six stanzas, the emblematic stanzas of the poem. The animal kingdom is one realm of these poems in which the spatial imagination—the stasis of the emblem, the vibrant stillness of the symbol—often gives way to movement, gesture, locomotion, the temporal sway. As real creatures Moore's animals have a poignant relation to their own emblematic function. Their comic, in the highest sense, behavior mellows and actualizes the moral ideals they have been adopted to innocently portray.

Moore's literal animals are part of the otherness of a world that both serves and resists our humanism. "They are what they seem to be," she said once. "There is something authentic about them, they have attractions and are not morally enigmatic."[16] We are the enigmatic, culpable, responsible ones who try for clarity and who make images of ideals. But Moore portrays her animals as literal and complex enough to bear and offset the simple emblematic roles we have assigned them. She is capable of imagining a world beside and beyond the human one, capable in her verse of transcending the humanistic perspective without breaking faith with human values.

After "Propriety," the 1944 definition poem that looks ahead to a renewed aesthetic concern, Moore published virtually no poems for three years, the demanding years of her mother's final illness. Then in 1947 one of her first new poems, "Voracities and Verities Sometimes Are Interacting," was published in *Spearhead: Ten Years' Experimental Writing in America*. Moore may well have raised an eyebrow at being recognized as experimental at the age of sixty, but one of the steadfast features of her verse is its continual change, a feature that is not often noticed and that finally necessitates developmental consideration of her work. Reading her poems in the order in which she wrote them, one comes to expect something new and to resist the temptation to generalize from a few pieces.

During the fifties, released from the preoccupation of the war and tuned to the music of translating La Fontaine's fables, she published original pieces in nearly every year of the decade. They include some of her most cryptic and some of her most personal poems.

6

Nonchalances of the Mind

During the mid-forties Moore's normally brisk pace of life, which had come to include a fair amount of travel for readings and talks, slowed down to accommodate her mother's advanced age and increasing infirmity. Mrs. Moore was bedridden, and paralysis of a throat muscle made the taking of even the slightest nourishment a difficult and exhausting process, which Marianne tended entirely by herself. "Work is a balm," she wrote to Hildegarde Watson in August of 1946; "it is the shadowy resistance of the inevitable, to our struggling minds, that harms us and must not be let harm us." In the same letter she recognized that "Mother's struggle is not temporary."[1]

The following May she confessed to Hildegarde, "I have not 'been to anything' for a year and more, but Saturday went to T. S. Eliot's lecture on Milton at the Frick Collection. . . . Mother had promised to do 'anything I told her' if I would just try the experiment of an outing and give no thought to any clinical cares."[2] The experimental outing was quite successful, but by the end of June Moore was again reporting, "None too good, these last weeks. In fact I can just say I know assistance *must* come to one so faithful and brave as Mole."[3]

It came on July 9, 1947, when Mary Warner Moore died at the age of eighty-five. She was buried in Gettysburg according to her wish, and Marianne wrote to Hildegarde from Bethesda, Maryland, where she was staying with relatives after the funeral: "How dear to us, your saying in these lines just now received, 'I thank God to have known Mole & been lifted by her tenderness, wisdom and grace over so many places it did not seem possible to endure.' " She added, "Warner has been sublime. His voice shook as he pronounced the benedictory words of farewell to mortal flesh, beside what is now her grave."[4] It was a staggering loss—not just of her mother but even more of her closest friend, her sternest critic,

133

and the voice that had stirred and joined her own in some of her finest poems.

After a visit to Ezra Pound in St. Elizabeth's Hospital and a stay in Maine, Moore returned to Cumberland Street to pick up the threads of her life there. Work remained a balm, and she resumed her labors on the translation of La Fontaine which she had begun in 1945. "I'd wake up at 6, work until 8, eat and then go on all day and all evening. I'd stop occasionally, go to market and buy a few things, then go on again. Early mornings in the winter, I'd work in bed. . . . The whole thing was done over completely four times."[5] After it was finished, she admitted with characteristic candor and respect for completeness, "It was fanatical of me to do them all. But I still feel that to have omitted some would be shabby."[6]

As enormous and possessing as this labor became, it still was often background music to visits with her fellow artists and friends, as she resumed the more active life she preferred. In the autumn of 1948 Moore, Elizabeth Bishop, Carlisle neighbor William Rose Benét, and others were photographed by *Life* magazine at the Gotham Book Mart reception for Dame Edith and Sir Osbert Sitwell. In the same letter mentioning this reception and her work on the fables, she tells of going to a dinner given for the Sitwells by W. H. Auden and the Lincoln Kirsteins, having Warner and Constance stay with her for five days, and attending Auden's lecture on "The Lyric of Condensed Experience" at the New School for Social Research.[7] She was by nature a curious and sympathetic person, who delighted in the rich cultural life that New York offered and was supported and refreshed by the company of friends. And in turn one of her friends from Bryn Mawr, Mary Case Pevear, once remarked of Marianne, "Well just simply anything you did with her was fun."[8]

Nor was the La Fontaine project always at center stage in her daily work. By 1951 Moore had prepared and brought out what probably remains her finest book, *The Collected Poems,* including nine previously uncollected pieces. The appearance of this volume immediately won her national acclaim and virtually every literary honor available in America. First came the Pulitzer Prize and the National Book Award, then the Bollingen Prize and the Gold Medal of the National Institute of Arts and Letters. Moore was no newcomer to prizes. Since the Dial Award of 1924, she had received the Helen Haire Levinson Prize from *Poetry* in 1932, the Shelley Memorial Award in 1941, the Harriet Monroe Poetry Award and the Contemporary Poetry Patrons' Prize in 1944, and by 1950 she had already been awarded honorary degrees by Williams, Mount Holyoke, and Smith Colleges. Nevertheless, the *annus mirabilis* occasioned by *The Collected Poems* confirmed her stature as one of the major American poets of the century.

And fast in the wake of these honors came the media, eager to transform the white-haired lady poet into their own kind of "literature," a marketable commodity. The mass media during the fifties and sixties offered a crash course on the public figure who had begun as a very private young poet and then earned the respect and affection of her peers as a poet's poet. For the final two decades of her life Moore managed to bear, usually with patience or amusement, various reporters' attempts to make some catchy, comprehensible sense of her grandmotherly appearance, her unusual personality, and her genius. They lit, of course, on her love of animal subjects and eventually her interest in baseball as quirks that would be accessible and endearing to the general public. Hilton Kramer has suggested that "she may very well have been the last spinster type created by the communications industry before the women's movement radically altered the terms of media mythmaking."[9]

It must have been both a tonic and an exhausting time for Moore. One of her responses to the sudden pressures of public attention was to strengthen her public persona by the adoption of the tricorne and black cape, a choice that had a touch of her mother's taste behind it. For the National Book Award dinner, she recalled, she wanted a new hat. "And as I was passing by in a bus I saw a tricorne in a 5th av. shop. My mother had bought a green straw tricorne in the 20s and I liked that, so I decided to try to find this new one."[10] By the time she found the shop, the tricorne had been sold; however, a Brooklyn hatter, Mrs. Klein, agreed to make one for her. " 'How do you want to look?' asked Mrs. Klein. 'Like Washington crossing the Delaware,' said Miss Moore."[11] And this persona suited many of the poems of the fifties and early sixties admirably, as we shall see.

The *Fables* were published in 1954, and *Predilections,* a selection of her prose, in 1955. By 1956 Moore had accepted three more honorary degrees, had been a visiting lecturer and recipient of the M. Carey Thomas Award at Bryn Mawr, and had published her seventh volume of original verse, *Like a Bulwark*. All the events of this crowded time—the loss of her mother, the years of translating La Fontaine, and her sudden national celebrity—had their various effects on the work that Moore produced in her sixties and seventies.

The poems of what I call roughly the fable years, the mid-forties to the mid-fifties, are in many ways a unique group within the larger company of Moore's later verses. First, their compression is even greater than that of the lyrics that precede them. The average length of these poems is twenty-two lines, down from thirty-eight lines in the early forties and about a third of the average length of seventy-six lines in the thirties. (This brevity lasts only during the years of the fables, however, for by the mid-fifties the verses are already expanding again toward an average of thirty-five lines in 1956–66.) A second distinctive feature of these poems is their use of end-rhyme. Over half of them rhyme three-quarters or more of their lines, whereas only a fourth of the lyrics of the forties and a fourth of the verse of the late fifties and sixties have such a high proportion of rhyming lines. And finally, this group of verses is set apart by a tendency toward abstract diction, uncentered construction, and a heightened internal musicality of rhyme.

Although they focus on many of the same types of subject as their predecessors, these poems of the fable years clearly reflect both the personal loss and the more public life to which Moore was adjusting. The five short pieces of 1947 and 1948—"A Face," "Voracities and Verities Sometimes Are Interacting," "Efforts of Affection," "At Rest in the Blast," and "By Disposition of Angels"—all have recurrent elegiac moments and share the dominant motifs of love and perseverance. In the poems of the fifties that followed these, we find (as we did among the lyrics of the war years) verses undertaking to define or concretize an idea, to anatomize a problem—"Armor's Undermining Modesty," "We Call Them the Brave," "Then the Ermine," "Style," "Logic and 'The Magic Flute,' " and "Blessed Is the Man." There is also a generous offering of poems written about artifacts and animals, such as "The Icosasphere," "Pretiolae," "Apparition of Splendor," "Tom Fool at Jamaica," "The Sycamore," and two pieces written on commission, "Rosemary" and "The Staff of Aesculapius." These poems on concrete subjects differ significantly from those of the thirties and forties, for in her work of the fable years Moore has shifted her customary balance of concrete and abstract materials toward a new texture, a more abstract emphasis than in her earlier work. Although it permeates nearly all the poems, this shift is most clearly noticeable in the pieces on artifacts and animals, for they can so easily be set beside similar subjects of the thirties and forties for comparison.

Nearly all of the qualities that distinguish Moore's work of the fable years are announced in the dozen lines of "A Face," one of the earliest poems of the group. The two halves of this piece, its first eight and last four lines, are a combination of the two epigrammatic styles that appear in the Bryn Mawr and Carlisle poems. These two styles are similar in texture to the two styles of imagery that we found in the lyrics of the forties, the fugal complexity of sensuous metaphors versus the hymnic simplicity of

plain statement of an idea. The two styles of the fifties, however, are both
ways of presenting ideas. In "A Face" the analytic spirit proceeds first on
its musically circuitous way through a thicket of abstractions:

> "I am not treacherous, callous, jealous, superstitious,
> supercilious, venomous, or absolutely hideous":
>> studying and studying its expression,
>> exasperated desperation
>>> though at no real impasse,
>>> would gladly break the mirror;
>
>> when love of order, ardor, uncircuitous simplicity
>> with an expression of inquiry, are all one needs to be!

The parade of abstract adjectives at the opening is reminiscent of the way
"To a Steam Roller" opens with its heavy abstractions,

> The illustration
> is nothing to you without the application,

and closes with its cacophanous alliteration of "conceive . . . question . . .
congruence . . . [and] complement." In "A Face" the end-rhyme and internal rhymes of "expression . . . exasperated . . . desperation . . . [and] im-
passe" is reminiscent of the rhyming abstractions of "Injudicious Gardening," in which

> the sense of privacy,
>> indeed might deprecate
>> offended ears, and need not tolerate
> effrontery.

The abstract, polysyllabic density of the first part of "A Face" is then
countered with "uncircuitous simplicity" as recommended in line seven:

> Certain faces, a few, one or two—or one
> face photographed by recollection—
>> to my mind, to my sight,
>> must remain a delight.

Here the music of internal rhyme is monosyllabic and even metrical in
the closing anapests. It reminds one of the early Bryn Mawr lines, "If you
will tell me why the fen / appears impassable, I then . . ." ("Progress") or
of the couplet from "In Distrust of Merits," "O / quiet form upon the
dust, I cannot / look and yet I must."

   Abstract language like that of the first part of "A Face" also appears in
the other three "love poems" of 1947–48, poems with a tone or an ex-

plicit theme of love. Even their titles are more complex than most of Moore's and attest to her abstract approach at this time—"Voracities and Verities Sometimes Are Interacting," "Efforts of Affection," and "By Disposition of Angels." Where the poetic voice of *What Are Years* and *Nevertheless* used ringing moral terms like "courage," "justice," "fortitude," and "humility," Moore now bypasses "greed" and "truth" in favor of "Voracities and Verities." Many lines of the later forties reach for fine distinctions like the final one of "Efforts of Affection":

> Thus wholeness—
>
> wholesomeness? say efforts of affection—
> attain integration too tough for infraction.

As in "A Face" this effect of abstract density is heightened by contrast with the simpler diction and rhythm of the preceding lines:

> Truly as the sun
> can rot or mend, love can make one
> bestial or make a beast a man.

Each of the key concepts of "Efforts of Affection" are stated twice, once simply and once in more Latinate conceptual form: "love's . . . stubbornness" becomes "efforts of affection," and "wholeness" becomes "integration." Likewise in "By Disposition of Angels," the center of each stanza turns on a repetition and re-inflection of abstract terms:

> Above particularities,
> these unparticularities praise cannot violate.
>
> . . . .
>
> Mysteries expound mysteries.
> Steadier than steady, star dazzling me, live and elate.

These two pivotal passages are connected across the stanza break by the rhyme of their unaccented endings.

Like the alliterative titles "Voracities and Verities" and "Efforts of Affection," many of the Latinate abstract terms in these four poems come to have a music of their own. Identical suffixes create an effect of echo on the upbeat, either immediately as in "treacherous, callous, jealous, superstitious" (in "A Face") or intermittently as in "distraction . . . integration . . . inspection . . . obsession . . . attraction . . . affection . . . infraction" (in "Efforts of Affection"). We have seen this music of syncopated syllables in the "unconscious fastidiousness" of "Critics and Connoisseurs" and in the "conscientious inconsistency" of "The Mind Is an Enchanting Thing," but during the fable years this sound is deepened from a passing verbal level to a structural level. The repetition of suffixes multiplies and seems to carry passages along in its own lilt. W. K. Wimsatt reminds us that the classical rhetoricians recognized this useful effect as *homoeoteleuton* or "like endings" (*homoeo,* similar, and *teleute* from *telos,* end).[12] As Wimsatt points out, this echo of like endings plays a very different role than does rhyme, a role that will support the growing emphasis on thought that underlies the abstract tendency of Moore's later work.

Wimsatt writes that, "Stylistic parallels or forms of meaning of this [homoeoteleutonic] sort seem to come fairly to the aid of logic."[13] Each echoing Latin suffix "has the same meaning, or is the same morpheme, and each supports the logic of the sentence by appearing in a certain place in the structure." In contrast Wimsatt points to the "alogical character of rhyme," especially when rhymed words clearly differ from one another in sense or part of speech. This "alogical character of rhyme," he concludes, when wedded to the logical sense of the passage, can "save the physical quality of words," a physicality of which we tend to lose awareness in "daily prose usage."[14] Certainly the physicality of words, the patterns and delight of speech sounds, is a fundamental resource for any poet. But particularly at this time in her career, when rhyme is highlighted more than at other times, Moore's work offers us a case study in what Viktor Shklovsky has called the "special dance of the organs of speech."[15]

First of all, we can see in these four love poems of the late forties that "like endings" is a different resource for the English writer than it was for the Latin writer. Like endings in English tend to produce an effect of abstract discussion, largely because of the kinds of words to which such endings are usually appended. As a language with far fewer suffixes of declension and conjugation than Latin has, English lends itself only in a limited way to homoeoteleuton. One is confined to such morphemes as *-ion, -y, -ness, -ence, -ing,* and *-ied,* which function largely as syntactic adjustments for our more abstract terms: simplicity, inquiry, steadiness, darkness, occasion, obligation. A majority of our concrete nouns do not usually carry such endings—face, mirror, mind, star, fir, hay, elephant-ears, diamonds—they do not carry the endings the declined Latin nouns do.

These first four poems of the fable years carry an especially heavy load of abstract terms with echoing endings. Their concrete nouns are fewer, and those are usually simple and unqualified by adjectives: the harp, the cattle, a saint, the sun. The effect is of basic or elemental things embedded in an elaborate composition of thought. Observation in these poems is transformed from description of visible objects to meditation upon intangible matters. And the delight of words themselves, their patterns of sound, becomes even more pronounced than it has been in Moore's work so far. In fact, it becomes so prominent that we are left with certain new difficulties in the realm of sense.

The abstract quality of what Wimsatt calls the "minimum rhyme" of word endings[16] contributes appropriately to the texture of "The Icosasphere" of 1950. The first rhymed sound, the long *e* occurring twice in each of the three stanzas, is carried down the lines by a chain of wholly abstract words, "density . . . efficiency . . . perjury . . . economy . . . geometrically . . . vertically." The poem contrasts wasteful greed with certain economical but mysterious feats of construction, and so its rather technological subject seems well enough served by such a web of conceptual terms. It is more telling, however, to find a similar chain of abstractions with echoing suffixes introducing the animal poem "Apparition of Splendor":

> Partaking of the miraculous
> since never known literally,
> Dürer's rhinoceros,
> might have startled us equally
> if black-and-white-spined elaborately.

And this poem's closing address—

> Shallow oppressor, intruder,
> insister, you have found a resister,

—displays both the internal rhyme (here in the last line of every stanza) and the polysyllabic music of this group of verses.

In fact, it is not easy to discern whether the creature intended as the "Apparition" is an egret or a porcupine or both. The grammatical subject of the second stanza is the shape of the bird—

> Like another porcupine, or fern,
> the mouth in an arching egret
> was too black to discern
> till exposed as a silhouette

—the "double-embattled thistle of jet" referring to its two long, pointed head-feathers. The pronoun of "Was it / some joyous fantasy" still refers grammatically to the egret, but "eider-eared" and "spines" suggest that Maine's animal intended here is the porcupine. This poem differs from the animal and artifact poems of the thirties in its emphasis on ideas at the expense of the visual clarity of its animal subject. We are not shown the habits and behavior of the egret or the porcupine in the way we are shown the behavior of the jerboa, the pangolin, or the ostrich. Compression moves the poem more directly past its images to its thought. "Apparition of Splendor," published in 1952, is actually a war poem, for the context of language like "double-embattled," "shot," "fight," and "oppressor" is the Korean War. "As Maine goes . . . " becomes the unspoken thrust of this poem about choosing not to fight. The "Splendor," the delicacy and fantastic quality of a peaceful creature, is of more concern to the poet than the literal actuality of the animal.

Other poems of the fifties show this new contrast with the animiles even more clearly. In "Rosemary," for example, the minimum rhyme of word endings reinforces the abstract nature of the poem's concern. All eighteen lines of the poem rhyme with the final long *e* of "rosemary":

> Beauty and Beauty's son and rosemary—
> Venus and Love, her son, to speak plainly—
> born of the sea supposedly,
> at Christmas each, in company,
> braids a garland of festivity.

Abstract rhyme-words predominate—"differently . . . originally . . . memory . . . legendary . . . pungency . . . reality"—while the few concrete rhyme-words are plain and unadorned: "Mary . . . sea . . . bee . . . tree." Only one line of this whole poem is devoted to description of the physical appearance of the plant itself, "With lancelike leaf, green but silver underneath," though reference is made to its "blue" flowers. But after the elaborately specified "blue-pink dregs-of-wine pyramids" of "Smooth Gnarled Crape Myrtle" and the "gray-blue-Andalusian-cock-feather" pansies of "Virginia Brittania," the adjective "blue" here is spare and general. It is clear that to Moore in the fifties the Christmas theme, the idea that the rosemary flowers imitate the robe of Mary, is more important than sensuous rendering of the special hue of the flower.

This is not to say that attention to sensuous detail has disappeared from the verses of the fable years. The familiar attributive metaphoric complexes depict the moth of "Armor's Undermining Modesty" with its

> backgammon-board wedges interlacing
> on the wing—

> like cloth of gold in a pattern
> of scales with a hair-seal Persian
> sheen.

And Tom Fool's "suede nostrils," the silk-shirted jockeys as "animated Valentines," and Fats Waller's "giraffe eyes" vivify the champions of "Tom Fool at Jamaica." But emphasis on the visual surface gives way to the thought and conceptual imagery in many of these poems, and their brevity does not allow them to wander the avenues of extended description or factual report.

A prime illustration and suggestive explanation of this conceptual turn is a poem of place, "The Web One Weaves of Italy." This poem has as enticing and musical a title as one could wish for, and it offers one of Moore's most haunting conceptual figures, the "nonchalances of the mind." But compared with earlier poems of place, with the perceptual fullness and variety of "New York," "An Octopus," "Virginia Brittania," or "Spenser's Ireland," these twelve lines make a very economical web. It would be a disappointing poem if one came to it expecting a continuation of the earlier plenitude and catalogues. In this 1954 poem, the web that leaves one "charmed" is not so much the country of Italy as the mind and its weaving. In fact, Italy is presented in an alliterative but very compact list of only five items:

> The crossbow tournament at Gubbio?

> For quiet excitement, canoe-ers
> or peach fairs? or near Perugia, the mule-show;
>   if not the Palio, slaying the Saracen.

Indeed, the advisability of attempting a fuller inventory of worldly multiplicity is doubted at the very outset of this poem, for the web "grows till it is not what but which, / blurred by too much." In this opening sentence Moore offers us a vital clue to a reason for her renewed insistence on compression in the lyrics of the early forties and especially in the early short poems of the fable years.

Observation of the external world, its sensuous and factual details, can extend indefinitely. We have witnessed how Moore's early compact style expanded in the twenties and thirties with accessibility to large new realms of experience in New York, with travels to the West Coast and Virginia. The plenitude of the world clearly had an exhilarating effect on the imagery of those poems, and it made their sense of value more open, genuinely inquiring, and generous. But sensuous detail, as enticing and infinite a resource as it may be, also poses the danger of distracting, even overwhelming, the susceptible observer. The mass of material, data, detail, and qualifications can grow till it is "blurred by too much," till it begins running away with a poem, spinning its imitations of inexhaustible nature on indefinitely, even past the realm of form. We may remember here Moore's repudiation of the two very long catalogue pieces, "Pigeons" and "Walking-Sticks," toward the end of the animiles, just before her return to compression in the lyrics of the early forties. This is part of the import of the lines "The Mind Is an Enchanting Thing / is an enchanted thing"—that there is peril as well as magic in the "power of strong enchantment."

At the center of "The Web One Weaves of Italy" is the mind. Moore quotes her own translation of La Fontaine's fable "The Monkey and the Leopard" in her third stanza of "The Web":

> One salutes—on reviewing again
>
> this modern *mythologica*
> *esopica*—its nonchalances of the mind,
>   that "fount by which enchanting gems are spilt."

La Fontaine's fable depicts the competition between the fancy-coated leopard and the quick-witted monkey, between body and mind, to capture a carnival audience, ending with the moral that

> Exterior diversity
> Can never charm as the mind can, to infinity—
> That sparkling fount by which enchanting gems are spilt.[17]

Moore recognized the poetic limits of "exterior diversity," and her poems of the fable years reflect her renewed allegiance to the "fount" of the mind. The blur of "too much" echoes her subtitle to the Romans' and Egyptians' material plenty in "The Jerboa," and she appears now to be aiming more at the "simplified creature" that is its counterpart.

We can discern, then, these two apparently contrary trends in the poems of the late forties and early fifties—on the one hand, a renewed severity evident in the brevity of the verse and the abstract nature of its diction, and on the other hand, a certain density of texture and heightened musicality of rhyme, especially of like feminine endings. The virtue of a certain severity was already on Moore's mind by the time she was finishing the animiles of the thirties, for in September of 1936 she wrote to a poet who had sent her his work for comment,

> Since there is severity at some points—of a kind natural to my imagination—the pages where there is not this severity are against my taste.[18]

We might well wish to see in the work she was commenting on the precise elements of the severity that Moore felt was "natural" to her imagination. But we have discerned some of its elements directly from this work of the early fable years: brevity, fine abstract distinctions, and two qualities which are only apparently contradictory—the cryptic and the didactic elements of her verse.

The cryptic nature of some of the verse of this time stems, as it does in the earlier Carlisle poems, from the poet's willingness to be private in public. In those early apostrophes and again in these verses, Moore refers to persons and situations that appear to be quite specific and yet unspecified. Whose is the "one / face photographed by recollection" that is the climactic image of "A Face"? The star of "By Disposition of Angels" is "like some we have known; too like her, / too like him," but we can only guess who they are. And practically all of "Voracities and Verities" seems prompted by offstage figures and circumstances. "Poets, don't make a fuss" makes us wonder which poets and what fuss, and is the fuss meant to be the "gratitude" that is "trying," and is that the same as the diamonds? "A tiger-book I am reading— / I think you know the one"—why would we know the one, or who is the "you" who would know it? Moore's note to this poem, printed at the foot of the page, attests to her supposition that the reader does not, in fact, know that she means James Corbett's *Man-Eaters of Kumaon.*

A tantalizing mystery is "Like a Bulwark" of 1948, which in its first published version states at its center,

> You take the blame
> And are inviolate—
> Down-cast but not cast
>
> Down.

Who is the "you" being addressed here, and what is the blame? It could be a third-person "you"—anyone taking any kind of blame—but the well-developed title simile is strongly reminiscent of the substantive metaphors of the Carlisle apostrophes. Stanley Baum has suggested that Moore's brother Warner was "her bulwark" but without overt reference to this particular poem.[19] The poem's early title "At Rest in the Blast" may provide a key, for it suggests that the poem may have been inspired by Ezra Pound, who at the end of World War II was brought to the United States under a charge of treason and incarcerated in St. Elizabeth's Hospital. *Blast* was the Vorticist magazine of Pound and Wyndham Lewis, which during the First World War printed its outspoken manifestoes that "blast" the bad and "bless" the good. Moore had read this magazine in 1915, and from its pages she had copied into her diary, among other lines, a motif concerning boats. She then incorporated these lines into an unpublished poem entitled "Ezra Pound" that ends with her own manifesto of praise for

> that page of Blast, on which
> Small boats ply to and
> Fro in bee lines. Bless Blast.[20]

During the mid-forties Pound was certainly "taking the blame" for his wartime broadcasts, but failing further extra-poetic clues, we may never know for sure whether this poem is indeed a statement of support for her friend.

Poems of this period can be cryptic in a richer, less severe way, too, not only through unexplained private reference but also through what T. S. Eliot has called "a very wide spread of association."[21] Certain associative links in these verses are made with more suddenness and less interpretation than is usual in Moore's work. "Elephants" explains its emblem, "His straight trunk seems to say: when / what we hoped for came to nothing, we revived." But in "Voracities and Verities" we move quickly into and past the image:

> Poets, don't make a fuss;
> the elephant's "crooked trumpet" "doth write";
> and to a tiger-book I am reading—

Here the logic remains implicit—that even the elephant can write, in a sense, and therefore poets should not make a fuss about such a natural thing as writing—and the poem moves through the image as swiftly as did the poet's associative mind. Veiled or oblique reference at its richest can overleap the gaps in our factual knowledge. This effect shares some of the uncertainty and intensity of a Symbolist poem moving through a series of private symbols and correspondences.

Such swiftness of movement, privacy, and intensity are even more evident in "Then the Ermine," as it goes from Clitophon's armorial device of the white ermine to the bat by daylight to Beaufort's motto *Mutare sperno*, "I don't change," to the *palisandre* settee to Dürer's violets. The typescript of a deleted stanza supplies some connotations for the closing image of the violets:

> Marine azures and heliotropes between
>   waves in motion, when effaced
> by wind reassemble, then
> die and again
>
> change.[22]

Thus the first part of the poem espouses the armorial attitudes of " 'rather dead than spotted' " and *Mutare sperno*, "I don't change," while the second half of the poem as it appeared in *Poetry* accepts the appearance of change embodied by the marine heliotropes effaced and reassembled, the chiaroscuro of velvet:

> Change? Of course, if the palisandre settee can express
>   for us, "ebony violet"—

> Master Corbo in full dress
> and shepherdess
>
> at once—

Master Corbo is La Fontaine's "Le Corbeau," whom Moore translates as "Master Crow" and "Sir Ebony." His " 'ebony violet' " and the implosive power of the "violets by Dürer" have a Symbolist-like intensity and mystery as embodiments of change. The "waves in motion" were dark counter-devices to the white, idealistic ermine.

What distinguishes this kind of poem from Moore's earlier work is its refusal to offer the reader an explicit center, an anchor in the form of a focal object or idea. The lines move as rapidly from image to image as those of "Nevertheless" or "The Mind Is an Enchanting Thing" or "Propriety" but without providing their kind of clearly unifying concept. The centering concept in "Then the Ermine" is change, but this word has been deleted from the final version of the last three stanzas. The negative force of "frighten," "Fail," and "foiled" is overcome by the beauty of " 'ebony violet' " and the "violets by Dürer; even darker." The images, the color, and even the paradoxical quality of the color does the work of expressing that "power," the possibility of overcoming fear and failure.

A similar intensity and mystery appear in "Logic and 'The Magic Flute,' " whose "winding stair" or "Wendeltrappe" and "theater" seem as if they are virtually inside the "abalonean gloom" of the wentletrap shell. A typescript of this poem affirms this new mode of imagery in its title— "Dream; or Dream: Logic and 'The Magic Flute.' " The dreamlike conflation of the shell and the theater of the "telecolor trove" is a visionary combination rather than a visual observation:

> Near Life and Time
> in their peculiar catacomb,
> abalonean gloom
> and an intrusive hum
> pervaded the mammoth cast's
> small audience-room.

Now that she is turning away from the blur of "too much" sensuous and factual detail, Moore's factual observation gives way to this highly compressed, even impressionistic vision—the "lightning . . . on thistlefine spears" in "Apparition of Splendor," the " 'ebony violet' " of "Then the Ermine," and the "abalonean gloom" of "Logic and 'The Magic Flute.' "

The turning inward of vision in these poems is accompanied by a distinct musicality of rhyme that is but one step away from the echoing feminine endings of the abstract terms. "Apparition of Splendor" with its internal rhymes is the most audible example, especially the fourth stanza with its

> "train supported by porcupines—
>   a fairy's eleven yards long"? . . .
> as when the lightning shines
>   on thistlefine spears, among
>   prongs in lanes above lanes of a shorter prong.

Triple rhyme reappears in "Then the Ermine," and a nearly quadruple effect is created by the simple and immediate echoes of "Logic and 'The Magic Flute' ":

> " 'What is love and
> shall I ever have it?' " The truth
> is simple. Banish sloth,
> fetter-feigning uncouth
>   fraud. Trapper Love with noble
> noise, the magic sleuth,
>   as bird-notes prove—
>   first telecolor trove—
> illogically wove
> what logic can't unweave:
>   one need not shoulder, need not shove.

This frequent, audible rhyme, both of the earlier abstract terms and of these strong monosyllabic chimes, is a feature of the verse of the fable years through the mid-fifties. Since it will disappear again in Moore's verse of the sixties, which is as lightly rhymed as much of the rest of her work, we should pause here to consider the meaning of this phenomenon.

It seems logical to assume that Moore's project of translating La Fontaine's fables influenced the frequency and audibility of the rhyme in her original verse of the time. As Laurence Stapleton has pointed out, "the pursuit of this difficult task gave birth to different energies in her own poems."[23] La Fontaine exploited the many like endings of French, a language with far more rhyme possibilities—a wider choice of words available for each rhyme sound—than English. Moore was also aware of the rhythmic difference between her own verse and the French she was working with. She wrote to Walter Pistole at Reynal and Hitchcock, the publisher for whom she began the translation, that "although in La Fontaine sentences end at the end of the line, mine constantly carry over."[24] Working with material whose end-stopped lines heighten the effects of readily available close rhymes must have tuned the poet's ear anew to a kind of rhyme sound which decades before she had chosen to de-emphasize in her own verse.

In *Marianne Moore: The Poet as Translator,* Rosalee Sprout has observed that "Nine years of struggling to find creative equivalents in English for La Fontaine's end-rhymes . . . had to have had some impact on Marianne Moore's approach to writing poetry."[25] Sprout finds the rhyme in the poems composed during and after the *Fables* "more regular, more musical," and she suggests how this came about:

> Her method of translation, her determination to imitate La Fontaine's rhyme patterns and to reproduce the *sounds* of his rhymes must have established a new habit of mind which I think is reflected in the kinds of poems she wrote after the *Fables*.

This influence, the force of the French original, must have been rather strong, especially as Moore's grasp of the sounds and nuances of that language grew with the project. But to have a full picture of Moore's writing during these years, we need to see the other side of this notion of "influence."

Influence assumes susceptibility, a passivity that can be swayed, a gap that can be filled. And surely there are many senses in which a work is written by its moment in history and by its predecessors, with the author as a consenting vehicle for the production. But just as surely, the writer is also an agent who writes down the material, the one who wrestles with its composition. If there is anxiety of influence, there is also the exhilaration of the act of making the poem—this particular poem, not just any. Each poem is an answer to anxiety by a thing accomplished, a transcendence of influence by the act of giving out or setting down the words. However far back the tumble of cause and effect, of pressure and choice extends, the poet also acts, writes down, deletes, makes choices that will—through this *kenosis* or relinquishing—recast the self as an author, as a name synonymous with its work.

Moore had many alternatives before her as she approached this project of translation. We know that she read and considered a number of quite different translations of the *Fables*: F. C. Tilney's prose translation for children (from which she had quoted "everything to do with love is mystery" in "Marriage"), Robert Thompson's reproductions of the fables' "contour and rhythm," Elizur Wright's rendition in Victorian diction, and Sir Edward Marsh's colloquial free verse versions with some end-rhymes.[26] From a whole array of different forms of fidelity and beauty Moore, like each of her predecessors, chose what kind of English work to make of the original, chose what to keep and what to sacrifice. La Fontaine's moral to "The Frog and the Rat" (IV,xi),

La ruse la mieux curdie
Peut nuire à son inventeur,
Et souvent la perfidie
Retourne sur son auteur,

Moore renders

Snares woven impeccably
Can be the weaver's executioner;
And how often treachery
Brings doom on its practitioner.[27]

She let go of literal equivalence and chose to keep another exactitude, not only the rhyme patterns but also the rhyme sounds of the original. This undertaking, to make the English version rhyme with the French as well as with itself, posed enormous difficulties, but it also placed the highest possible premium on sound as a distinctive element of a poet's work. To render La Fontaine, Moore temporarily surrendered her own allegiance to enjambed and inaudible rhyme and placed herself in the service of the Frenchman's audible, end-stopped rhymes. Moore's interest in rhyme conditioned her translation as much as the translation conditioned the rhyme of her own poems.

Moore's strategy places more emphasis on rhyme than even the usual rhymed translation does: it assumes that there is a value to be preserved not only in the rhyme pattern but also in the sounds that carry the pattern. In other words, the poet's assumption here seems to be that the sounds themselves are a sufficiently autonomous element of verse to be actually transferable, and worth transferring, from one language to another. Perhaps "autonomous" has the wrong implications here: Moore's strategy may assume rather that sound qualities are so integral to the sense of a poem that they too must be rendered if the sense is not to be diminished. Sound is the non-conceptual component of sense.

Modern theorists of rhyme as an irrational or transrational phenomenon are thinking in terms of traditionally audible rhyme. In insisting on the "alogical character of rhyme," Wimsatt distinguishes between "melodies" and "ideas," assuming that rhyme is sensory, audible.[28] Emphasizing the necessary "wedding of the alogical with the logical," Wimsatt calls the words of a rhyme "the icon in which the idea is caught."[29] This recognition of the "wedding" of sound and sense in a poem is not beside the point, for two decades earlier the Russian formalists had effected something of a divorce on this traditional marriage by positing an "opposition between 'poetic' language and 'practical' language."[30] Sounds in poetic language, the formalists claimed, have a certain "autonomous value."

Viktor Shklovsky wrote, "It may very well be that a large part of the pleasure poetry gives us stems from its articulatory aspect—from a special dance of the organs of speech."[31] Shklovsky continues, "Poetic language is distinguished from prosaic language by the palpableness of its construction,"[32] and it is partly this "palpableness," this foregrounding of the medium of words themselves as sensory things, that results in the defamiliarizing effect of art.

Marianne Moore's inaudible rhyme, however, does not entirely submit to this distinction of sound from communicative sense, for inaudible rhymes are perceived with the eyes on a written text or not at all. They are not available to the ear alone, and hence do not affect the spoken rhythm of the lines, as we have already seen. Instead, they discover for us the rhymes hidden in practical language without audibly or rhythmically foregrounding those rhymes. The difference in sound before and during the *Fables* becomes clear in two poems published only six years apart on similar subjects, "His Shield" of 1944 and "Armor's Undermining Modesty" of 1950. All of the lines of each of these poems are rhymed, but the rendering of a stanza from each in a prose format will demonstrate the change in sound. In 1944 Moore wrote, "Pig-fur won't do, I'll wrap myself in salamander-skin like Presbyter John. A lizard in the midst of flames, a firebrand that is life, asbestos-eyed asbestos-eared, with tattooed nap and permanent pig on the instep; he can withstand fire and won't drown." The ear does not readily pick out the rhymes of "wrap" with "nap," "John" with "on," and "firebrand" with "withstand." In 1950 she wrote, "Arise, for it is day. Even gifted scholars lose their way through faulty etymology. No wonder we hate poetry. . . ." Here one can hardly miss the chiming of "day" and "way," "etymology" and "poetry."

Moore's inaudible rhyme has thus been a way of overcoming the distinction between poetic and practical language in the poem as spoken, while preserving that distinction in the poem as a written text. The verse patterning is visually but not audibly stanzaic; its sensuous "dance" takes place outside, and often in tension with, the stanzaic pattern. At the same time, we are finding that so-called "practical" language can be far more sensuously patterned than the formalists' distinction would suggest. In the formalist view, sensuous patterning is incidental in practical communication, while it is integral to poetic utterance. But Moore's distinctive art has been to make the incidental patterns of practical language into a liberating principle of her verse.

We may now understand better why, after three experiments in audibly rhymed couplets in 1956 and 1957, Moore will virtually abandon for serious purposes the audible, end-stopped rhyme of the fable years and return to her own hidden patterns and to freer verse forms. Of those three experiments—"Values in Use," "Hometown Piece for Messrs. Alston and Reese," and "Enough: Jamestown, 1607–1957"—the last is the most serious undertaking and thus shows most clearly the alien nature of the idiom that henceforth Moore would reserve only for light verse. The central descriptive interlude of "Enough: Jamestown" has an Audenesque plain music that the poet never returned to after this piece:

> The crested moss-rose casts a spell;
> and bud of solid green as well;
>
> old deep pink one with fragrant wings
> imparting balsam scent that clings
>
> where redbrown tanbark holds the sun—
> path enticing beyond comparison.

This has more of the sound of poetry-in-general than of Marianne Moore. Auden confessed to having "stolen a great deal" from the "endless musical and structural possibilities of Miss Moore's invention."[33] But he did not stay with his syllabic experiments any longer than Moore stayed with her serious venture into audible rhyme.

This venture may be compared in some ways with Moore's venture into free verse during the early twenties. Both strategies proved to be relatively short-lived detours that expanded the dimensions and enriched the musicality of her verse beyond what Moore eventually saw as compatible with her intent. The model she established in 1958, immediately after "Enough: Jamestown," is the artist "Melchior Vulpius," a composer of chorales, hymns, and anthems. "We have to trust this art," she writes in the enjambed stanzas, slant rhymes, and unrhymed lines that resume the spare sound of her work before the fables. From now on, when the poet is writing playfully, as in "To Victor Hugo of My Crow Pluto" or in "Occasionem Cognosce" (retitled " 'Avec Ardeur' "), audible rhymes are part of her irony of technique. They press the lilt of poetry-in-general into the foreground, even while the poet assures us in " 'Avec Ardeur' " that "This is not verse / of course."

Already by the poem "Style" of 1956, Moore's familiarly enjambed and inaudible rhyme is returning. Once again one can hardly hear the line breaks when they are not visually present: "There is no suitable simile. It is as though the equidistant three tiny arcs of seeds in a banana had been conjoined by Palestrina; it is like the eyes, or say the face, of Palestrina by El Greco." One does not hear the distant, unaccented rhyme of "though" with "El Greco"; and the immediate but unaccented rhyme of "banana" and "Palestrina" is less noticeable than the chance internal chime of "simile" and "three." None of these sounds are strong enough to press the rhythm of the utterance toward an end-stopped pattern. The sound of "Style" is Moore's syncopated alliteration—"Escudero's constant of the plumbline / axis of the hairfine moon" and Soledad's "black-clad solitude that is not sad"—a sensuous prose that audibly overrides the poem's end-rhyme pattern.

Just as the venture into free verse during the twenties ended with a return to the syllabic stanza form, so the venture into audible rhyme ends with a reaffirmation of the "unaccented syllable," the light rhyme. In each case, the poet appears to be reasserting the strategy that preserves the tension between the poetic and the non-poetic, making something that looks like verse sound like the richest kind of practical language. Moore's characteristic syllabically shaped, inaudibly rhymed stanza is a verse that defies certain of our expectations of verse. In fact, the work of every distinctive poet is a construction in verse that deconstructs some other idea of verse. The purpose is to make the lines feel instead more like a song, a speech, a prayer, like ordinary talk or the newspapers or the muttering of the mind or, in Moore's case, educated writing and speech. The writing of verse is, in part, an act against itself, a doing that must undo itself if it is to result in anything more than poetry-in-general, that ground against which each poem must detach itself as a figure.

Verse must be written against itself because intertextuality is not only a fact; it is also a closed, circular, and therefore limited system. Language refers and responds not only to other language. The whole network of language in use operates at a frontier, at the border of the speechless. Utterance is a threshold. One cannot prove in language the existence of a non-linguistic realm or substance, nor can one prove its non-existence. We are left, with Dr. Johnson, kicking the stone—left, as Edward Said puts it, with a "worldliness [that] does not come and go," but stays ineluctably.[34] And wordless actuality, that "ultimate subtext," is by definition non-textual.[35] It is the changing nature of this non-textual actuality that makes, that *is,* the particularity of the text. The poet resists poetry in order to make the poem more than just "poetic language"; or, the text also attempts to serve its own ultimate subtext. The point is the same: verbal art takes words, textuality, as its materials, but what makes anything an art is that to us it is so much more than its materials.

Finally, then, Moore's poems of the fable years bring us back to the issue of value in a new way. In 1957 *The Saturday Review* carried this observation by Winfield Townley Scott on *Like a Bulwark:* "It has been remarked, but not sufficiently, that there is a strong streak of didacticism in Miss Moore's poetry. . . . There is the didactic so concentrated as to force moral statement into poetry."[36] It is not quite clear whether Scott means by his final phrase "forcibly insert moral statement into the poem" or, let us hope, "press moral statement to the point at which it becomes art." One thing which prompts recognition of the moral dimension of these poems is the more than usually prominent role played in them by imperatives. In Moore's earlier work we have encountered the imperative form in various rhetorical contexts that tended to mitigate its tone of command. In "To a Chameleon" the verb is actually descriptive in effect: "Hid by the august foliage and fruit of the grape vine / Twine / Your anatomy / Round the pruned and polished stem." We find quoted instructions in "Camellia Sabina"—" 'Dry / the windows with a cloth' "—and mottoes in "The Frigate Pelican"—"Make hay; keep / the shop . . . Be gay / civilly." The poet's editorial hand guides our glance in "Virginia Britannia"—"Observe the terse Virginian, / the mettlesome gray one." And the imperative form has the force of a prayer in the lines of "In Distrust of Merits"—"Be joined at last, be / joined."

Some of these strategies appear in the work of the mid-forties to mid-fifties. "Armor's Undermining Modesty" includes the motto, "Arise, for it is day," of the John Day Company, a sixteenth-century printing house that incorporated the words into its title-page device, and "Voracities and Verities" offers the professional advice, "Poets, don't make a fuss." But we find also in the poems of the fable years a number of quite definitely moral imperatives, particularly in "Tom Fool at Jamaica":

> Be infallible at your peril, for your system will fail,
> and select as a model the schoolboy in Spain
>   who at the age of six, portrayed a mule and jockey
>   who had pulled up for a snail.

The counsel of "Logic and 'The Magic Flute' " to "Banish sloth" is borrowed from Ovid, but it is not presented as a found moral like those of "The Frigate Pelican." The advisory voice continues to the poem's end, "one need not shoulder, need not shove." We might at first wish to attribute this admonitory strain to Moore's long sojourn in the moral atmosphere of the fables, but in fact we saw this turn toward moral imperative in 1944 work that was completed before the work of translation was undertaken. "His Shield" urged us with the finality of a closing note to "be / dull. Don't be envied or / armed with a measuring-rod."

Rather it is to the poet's early practice that we must look for the source of this imperative note, just as we looked there for her first experiments with close audible rhyme. The couplet containing the imperative in "To a Prize Bird" reminds us of both the rhyme and the judgmental strain that were Moore's point of departure:

> Pride sits you well, so strut, colossal bird.
> No barnyard makes you look absurd.

Perhaps it would be most accurate to say that the work on La Fontaine prompted the poet to try pressing some of her earlier techniques farther than she had in the past. The imperatives of the fable years are like a generalizing of the specific judgments of the Carlisle years. They are implicitly addressed to a second-person "you," but this time not to an individual but to a universal "you"—to a reader rather than to the poem's subject.

Furthermore, the aphoristically moral titles of certain poems of the fable years are reminiscent of the aphoristic titles of a number of Bryn Mawr and Carlisle poems. The early adopted mottoes of some of her college poems—"Qui S'Excuse, S'Accuse," "Tunica Pallio Proprior," "Things Are What They Seem"—are followed by the longer and wittier title aphorisms of *Observations* like "Diligence Is to Magic as Progress Is to Flight," "In This Age of Hard Trying, Nonchalance Is Good and," "Nothing Will Cure the Sick Lion but to Eat an Ape." This practice largely disappears during the thirties when inquiry and ambiguity are undercutting such set maxims. And when aphoristic titles return in the lyrics of the war years, they have a new directness and simplicity: "What Are Years?", "Light is Speech," "The Mind Is an Enchanting Thing." In comparison with those, we can now see that the aphoristic titles of the fable years have a distinctly moral emphasis: "Voracities and Verities Sometimes Are Interacting," "We Call Them the Brave," "Blessed Is the Man." When we remember that "Tom Fool at Jamaica" is actually Howard Moss's title and that Moore had written and submitted the poem with the title "Letter Perfect Is Not Perfect," the larger admonitory context of its imperatives becomes clear.[37]

A clue to the significance of this temporary cluster of imperatives and moral aphorisms lies in the generally negative form of most of the advice and precepts. "Don't make a fuss," poets are advised; "Letter Perfect Is Not Perfect"; "Be fallible at your peril, for your system will fail"; and "Blessed Is the Man" who

> does not sit in the seat of the scoffer—
> the man who does not denigrate, depreciate, denunciate:
> who is not "characteristically intemperate,"
> who does not "excuse, retreat, equivocate; and will be
> heard."

This admonitory strain is probably another face of the moral feeling that was often expressed ironically in the animiles and in heroic terms in the war lyrics. Inquiry and ambiguity went only so far before the extremities of the war years gave detachment an inhuman air. The admonitions of the fable years are the reverse side of the appreciations for which Moore is so well known. But unlike the pointed judgments of her early work, the admonitions here are general in form, while the appreciations—of Tom Fool and Fats Waller, of Escudero and Etchebaster—are quite specific. She has praise for the person and warning of the universal pitfalls. Thus the return of the poetic voice's confident pronouncements is accompanied by a growth in generosity, a selective gentleness.

The judgmental and the admonitory are passing phases in Moore's ongoing development, but the appreciative is a constant. And the celebrative air of the last two volumes that she published will take us into a discussion of the wider import of aesthetic values in her work. There we shall leave behind several of the difficulties peculiar to the poems of the fable years—the occasionally extreme compression, the abstract diction and emphasis, the heavier than usual texture of rhyme, and the cryptic quality that balances this verse between its private reference and its public performance.

As "The Sycamore" reminds us, "there's more than just one kind of grace." And in a way this poem is a parable: it guides us to the values and implications of the work around and after it. The unusual and towering "chamois-white" sycamore seems to afford the occasion for the poem, but the "little dry thing from the grass . . . retiringly formal" is the subject of the closing model stanza, Moore's determinant of form here. The graces of the grand and of the humble are joined by the graces of the living and the dead, of the flowers that "must die, and nine / she-camel-hairs aid memory." These graces of art are reciprocal: that the little dry thing from the grass is "worthy of Imami," the Persian miniaturist painter, places nature in the service of art; that art is memorial places it in the service of life.

7

The Celebrative Air

As she entered her seventies, Moore must have found writing as a celebrity a very different business from her efforts in Carlisle and the early years in Brooklyn with Mole to guard the door and censor anything less than her best. Frequently in her later years she was asked to write verse for a specific occasion or publication, and sometimes she deplored the result. In 1956, just home from a visit to Harvard, she wrote to Hildegarde Watson with characteristic verve, "Have been in a frenzy, like a wild cat in a waste-basket, diagnosing MSs—3 of them—and struggling with a piece about the Dodgers, that I was urged at Harvard to produce for the Hudson Review by August 16th. . . . The whole thing," she lamented, "may seem too infantile to print. I can't *imagine* submitting it to Sibley and Scofield."[1]

Without her mother's ruthless "It won't do,"[2] Moore sometimes shuddered at what she consented to publish. The two early poems, "I May, I Might, I Must" and "A Jelly-Fish," which she included in *O to Be a Dragon* she by now considered "so slight, I hide under a leaf"; of "Melchior Vulpius" she said simply "I am embarrassed"; and in her Conversation Notebook she would eventually admit, "I don't care for the books that were not worked on by her."[3] But she persevered—"A blessing should rest on us all for our ardor," she exclaimed, "I write like a donkey, a gosling, a wasp bound it will get out of a bolted French window"[4]—and we may be glad that she did for the sake of the very good moments embedded in the last two volumes.

After the success of *The Collected Poems* Moore branched out into new genres, as if she felt somehow liberated by her accomplishment. Of her 1954 play *The Absentee,* based on Maria Edgeworth's novel, she said, "Nothing may ever come of it [it was published in 1962] but I had immense fun working on it."[5] And in 1963 Macmillan published the three

156

Perrault fairy tales, *Puss in Boots, The Sleeping Beauty, and Cinderella,* which she had translated from the rare original manuscript edition of Perrault's tales in the Pierpont Morgan Library.[6] "I'm a happy hack as a writer," she told *Life* magazine,[7] but there were also times when she felt overwhelmed by the multitude of requests that arrived in the mail and over the telephone.

Moore traveled extensively in the United States during these later years, giving readings and talks, accepting further honors. In desperate need of a respite from her admiring public, she accepted her Bryn Mawr friends Frances and Norvelle Browne's invitation to accompany them to Italy and Greece in 1962, and in 1964 she toured England and Ireland with them and a third friend. On this last visit she had luncheon with her old *Dial* cohort Alyse Gregory, whose description of Marianne affords us a vivid glimpse of the personal qualities behind the magazine photos of the white-haired poet visiting the zoo or strolling through Washington Square Park in her cape and tricorne:

> What did most continually and penetratingly come home to me was the rarity, the utter unimpressiveness of our Marianne, from her very first appearance in her dress, all winnowed but [her] so refined and exquisitely responsive face under that enormous black straw hat . . . what a combination of total outgoing almost heedless naturalness and most delicate and minute observations. . . . She says no one will believe how naive she is or how torpid (not with the word) – but what remains as my final impression is one of a combination of extreme fragility and vulnerability, combined with a firmness and fineness of texture and an intrepidity of spirit and a generosity of heart that I found deeply moving.[8]

The description omits Moore's prodigious energy, which anyone can vouch for who has had the honor of escorting her around the Bryn Mawr campus at reunion time, hurrying to keep up with her. While sometimes deploring "this rushing inadequate dearth of leisure," she did also often seem to relish the "simply scandalous" pace of her life, as long as it did not prevent her entirely from writing.[9]

The late poems of almost any long-lived poet are bound to have a certain testamentary quality for us. And Marianne Moore's last two volumes of verse, *O to Be a Dragon* of 1959 and *Tell Me, Tell Me* of 1966, offer a fairly clear picture of where she believed poetry belongs and what it is meant to do. In fact, the dominant concern of these late poems is art itself: a full half of them focus on artists, performances, styles, and the role of art. We find poems that are concerned with art centrally—"In the Public Garden," "An Expedient—Leonardo da Vinci's—and a Query," "The Mind, Intractable Thing," "Tell Me, Tell Me"—and peripherally—"Blue Bug," "Baseball and Writing," "Saint Valentine." For Moore, of course, art was a natural lifelong interest, and in the decade of her seventies it comes into the foreground of her work in a way it has not since the criteria poems of the twenties like "When I Buy Pictures" and the early animiles of the thirties like "Nine Nectarines." But now the poet does not primarily judge or analyze—she celebrates. And the wider, even ethical, import of aesthetic value is the issue to be raised in these meditations and late celebrations.

Another prominent concern of these late poems is echoed in the cape and tricorne hat that Moore had adopted after the fashion of George Washington. In 1938 *Twentieth Century Verse* sent out an "enquiry" to a number of "older" American poets. To the query, "Do you regard yourself as part of the American tradition, as an American poet?" Moore replied, "Yes; as implied above, an American chameleon on an American leaf."[10] And indeed, Moore's last two volumes reflect more of contemporary America than we have found in her work for some time. From an early preference for British subjects like Yeats, Browning, Disraeli, and Shaw in the Carlisle poems, we can see a clear shift in her focus toward the plenitude and local color of "Dock Rats" and "New York" that followed the Moores' move to New York City. For many years Moore balanced American subjects like "An Octopus," "The Steeple-Jack," "Virginia Brittania," and "Tom Fool at Jamaica" with depiction of foreign scenes and cultures in "England," "Camellia Sabina," "A Carriage from Sweden," and "Spenser's Ireland." But during the decade of the late poems, 1956–66, only one out of thirty-two pieces really uses a foreign culture in a central way—"Combat Cultural" focusing on the dances of Old Russia. The occasional British subject like W. S. Landor is outnumbered by the homegrown Messrs. Alston and Reese of the Brooklyn Dodgers, Yul Brynner, Yvor Winters, dancer Arthur Mitchell, and the "Master Tailor" Ben Zuckerman. The American idiom and setting dominate a good third of the late poems from the two baseball pieces to Jamestown to Vermont's "Arctic Ox," Boston's "Public Garden," and New York's "Carnegie Hall," "Old Amusement Park," and the "Granite and Steel" of the Brooklyn Bridge.

Thus many of these late poems share with the lyrics of the war years a certain immediacy, a sense of immersion in a stream of public events. But the stream of events of the fifties and early sixties appeared in many ways less tragic, less dire than that of the World War II years. The American national consciousness, as yet untouched by the anguish of Vietnam, often seemed buoyant with prosperity and even pride. It was a good time for the celebration of excellence in general and for pleasure in local excellence in particular. It may be difficult for us now to recapture the confidence of the fifties, just as it was difficult for modernists of the twenties to feel sustained by the sense of moral order that, prior to World War I, made judgment possible and desirable.

In *Making, Knowing and Judging,* W. H. Auden said of the poet, "Every poem he writes involves his whole past."[11] This is true in a technical sense for, as we shall see, the voice, rhyme, and metaphors of Moore's late poems exhibit the variety of half a century of experimentation and growth on which she could draw. These two volumes contain more diversity of technique than any original collection Moore published since *Observations.* And Auden's remark is even truer of the emotional and contemplative dimensions of a poem, for feeling grows in part out of memory, and understanding involves past views of things as much as the momentary insight. What is absent from any one poem is still present as the field of possibility on which the actual utterance stands out, sometimes a rather palpable field. The approaches to value that have characterized Moore's work of earlier periods—judgment, criteria, inquiry, advocacy—are each reclaimed in these late poems and become part of their diversity. They are also the field for a new form of gravity to be found here beside the playfulness—a vulnerable self and its labor of affirmation.

It may appear at first as if Moore is simply picking up an early strategy here, for the dominant voice of these late poems is a modification of the early interaction between an "I" and a "you." The "we" of the thirties and the morally problematic "I" of the war lyrics recede here in favor of an imagined meeting of first and second persons, and the third-person or reader-oriented "you" of the twenties, thirties, and forties gives way here to the "you" addressing a figure within the poem, a vocative in some ways reminiscent of the Carlisle apostrophes. "I don't know how you got your name," she says to the polo pony "Blue Bug," and to his "bug brother," the dancer Arthur Mitchell,

> Your jewels of mobility
>
>   reveal
>   and veil
>   a peacock-tail.

However, unlike the early, very short apostrophes, these late poems incorporate their "you" address into a longer poem of more varied texture and often multiple subjects. "Blue Bug," for instance, moves from the photograph of the polo ponies to a dragonfly to "an ancient Chinese melody" to the movement of the eye to the acrobat Li Sian Than. Thus the address of Blue Bug happens in passing rather than being the central determinant of the poem's rhetorical stance.

Another second-person poem, "The Mind, Intractable Thing," the most poignant piece of the late collections, addresses more than one auditor. The ongoing conversational address to the mind, "You understand terror, know how to deal / with pent-up emotion," is punctuated by the supplicatory "O Zeus and O Destiny!" The same kind of changing address appears four-fold in "Baseball and Writing," which turns first to the reader ("You can never tell with either / how it will go") then to Mickey Mantle ("you'll be tough, premature prodigy") then to the owners ("Mr. Houk and Mr. Sain . . . don't sell Roland Sheldon") and finally to the whole team ("O flashing Orion, / your stars are muscled like the lion"). This multiple and shifting address turns the confrontational to a more conversational mode that serves the appreciative spirit of these late pieces.

An even broader diversity than that of voice is exhibited in the rhyme in these two volumes of work. We find the early style of very light and unaccented rhyme in "Baseball and Writing":

> "Going, going . . . " Is
> it? Roger Maris
> has it, running fast.

We find also the combination of a more audible and a less audible, accented and unaccented rhyme in the same stanza in "Saint Nicholas":

> might I, if you can find it, be given
> a chameleon with tail
> that curls like a watch spring; and vertical
> on the body—including the face—pale
> tiger-stripes, about seven.

Homoeoteleuton, the like endings that appeared in some of the more abstract poems of the fable years, contributes to the unaccented music of "In the Public Garden":

> Boston has a festival—
> compositely for all—
> and nearby, cupolas of learning

(crimson, blue, and gold) that
    have made education individual.

This Latin style of echoed endings proves itself a versatile and lasting
mode of unaccented rhyme, providing a leitmotif for even the rhapsodic
lines of "Granite and Steel": "Enfranchising cable, silvered by the sea . . .
Tyranny . . . ingenuity . . . priority . . . harmony . . . perspicacity . . .
composite span—an actuality."

Another strategy preserved from the fable years is the audibly rhymed,
end-stopped couplet of "The Arctic Ox (or Goat)," a light verse whose
playful tone distinguishes it from the animiles of the thirties. The aphorism providing the final rhyme for many of its stanzas underlines the neat
fit between the creature and the moral. The tidy sound and final position
of the unchallenged aphorism keep the tone of this animal piece lightly
witty and even jaunty:

                        sweater;
        your coat is warm; your conscience, better.
        · · · · · · · · · · · ·
                Procrustes' bed;
        so some decide to stay unwed.
        · · · · · · · · · ·
                If we can't be cordial
        to these creatures' fleece,
        I think that we deserve to freeze.

Alongside these more lately adopted strategies, we also find combina-
tions of end- and internal rhyme like those that appeared in "Those Various Scalpels" and "A Carriage from Sweden" where, as now in "The
Mind, Intractable Thing," the first syllable of the line rhymes with the
last syllable of the line: "O imagnifico . . . a bird—Arizona . . . Unafraid
of what's been done." In short, the diversity of this period suggests that
Moore is now orchestrating all of her familiar strategies rather than pursu-
ing experiments in a new technique.

"Rhythm and rhyme, of course, are magic and mesmerizing," said
Moore in her August 1950 speech at Harvard.[12] But her notes and notebooks of subsequent years of that decade suggest that after the *Fables* had
been completed, she engaged in something of a reconsideration of the pitfalls attending this magic. In a 1955 talk called "Words and Modes of Expression," Moore seems wary of audible end-rhyme as she notes that in
some lines she is reading, "who which comes at the end of the line is
rhymed with 'yew' (dangerous practice, but I approve of it here)."[13] Two
years later she writes in her notebook,

> Rhyme is an outrageous thing—
> able to damage anything verbal—
> But if it weren't
> could "success" be anything but partial?[14]

The "dangerous" and "outrageous" qualities of rhyme lie precisely in its "magic" and "mesmerizing" delight in that "special dance of the organs of speech," in its foregrounding of the sensuous nature of words over their sense.[15]

Finally, in a notebook entry of 1959 Moore gives a name to the principle that underlies her distinctive practice of syncopated alliteration and swiftly enjambed, virtually internal rhymes:

> like Braque and his
>   trees at Estaque
>
>   the rhyming incidental.[16]

Unaccented, enjambed, and internal rhymes tend to seem more "incidental" to the ear than do audible, end-stopped rhymes. But to the eye scanning a written text, unaccented rhymes form as much of a pattern of artifice as the more traditional ones do. In "Saint Nicholas" Moore describes Marées's St. Hubert,

> erect—in velvet and tense with restraint—
> hand hanging down: the horse, free.
> Not the original, of course. Give me
> a postcard of the scene—huntsman and divinity—
>   hunt-mad Hubert startled into a saint.

Here the enjambed rhymes "free . . . me . . . divinity" are no more audible than the incidental internal pauses on "horse . . . of course." The pattern of rhyme originates in the utterance of the model stanza in which the verse germinated, but in the rest of the poem both rhyme and alliteration may be seen, if not heard, intersecting the utterance.

Rhyming "who" immediately with "yew," or "sweater" with "better," "tail" with "pale" can interfere with the sense of a passage in a positive, heightening way or in a negative, distracting way. "Don't speak in rhyme," warns the poet of "Enough: Jamestown" of "maddened men in starving time." She subsequently followed this advice by depicting, for instance, the desolation of Leonardo with less audible, unaccented rhymes and like endings in "An Expedient—Leonardo da Vinci's—and a Query":

> Could not
> the Leda with face matchless minutely—
>   have lightened the blow?
>   "Sad" . . . Could not Leonardo
> have said, "I agree; proof refutes me.
> If all is mobility,
>   mathematics won't do."

Here the alliteration of "matchless minutely . . . me . . . mobility, / mathematics," of "Leda . . . minutely . . . agree . . . mobility," and of "Minutely . . . proof refutes . . . won't do" is Moore's syncopated alliteration again markedly overriding the simpler, less palpable pattern of end-rhymes. In other words, the texture of the utterance as practical language within the lines is more audible than the pattern that demarcates it on paper as verse.

This texture, or what I am calling syncopated alliteration, bears a certain resemblance to Gerard Manley Hopkins's practice of unravelling alliterative patterns, primarily of consonance, as in "Spring," "When weeds, in wheels, shoot long and lovely and lush; / Thrush's eggs look little low heavens." Moore's alliterative texture is usually more loosely woven than Hopkins's is, her echoes spaced farther apart, like the ones in "An Expedient—Leonardo da Vinci's" that are spread over five or six lines. But in a late and very musical poem like "Rescue with Yul Brynner," the texture can be quite dense, with the "th," "h," "w," and "s" sounds shifting around the reiterated "ill" syllable:

> There were thirty million; there are thirteen still—
> healthy to begin with, kept waiting till they're ill.
> History judges. It will
> salute Winnipeg's incredible
> conditions: "Ill; no sponsor; and no kind of skill."

We know that Moore read Hopkins carefully at least as early as the thirties. In September of 1933 she wrote to Sister Mary James, "more recently I have been influenced somewhat, I think, by the poems of Gerard Manley Hopkins."[17] Some of the sounds of the Old English alliterative line and of the Welsh *cynghanedd* (king-hah-neth´), a shifting pattern of consonants bearing repeated vowel sounds, have re-entered modern poetry largely through Hopkins.[18] Well before her recognition of his influence, however, we find a light, germinal form of syncopated alliteration in the poem which Moore selected to close her final volume—" 'Sun!' " of 1916. "Splendid with splendor hid you come," she wrote half a century ago, like a device

of Moorish gorgeousness, round glasses spun
to flame as hemispheres of one
great hour-glass swindling to a stem.

Already in this early work, the echoes of "d," "m," "g," "ou," and "em"
nearly override the end-rhymes.

In general, the poet is the artist for whom language is the sensuous medium of communication, language both as text (visual and lasting) and as
voice (audial and evanescent). In certain radically abstract poetries such as
those of Gertrude Stein or the *Façade* poems of Edith Sitwell, poetic language does very nearly cease to function as practical language. In a line
like Stein's "Why while while why while why why identity identity why
while why. Why while while while while identity," the referential and
logical dimensions are almost wholly suspended—but not quite. As Stein
recognized, our conceptual processing of words can only be suspended
by some strategy that disengages the mind, such as monotonous repetition sustained out of all proportion to the yield of meaning, until the sensuous dimension of language takes over with its own forms of play. Sitwell, less radically, uses an unlikely variety of language similar to that of
nonsense verse. Sense becomes a non-logical, atmospheric adjunct to
sound in a passage from her "Four in the Morning" like "Mr. Belaker /
The allegro negro cocktail shaker."

But in most poetry, and especially in Moore's, poetic language does
not cease to perform the conceptual and referential roles of practical language. It is because poetic language retains its practical function that we
even begin to respond to a poem, if we do, as anything more than an arrangement in lines of letters and vocal noise. Even in such a prominently
euphonious poem about music as "Rescue with Yul Brynner," the referential, conceptual action of words is heightened rather than suspended by
the sensuous artistry with which they are deployed. The syncopated alliteration of Brynner's "face / of milkweed-witch seed-brown" is a
stronger, more audible music than the end-rhyme of "face" with "palace," but the image it conveys of an earthy brown color is also an integral
part of the configuration of images and thoughts that constitute the sense
of the poem. The poetry resides in the tension between the "special dance
of the organs of speech" and their meanings, between the sensuousness
and the sense.

The temptations of the sensuous surface of words appear to have been
more real for Moore in these late poems than at any other time, and she
appears to be more conscious of them in the verses themselves. The poems' pervasive concern with art is often self-challenging, as in the ironic

lines of the deceptively playful "Dream," where the richly alliterative texture of "m," "p," "t," and like endings heightens the irony of the subsequent tag:

> For his methodic unmetronomic melodic diversity
> contrapuntally appointedly persistently
>   irresistibly Fate-like Bach—find me words.

The lines turn on the seeming inadequacy and yet availability of such a sonorous array of words, the Bach-like music of language preceding the plea to "find me words." This passage echoes the similar closing irony of the earlier poem "Style," in which the complaint of "no suitable simile" is followed by three quite remarkable ones:

> There is no suitable simile. It is as though
> the equidistant three tiny arcs of seeds in a banana
> had been conjoined by Palestrina;
>   it is like the eyes,
> or say the face, of Palestrina by El Greco.

These poems are both aware of, yet unimpeded by, the limits and inadequacies of language. Those limits are ironically belied by the pleasing, even virtuoso, surface of the words.

The motif of the limits of words spills over, however, into a concern in the late poems with the limits of the poet, of the artist as a person. This concern and its newly somber tone distinguishes the late poems about art from earlier such poems and offsets the playful atmosphere of these volumes. For instance, from an earlier period the 1944 poem "Propriety" exhibits the streamlined directness of many of the war lyrics. It defines its central concept by cataloguing embodiments of it—"a not long / sparrow song . . . the fish-spine / on firs"—along with the names of its component virtues, "reticence . . . rigor . . . resistance." In contrast with this upbeat brevity, "Style" of 1956 shows the denser verbal texture and homoeoteleuton of the fable years. We see both of these here in the pattern of "b," "v," "d," and the "-er" endings describing Soledad:

> As if bisecting
> a viper, she can dart down three times and recover
>   without a disaster, having
> been a bull-fighter. Well; she has a forgiver.

The poem again defines a concept by embodying it, but this task is virtually eclipsed by the celebrative spirit, by appreciative description of the performers and athletes who epitomize style.

In contrast with both of these pieces, the 1965 poem "The Mind, Intractable Thing" expresses in an unusually personal, lyrical voice the vulnerability of the artist. The title turns its predecessor, "The Mind Is an Enchanting Thing," to the somber note of an "Intractable Thing" that

> even with its own ax to grind, sometimes
> helps others. Why can't it help me?

The definition of the poet as a "wizard in words" in this poem takes us back to the 1915 Merlin piece titled "The Wizard in Words" and beginning " 'When I am dead,' the wizard said. . . . " This echo and the inclusion of the 1909 and 1916 verses in these two late collections remind us that Moore is looking back over her whole work, which is not a surprising perspective for her seventies. But we shall see that there is also a thematic reason for this retrospect. The sensuous, attributive metaphoric complex is absent from this poem, for sight has given way to insight that is less sensuous and more abstract. As in many of the poems of the fable years, observation is now a thought process rather than a garnering of sense data. The central metaphor of "The Mind, Intractable Thing" is substantive and conceptual—"my eye's half-closed triptych"—and it continues Moore's tendency to internalize her vision.

But the most important element of this poem is the relation it develops between the mind, poetry, and the self. The mind is identical with the poet, for it is addressed as "O imagnifico, / wizard in words—poet . . . "

> you, imagnifico, unafraid
> of disparagers, death, dejection,
> have out-wiled the Mermaid of Zennor,
> made wordcraft irresistible.

And yet the mind-as-poet remains distinct from the subjective self, the "I" of the poem: "You understand terror, know how to deal / . . . I don't." The wordcraft of which the mind and poet are the wizard is a "craft with which I don't know how to deal." Thus the personal self is distinguished from the authorial mind, and the first, last, and central motif of the poem is the vulnerability of the personal self to those forms of defeat by which the authorial mind is "undeterred."

The vulnerability in "The Mind, Intractable Thing" is unusual in Moore's late work, for more often the dilemma of the artist's personal dejection is solved by the saving consolations of art. Like Ben Jonson, the poet of "No Better than a 'Withered Daffodil' " confesses " 'O I could . . . drop, drop, drop, drop.' / I too until I saw that French brocade / blaze green. . . . " That "work of art," Sidney's green jacket in the Elizabethan miniature painting, revives the speaker of the poem.

The "insupportably tiring" problem of "Charity Overcoming Envy" appears to be resolved by the elephant in the tapestry, who "convinces the victim / that Destiny is not devising a plot." "Tell Me, Tell Me" provides a refuge from egocentricity in the "absorbing / geometry of a fantasy" such as the work of Henry James or of Beatrix Potter, the fictions that "rescued a reader." And the consolations of art in "An Expedient—Leonardo da Vinci's—and a Query" are perhaps most movingly evoked by the closing query, once Leonardo has "succumbed to dejection": "Could not / the Leda with fact matchless minutely—have lightened the blow?" The opening of that poem, moreover, suggests that memory of the past could help "lighten the blow,"

> so that "great wrongs
> were powerless to vex"—
> and problems that seemed to perplex
>   him bore fruit, memory
> making past present.

The artist can make his own consolation by involving, as Auden says, "his whole past," as Moore appears to be doing in her retrospect of techniques. And in the work of the very end of her career, we shall see how the commemorative function of art contributes to its creation and preservation of a sense of value.

We can now understand why the two longer gift poems, "Saint Nicholas" and "Saint Valentine," highlight the special gift of a work of art. The gift poem in general, including the shorter "For February 14th," is a version of the earlier catalogue poem, an inventory or list of things, whose ordering principle here is value or desirability. Thus in "Saint Nicholas," after the chameleon, the *qiviut* dress, and the moonlight's "dim marvel," we come finally to an artwork, "the most / prized gift that ever was"—the reproduction of Hans von Marées's painting of St. Hubert kneeling in reverence before the stag with Christ "entined" in its antlers. Likewise in "Saint Valentine," the two main gifts are "a replica, framed oval" of El Greco's painting of his daughter Vera and "verse—unabashedly bold" and yet "as neat / as the most careful writer's '8.' " The value of these gifts lies in the profoundly inspiriting nature of art as Moore understood it. In her last volume, *Tell Me, Tell Me*, she quotes a fellow American author: "Writing is a fascinating business. 'And what should it do?' William Faulkner asked. 'It should help a man endure by lifting up his heart.' " And Moore adds with emphasis that indeed, "*It should.*"

Another kind of verse that, like the gift poems, appears as new in the fifties and sixties is the group of dance and sports poems, seven pieces celebrating physical agility, the artistry of the body. "Tom Fool at Jamaica" and "Blue Bug" both commemorate champion horses and juxtapose their qualities with the human physical skills of musicians and acrobats. "Style," "Combat Cultural," and "Arthur Mitchell" honor dancers, and the two New York baseball poems, "Hometown Piece for Messrs. Alston and Reese" and "Baseball and Writing" share with the others of this group an explicit admiration of strength and ease, zest and modesty. Since the baseball poems in particular have become such a sentimentalized part of Moore's public image, it is worth our while to examine briefly their place in her overall late poetic endeavor.

The early "baseball fan," whose role in "Poetry" of 1919 was to rhyme inaudibly and ironically with "statistician," was long ago claimed as one of the legitimate "phenomena" of poetry. The poet as fan is the poet moving in the mode of pure zest. While she was at work on the second of the two baseball pieces in October of 1961, Moore wrote to Katherine Sargeant White at *The New Yorker,* "(Am reprehended for writing about the Dodgers) but urged on by T. S. Eliot and even if he discouraged me, I couldn't forsake my catcher and fielders."[19] The personal involvement indicated by this passage may reflect a poetic reason for the composition of "Baseball and Writing" in addition to the personal one of transferring her loyalties from the ex-Brooklyn Dodgers to the New York Yankees. "Baseball and Writing" does not repeat "Hometown Piece" but rather significantly improves on and matures three elements of the earlier poem. It transposes the somewhat assuming "we" into the more personal "I-you" form, the straight rhymed couplets into stanzas of immediate and distant, accented and unaccented rhymes, and its simple urge to win into a deeper appreciation of excellence bought by training and discipline.

The sports poems—the pieces on both baseball and horses—occasionally break out of the spatial mode into a time stream of narrative motion. Gil Hodges "lengthens up, leans, and gloves the ball," and the polo pony Blue Bug is imagined as

> bug brother to an Arthur
> Mitchell dragonfly,
>   speeding to left,
>   speeding to right.

Most of the dance and sports poems, however, maintain a spatial mode of presentation that is surprisingly still and pervasive for depictions of physical action. "Tom Fool" has "a chiselled foot," and even in the midst of his "harmonious rush" on the race track, we see, as if they were still points, his "nose rigid and suede nostrils spread, a left hand on the rein." In "Style" the dancers and athletes are all captured in still configurations—skater Dick Button's "classic silhouette," Spanish dancer Soledad's "black-clad solitude . . . [like] S soundholes in a 'cello / set contradictorily," and tennis champion Etchebaster's "mousing pose"—identifying the spatial as the mode for the perception of style. The arrested quality of all these physical images is epitomized in this poem by the radically spatial simile of the "equidistant three tiny arcs of seeds in a banana." All that movement and skill in dance and athletics is "like the eyes, / or say the face, of Palestrina by El Greco"—not so much like music as like the painting of a face. The presentation of motion as still shape—the Yankees as the stars of Orion, polo as "Yellow River- / scroll accuracies"—is a preservation of the momentary as permanent. And it is this lasting element, the shape of the momentary preserved in the ritual repetitions of memory, that is the material of the symbolic. "Combat Cultural" reaches toward that mode in its last stanza:

> These battlers, dressed identically—
> just one person—may, by seeming twins,
> point a moral, should I confess;
> we must cement the parts of any
> objective symbolic of *sagesse*.

In general the dance and sport poems do not translate their spatial images in such an explicit way, but the stillness of those images encourages a reader to consider them as translatable, significant.

What Moore was looking for in these poems on the artistry of the body is suggested in her letter to Mrs. White while at work on "Baseball and Writing." "Have a thousand details garnered—," she says, "of vernacular and virtuosity."[20] This paradoxical interest in the naturalness of vernacular and the artistry of accuracies is reminiscent of Moore's earlier oxymoron "unconscious fastidiousness" in "Critics and Connoisseurs." The animal and the body are the most natural subjects of art, and Moore evidently felt that the "virtuosity" of the athlete had as much to do with her art as the "mastery" of Melchior Vulpius or the "pure glory" that Cocteau dreams of in "Carnegie Hall: Rescued." If the vernacular of the baseball poems remains garnered detail, the celebration of the champion's style still contributes to these two volumes' larger theme of praise for excellence of all kinds.

Moore's emphasis on performers and the arts in the late poems makes clear the role that art has played in her own work, a subject of considerable import. Both of the Boston poems, "In the Public Garden" and "In Lieu of the Lyre," express Moore's view of art and especially of poetry. In the latter piece, the poet depicts herself as a

> verbal pilgrim
> like Thomas Bewick, drinking from his hat brim,
> drops spilled from a waterfall.

The image suggests that the poet as "verbal pilgrim" takes in a few drops from the larger stream, from what "In the Public Garden" calls the "word-waterfall of the banal." Both of these poems excuse themselves explicitly from the traditional categories of poetry. The "Lyre," the harp used to accompany the reader of older poetries, suggests those traditional rhythms and regular musical lilt that Moore deliberately avoided. And the poem she reads "In the Public Garden" to the Boston Arts Festival of 1958 also declines the musical categories:

> And I? This is no madrigal—
> no medieval gradual.
> It is a grateful tale—
> without that radiance which poets
> are supposed to have—
> unofficial, unprofessional.

Moore must have quietly enjoyed the irony of arriving at Boston Common as the "Poet" to read a poem that declines, in a sense, to be a poem but that speaks nevertheless about the nature of poetry.

This oblique approach, this "unpoetic" poetry about poetry, reveals a new perspective in Moore's later work, a not surprising tendency to contemplate the role her audience hands her as a public poet. "In the Public Garden" is a compendium of many of her gradually accrued techniques and concerns: her familiar unaccented rhyme, the catalogue of concrete observations prompted by exposure to a new environment, the war years' theme of "freedom for . . . 'self-discipline,' " the homoeoteleutonic endings (here the "-al") of the fable years, and her recent preoccupation with art. The poem's conclusion, "that Art, admired in general, / is always actually personal," is usually accented on the final word "personal." And her work has indeed demonstrated that writing need not confess indelicate secrets in the first-person singular to be intensely, even cryptically, personal. But toward the end of her career, Moore came to place a special emphasis on the sense conveyed in that penultimate word, "actually." The significance of "an actuality" is at the heart of her last great and provocative poem, "Granite and Steel."

In 1965 when Moore offered *The Harvard Advocate* some "reflections . . . / in lieu of the lyre," she had already read Alan Trachtenberg's book, *Brooklyn Bridge, Fact and Symbol*. Perhaps the establishment of the bridge as a national monument in 1964 brought her attention back to it and led her to quote from Trachtenberg in the poem for Harvard in the following year. Thus in "In Lieu of the Lyre" she offers two useful axioms from Trachtenberg's text as alternatives to "the waterfall, pilgrim and hat-brim" style of poetry:

"a force at rest is at rest because balanced by some other
force,"
or "catenary and triangle together hold the span in place"
(of a bridge).

She reminds us also of "Roebling cable . . . invented by John A. Roebling," but she does not mention the Brooklyn Bridge, which Roebling designed, to her Boston audience. In fact, neither does she mention the bridge itself explicitly in "Granite and Steel," even though that structure is her central visible subject. However, in "Granite and Steel" she does make pervasive use of Trachtenberg's account of the design, building, politics, and literary portrayals of the bridge.

Her most immediate and luminous predecessor for this poem, of course, is Hart Crane, whose major poem "The Bridge" Moore considered "a grand theme."[21] Her title phrase "Granite and Steel" appears in the "Atlantis" section of Crane's poem—"Up the index of night, granite and steel"—a line that Trachtenberg quotes in his chapter on Crane.[22] Moore also adapted a later line from that section, "(O Thou whose radiance doth inherit me)," to make her simpler exclamation "O radiance that doth inherit me!" Her title phrase provides a key to the contrast between Crane's poem and Moore's and also to the import of Moore's poem as an aesthetic statement.

To Hart Crane, Brooklyn Bridge was both a fact of everyday life and a symbol, "Deity's glittering pledge." He lived for a time, as Trachtenberg reminds us, in Brooklyn Heights near what he considered "the most beautiful Bridge of the world" and what he called the "delicate ambassador" (BB, 144). In April of 1924 he wrote that he was "living in the shadow of the bridge," for he had moved into "the very house, and later, the very room" from which fifty years earlier the crippled Washington Roebling had overseen the actualization of his father's dream and design (BB, 144). Thus Crane knew well both the daily reality and the difficult history of the bridge, and still he chose in his poem to emphasize the ascendancy of the bridge as a symbol.

Both his opening poem "To Brooklyn Bridge" and his closing "Atlantis" move swiftly from observed actuality into the rhapsodic, symbolic mode. The passage containing Moore's title phrase is a good example of his nearly immediate conversion of the material into the mythic:

> Up the index of light, granite and steel—
> Transparent meshes—fleckless the gleaming staves—
> Sibylline voices flicker, waveringly stream
> As though a god were issue of the strings.

And the visionary richness, the ecstasy, of much of the rest of "Atlantis"— "O choir, translating time . . . O Thou steeled Cognizance . . . O Answerer of All, Anemone . . . One Song, One Bridge of Fire!"—confirms Trachtenberg's claim that "Hart Crane completed the passage of Brooklyn Bridge from fact to symbol" (BB, 167).

In a sense, then, one might expect Moore's poem to be a move to reverse that passage and re-establish the bridge as a fact. She opens with a title emphasizing the materials of which the bridge is constructed, the weighty strength of granite and steel. She counters Crane's mythic invocations with the material invocations "O steel! O stone!" And she closes with that category, "an actuality." Moore too had lived in Brooklyn: she was there from 1929 until 1965 when, the year before her poem appeared, she moved back across the East River to Manhattan. If any modern poet is known for sharp observation, for counting the stripes in the tulip, it is she. And yet this last published poem of her last single volume of work is not primarily a poem of observation at all. Crane wrote a poem about the bridge; Trachtenberg wrote a book about the bridge and about Crane's poem; and Moore wrote a poem from Trachtenberg's book about the bridge and Crane's poem.

Actually Moore's poem is about certain ideas treated in Trachtenberg's book, and in the service of these ideas the poet uses half a dozen passages from that book and echoes of related literature. In addition to her adaptations of lines from "Atlantis," Moore follows Crane in opening her poem on the contrasting motifs of "the chained bay waters Liberty," which she renders

> and Liberty dominate the bay—
> her feet as one on shattered chains.

A source common to both Crane and Moore is Edgar Allen Poe's poem "The City in the Sea," perhaps referring to the lost ideal city of Atlantis. Poe appears in Crane's descent in "The Tunnel," where Crane's speaker says to him, "of cities you bespeak / subways, rivered under streets." And Poe is echoed in Moore's line "as if probity had not joined our cities / in the sea." It is rare, in fact virtually unique, for Moore to draw so extensively on poetic sources in a single poem. Except for this and her brief echo of Wordsworth (like Poe a romantic) in "Virginia Brittania," her borrowings are distinctively non-poetic in their reliance on newspapers, magazines, technical reports, and non-fictional prose. The presence of so many literary echoes in "Granite and Steel" highlights her special concern with the literary or conceptual dimension of the bridge, the ways in which poetic visions of it have already been textualized.

Moore's use of the material in Trachtenberg's book provides a fascinating study in her practices of quotation and paraphrase. We can see in her copy how she has collected material for the poem in her many notes, quotations, and page references handwritten into the inside front and back covers of her book. And interestingly the passages that she chose to use are all passages in which Trachtenberg quotes from a prior text, as if she were reaching back through his book toward a "source." For instance, her first borrowed image, the "Caged Circe of steel and stone," is derived, as her note tells us, from a story that Trachtenberg reports from Meyer Berger's *Modernized Brooklyn Bridge*. As Trachtenberg tells it,

> A young reporter in the 1870's felt a profound longing for the still unfinished bridge, "unaccountably drawn to it, almost as to a woman warm and pulsing." One night, as though lured to it . . . he climbed one of the cables to the summit of the Manhattan tower. "The siren held him." But then the spell broke, and terrified, he cried for help. None came till morning. Shaken with fear, he was removed. But the fascination continued: "To him she was always a Circe made of steel and granite, but irresistible." (BB, 137)

So Moore's Circe is borrowed from Trachtenberg, who borrowed it from Meyer Berger, who borrowed it from the young reporter, who borrowed it via who knows whom from Homer. The genealogy of the line is emphatically literary and textual.

Likewise, the second and third borrowings from Trachtenberg appear in the second and third stanza of the poem as more explicit appropriations of sources twice removed. The "catenary curve" of cable that runs from each high tower down to the pier on shore is lifted from Trachtenberg's account of what John Roebling considered the "true theory," the ideal solution to the problem of long spans. The "catenary curve," he writes and Moore's note quotes in part, "formed by a rope or cable hanging freely between two fixed points of support," is the answer to the "problems of the greatest strength, greatest economy, greatest safety, of perfect equilibrium and consequently also of perfect stability" (BB, 69). And the quotation in line 18, "O path amid the stars," Moore discovered in a footnote (BB, 137) in which Trachtenberg gives excerpts from Dorothy Landers Beall's verse drama "The Bridge," including her line, "this path among the stars."

The fourth, fifth, and sixth passages in debt to Trachtenberg's text are clustered in Moore's final stanza, and they too are twice removed, her rendering of his quotation of a prior text. The self-echoing opening of that stanza presents the doubleness of a thing that is first potential and then actual:

> Untried expedient, untried; then tried;
> way out; way in; romantic passageway
> first seen by the eye of the mind,
> then by the eye.

What John Roebling wrote and Trachtenberg quoted was that, "Before the sculptor can embody his spiritual or ideal conception into marble, he must have spiritually created the statue in his mind" (BB, 68). Roebling's essay "Life and Creation" of 1864 was, as Trachtenberg notes, inspired by Henry James, Sr.'s *Shadow and Substance*. This understanding of conception and creation led Moore to her next borrowing, a puzzling line when read apart from its source in the parent text:

> Climactic ornament, a double rainbow,
> as if inverted by French perspicacity,
>   John Roebling's monument,
>   German tenacity's also;
>   composite span—

One may well wonder what "French perspicacity" has to do with the Brooklyn Bridge. And the answer lies in a speech delivered by the Reverend Richard S. Storrs at the Opening Ceremonies of the bridge in 1883. As Trachtenberg reports, Storrs described the bridge as an emblem of peace: "Built by a German, it stands next to the figure of Liberty, the work of a Frenchman; it 'represents that fellowship of the Nations which is more and more prominently a fact of our times' " (BB, 126).

And in her final borrowing, the "composite span" that represents "that fellowship of the Nations" is finally proclaimed by Moore "—an actuality." That word "actuality" appears to have entered the poem through a series of four sources—from Hegel via Roebling via his biographers Schuyler and Steinman via Trachtenberg. While studying at the Royal Polytechnic Institute of Berlin during the 1820s, Roebling attended Hegel's highly popular lectures at the University of Berlin and became, "according to family legend, a close friend and favorite student of the philosopher" (BB, 42). Hegel's view of America as "the land of the future" contributed to Roebling's eventual decision to emigrate (BB, 44). And as Trachtenberg demonstrates, Roebling's manuscripts reveal his desire that the bridge he was designing should fully possess that "Hegelian trait of actuality or *Wirklichkeit*. 'Actuality,' Hegel had written, 'is the unity of essence and existence, of the inner world of life and the outer world of its appearance' " (BB, 68). The key thematic word of the poem is thus Hegel's, Roebling's, Trachtenberg's, and finally Moore's.

The discontinuity in this kind of textual excavation appears at the verge of the poem. Up to that point each text incorporates an acknowledgment of its source, so that Trachtenberg attributes words, for example, to Meyer Berger, who attributes them to the young reporter. But this kind of explicit genealogy of language and ideas is only sketchily suggested by Moore's notes, and it is virtually absent from the poem itself. Apart from three or four quoted lines, the poetic language appears to be pristine. The impression of the originality of most of the poem is actually heightened by the few quoted passages, since we are led by them to assume that borrowings are going to be signaled visibly. But as we have seen so often, what Moore calls her "hybrid method of composition" goes far beyond a few drops from the waterfall, a few choice phrases embedded visibly in the poem like "flies in amber."[23] The passages we have just examined in which "the chief interest is borrowed" constitute eighteen of "Granite and Steel's" thirty lines, three-fifths of the poem. What, after this holiday of textual digging, are we to say about such a largely borrowed poem's relation to the world, to a non-textual world, if we may speak at all of such a thing? An earlier poem will put the answer to this into context.

When Moore and her mother first moved to New York City in 1918, Moore's verse was undergoing a radical change from the compressed, judgmental apostrophes of the Carlisle years to the plenitude, the expansive catalogues of the later "observations." One of the first poems to display the effect of New York's impressive "accessibility to experience" was "Dock Rats," which Alfred Kreymborg published in his annual, *Others for 1919*. The characteristics of many of the later "observations" are present in this piece. In particular, the plurality of subject matter, of types and groups of things, is evident in its catalogue of ships and cargoes:

> the square-rigged four-master, the liner, the
> > battleship, like the two-
> thirds submerged section of an iceberg; the tug—strong
> > moving thing,
> dipping and pushing, the bell striking as it comes; the
> > steam yacht, lying
> like a new made arrow on the

> stream; the ferry-boat—a head assigned, one to each
> 　　　　　　　　　　　　　　　compartment, making
> 　a row of chessmen set for play. When the wind is from
> 　　　　　　　　　　　　　　　　　the east,
> 　　the smell is of apples; of hay . . . .

The figurative language here is visually oriented, the catalogue of aromas sensuous. Also characteristic of the work of these early New York years is the explicit emphasis on perception—the "human beings who seem to regard the place as craftily / as we do"—and the shift away from evaluating a subject to presenting it in its multiplicity. The rich variety of literal particulars in these early Manhattan poems justifies their title, *Observations,* and the enthusiasm of an example like "Dock Rats" is not yet tempered by awareness of the problems inherent in the program of "art as exact perception."

　The ironies of perception become clear in a later "observation" like "An Octopus," where the poet allows the confident perceptual motifs to be continuously challenged by an equally pervasive recognition of the blindness and error of the onlooker. And the program of "art as exact perception," as presenting the things of this world to the reader in an objective way, has led the poet twice, in the twenties and in the thirties, into an expansiveness that she soon felt obliged to rein in. Poetry as observation and a record of sense data has its own built-in limits: the phenomenological enterprise of inspection of appearances runs up against its own endlessness. The piling up of sensuous details, facts, lists and lists of lists, namings, qualifications, vivifications of thing after thing eventually outstrips artistic form and human patience. Like Mt. Rainier, the world always transcends the observer and reminds us of the limits and fallibility of our powers of perception. Eventually, as we have seen, Moore moved away from the project of sensuous observation, of exact perception of the details of the external world, that "web one weaves" that "grows till it is . . . blurred by too much."

　What, after all, can one say about material actuality in itself? One can represent it, plainly or cleverly, caress it, so to speak, acclaim it, even affirm its elusiveness, but the thing itself remains primary and superior to the artist's copy or imitation of it. The artistic entity is secondary, a mere reflection, however skillful. It becomes the equal of the copied thing only when it ceases to be a copy and becomes a thing itself, something existing in its own right rather than as a window onto something that transcends it. The danger for the art object as a thing itself is that, in order to be released from its secondary, imitative role, it has to sever a certain relation with that world on which it might have been a window. It must turn its back on that world, in a sense, in order to take its place as an entity in its own right and not just a reflection parasitic on something else. The only way in which art can be purely autonomous, wrapped up in itself and not reflective of the world, is by becoming purely formal, at which point it risks trivializing itself.

Thus the literature of material actuality either serves the world by remaining in some sense secondary and outside of things in an attempt to reproduce and represent the world, or it repudiates that imitative status in order to take its own primary place as an object in the world like any other with its own structure and texture. This either/or, however, is actually the logical clarification of a both/and. We make the distinction in order to see more clearly the multiple facets of verbal art, just as we divide it up into speech and writing in order to amplify its heard and its seen virtues, its evanescence and its duration. Likewise we divide the inside from the outside of a poem, the signifier from the signified, the text from the world. The intertextual dimension of literature appears to escape worldliness because of our romantic conception of the world as nature versus the text as something other than nature—that is, culture, which is the human attempt to improve on or learn from nature and, when that fails, to comment on it, to have the last word.

Moore's two Manhattan poems, the early "Dock Rats" and the late "Granite and Steel," offer us a convenient contrast between these two functions of poetry in its relation to the world. We may say that "Dock Rats" seems to bring to us some material world, the vessels and cargoes of shipping, or it seems to bring us to them. It is a poem of delight in things; that is its theme and reason:

> a monkey—tail and feet
> in readiness for an over-
>
> ture. All palms and tail; how delightful!

Its brief opening and closing remarks are a frame for perceiving, naming, reproducing the marvelous multiplicity discovered at the edge of this city, where the whole exotic world pours into it. "Granite and Steel" seems, after its first few lines, to bypass such perceptual reporting and delight, for it enters instead into relation with literary or textual entities, representing the language and ideas of a series of texts.

We might be tempted to say that "Granite and Steel" turns away from the world toward textuality, in the sense in which people sometimes suggest that literature is not life or that education is not the real world. But worldliness, as Edward Said has already reminded us, "does not come and go, nor is it here and there."[24] One can temporarily seem to escape "the world" in one of its narrow senses, the rat race or commercialism, the façades of politics or the grimness of war. But actually "the world" should not have the particle "the" before it, suggesting its thing-hood, for it is no such thing but rather the partly transcendent pole of human awareness. Both of these Manhattan poems are transparencies, windows on the world, and both are opaque literary entities with their autonomous formal characteristics. What "Granite and Steel" claims on behalf of Moore's whole work is that the world is not only sensuous but also and just as legitimately textual. It is nature and culture both. It is perhaps true that all poems are about other poetry, even if only implicitly, but it is also true that all poems are about our world, even if only explicitly. Their function as art is to be formal, self-absorbed, and also to be more than merely artful, that is, to have the audacity to try to tell us something about the world. Art is self-transcending or, if not, it is at best a preliminary exercise.

We can now see why for Moore the project of observation eventually proved to be but the starting-point. The poems of experience gave way gradually to the poems of authority, of reports from the texts of the experts, the travelers, the observers in the field—those who return from the mountain still capable of speech. Those poems of the twenties and thirties taught us that the fact, for all its fascination, is a cultural phenomenon, a relative form of knowledge shot through with the subjective "authorities" of perception, imagination, hearsay, habit, and desire. The romance of the text is its quest for certainty and truth, its voyage of discovery that always finds something other than Cathay. Moore understood this romance ironically, having recognized it by recognizing the partiality and fallibility of any text. She did not, however, remain identified with that irony, for the irony does not destroy the romance but rather requires it, just as the deconstruction needs and preserves a certain intention of sense.

Perhaps in the twenties and thirties Moore might have countered Hart Crane's symbolically apotheosized Brooklyn Bridge with a poetic reconstruction of its facts—details of design and dimensions, the tragic history of its construction, and the daily convenience to the traffic of Brooklyn and Manhattan. But at the age of seventy-nine she chose instead to make the bridge just barely visible in her poem, a metaphor for probity and peace whose climactic attribute is actuality, the sense of a dream come true. The poem is a metonym of her art, that could see through the postures of our texts and yet show them to us as luminous.

8

A Magician's Retreat

By the mid-sixties Moore's Brooklyn neighborhood had changed radically for the worse from 1929, when she and her mother had moved there and "decorum marked life on Clinton Hill."[1] The streets and subways, which she insisted on using, had become dangerous; every apartment in her building except hers had been burglarized at least once; and no agent would insure anyone living on Cumberland Street. Reluctantly Moore bowed to the insistence of Warner and her friends—principally the Watsons and Louise Crane—that she find a safer place to live. Marianne's niece and namesake, known as Bee, spent the summer of 1965 helping her aunt to pack and prepare, and in November Warner, Constance, and both of their daughters, Sallie and Bee, moved her back over to Manhattan into a pleasant apartment at 35 West Ninth Street.

From this new headquarters, which she once dubbed "35 West Ninth Meadowlark Meadow," Moore remained active.[2] She vacationed in Florida with Frances and Norvelle Browne, traveled to Wellesley, St. Louis, Peterborough (New Hampshire), and Princeton to read and be honored, and on one occasion was curiously cited as "Marianne Craig Moore, D.LET., poet. An aristocratic lady with a high sense of comedy and a fine taste in hats."[3] She celebrated her eightieth birthday in 1967 by dining out with Warner and Constance and her longtime friends novelist Glenway Wescott and Monroe Wheeler, the original publisher of her poem "Marriage" in 1923 and now counselor to the Trustees of the Museum of Modern Art. In 1968 she received the National Medal for Literature, and that spring she threw into the field at Yankee Stadium the most poetically famous baseball since Casey's third strike. In May of 1969 she attended her sixtieth class reunion at Bryn Mawr and in June accepted an honorary degree from Harvard University, an institution that held a special place in her affections.

By the end of that summer of 1969, Moore had suffered the first of several strokes that would impair both her mobility and her speech. The remarkable flow of polysyllabic talk that Kreymborg had compared with "the rapids of a beautiful stream" slowed to a trickle. She was cared for at home by two nurses, her family, and friends, and on Saturday, February 5th, 1972, at the age of eighty-four, she passed away in her sleep. The next day, her colleague from *The Dial* offices Kenneth Burke wrote, "She was so unusual, it took me a long time to realize that her greatest ambition was to be totally ordinary."[4] And Elizabeth Bishop echoed the sentiment, "She looked like no one else; she talked like no one else; her poems showed a mind not much like anyone else's."[5] It was her originality, precipitated by her courage to be natural, that was instrumental in changing the course of poetry in the English language.

It is not at all surprising that Moore's last poem to appear in *The New Yorker,* "The Magician's Retreat" of 1970, is a meditation on the essential nature and public persona of the artist. These fifteen lines also offer as suggestive an image of the nature of the self as one is likely to find in poetry. And several others of this final dozen "hitherto uncollected" verses give us the chance for a closing perspective on the personal voice and the process of creating and reflecting value in poetry.

To begin with, "The Magician's Retreat" is a triple-layered title. It appears that Moore discovered the phrase identifying a drawing by one of the "Visionary Architects of the 18th Century," Jean-Jacques Lequeu, introducing that cover article in *Arts Magazine* for December/January of 1967–68.[6] Moore saved the article and the drawing of the classic façade which Lequeu had labelled "Repaire des Magiciens"—the magicians' den. Lequeu's ironic contrast between the bright elegance of the façade and the darker, more hidden sense of a "repaire" as a lair, den, or haunt was lost in the English translation as "retreat." But intentionally or not, Moore restored some of this original sense of darkness and hiddenness by applying the translated title to a painting by René Magritte. Above one of Magritte's versions of "Domain of Lights," reproduced in *The New York Times Magazine* for January of 1969, Moore penciled in "The Magician's Retreat." The painting shows a "black tree mass" rising over the very dark façade that she describes as showing "a yellow glow / from a shutter-crack" and "a blue glow from the lamppost." Magritte's house is even more "consummately plain" than the ironically elegant façade of Lequeu's "repaire," and Moore's poem is both plain and, in its own way, visionary.

The magician of these three works is nowhere visible, and yet this unseen figure is at the center of each title and presumably at the inner center of each structure depicted. The resident of the house is everywhere spoken of and nowhere manifest. In Moore's vocabulary, we have already seen that the magician is the poet: in "The Mind, Intractable Thing" she addressed the "imagnifico, / wizard in words—poet, was it, as / Alfredo Panzini defined you." The image of the retreat or den suggests that the *magicien,* the mind as poet, may be thought of as enclosed or hidden, as residing within the given structure, be it the house or the poem. The architectural or aesthetic structure is a refuge secluding its resident; the public façade eclipses the privacy that is its other face.

In 1922 Moore had considered in a literal way this theme of the relation between the person and the place. In writing of "People's Surroundings," she began, "They answer one's questions." She described surroundings as "non-committal, personal-impersonal expressions," for they are objects expressive of the people who have made or assembled them. The subjective overtones of such objects are apparently as close as Moore felt one could get to grasping the subject verbally: "we see the exterior and the fundamental structure." The subjective self may not show up as a concrete thing in the poem but rather must be assumed, imagined as absent merely from the surface and therefore present, if at all, inaccessibly. The retreat—the poem—is the only evidence we have of the nature of this elusive inhabitant, whose trace is the visible form. And if the *magicien* or poetic mind is elusive, how much less comprehensible must be the personal self, the whole dimension of possible awareness in the world?

Moore notes in the poem that the visible image in Magritte's painting is "above all discreet," and this statement is both descriptive and prescriptive. The black tree mass that darkens the outside of the retreat is inevitably an image of reserve, but the reserve that it embodies may also be considered desirable. Reserve may signal what cannot be exposed without betrayal or distortion, a dimension of mystery, and any image objectifying the subject remains a partial betrayal of the subjective self. This is one of the lessons of the judgmental Carlisle apostrophes. Here Lequeu's and Magritte's designs are reverse images of one another, the eighteenth-century drawing showing a light façade with blackness inside the open window, Magritte's house shrouded in darkness with light in two unshuttered windows. Moore selected for her poem Magritte's dark exterior "but bright inside / like a moonstone." The discretion of the façade does not mean that it is closed and utterly impermeable, but rather that it is open in an unpretentious way. The translucence of the moonstone as a gem, of the moon as a light in darkness, is an image of value, for by this sign of life the house is illumined without violating the seclusion of the retreat.

The majority of Moore's poetry is appropriately described by this late image, for her sense of the privacy of the poet as a person is more aptly captured by Magritte's glow of brightness inside, by the moonstone and the cat's eye, than it would be by Lequeu's light façade over darkness. Her poems are not impersonal but personally private, permeated by the sense of one individual's reticent intensity. Moore was selective about what she put into her poems, but she did put herself into them, even if they sometimes leave us puzzled and confronted with mysteries. In her own way, she has done a service to that dimension of the human personality which resists exposure, objectification, and the fiction of the complete grasp. The pronoun "I," the image for the self, and the writer as subject of her own writing are all reductions, because of the inevitable discrepancy between words and the evanescent individuality of whatever they speak of. The determinate nature of signification demands a network of fictively finite meanings, and poems have to operate from within this network, even when they end by transcending it. The dimension of personality that is present as absent, the *magicien,* cannot offer itself up directly to scrutiny without diminishing itself. Thus in Moore's work the poet becomes manifest not as the witnessed but as the witness—"I have seen it," she says in "The Magician's Retreat." The self is given in the gift of writing about its world.

Moore's early private poems and her late, more public verse both suggest something similar about her conception of the place of the poem in its culture. The anecdotal epigrams of the Carlisle years, like "To a Man Working His Way through a Crowd," are responses to specific behavior and events which confronted the poet in the course of daily life. They are occasional in a private sense—that is, circumstantial—while a significant number of her later poems are occasional in the public sense of addressing a communal cultural moment. Clearly some of these later pieces are of greater interest than others, for Moore was at times more obliging than the muse was to her importunate admirers, with the result that she printed some ephemeral lines, such as "Velvet Mat" or "Santa Claus," that are better passed over as courtesies.

The presence of more memorable occasional pieces in her work, however, indicates both this poet's and the public's notion of verbal art as commemorative. Moore offered, and her readers requested, poetry for holy days and holidays—"Rosemary," "Saint Nicholas," and "Santa Claus" for Christmas, lines for Advent and for St. Valentine's Day, and verses celebrating the Jamestown Tercentenary and the preservation of the landmark Carnegie Hall. The general public continues to consider poetry appropriate to such socially shared moments, whether they are repeated or unique. We invite our modern poets to contribute their work and presence to Presidential Inaugurations, arts festivals, political rallies, honorary dinners, and even (unbelievably) to a national Pencil Week.[7] However august or trifling the event, verse helps to constitute it as an occasion by creating a memorial to it while it is still in progress. By formally textualizing its significance in the midst of the event, verse delivers the sense of the moment up from the flux of time. And in turn, much occasional verse is overtaken by that flux and floated mercifully downstream.

What we ask the commemorative artist to do, essentially, is to confer a certain value on a moment or to embody its accepted value in a renewed form. The formal aspects of poetry are a counterpart of ritual, and its referential aspects identify and, most importantly, enlarge the reason for the ritual. This enlargement or amplification is where the poem both serves its subject and borrows some of its glory. In March of 1966, for instance, Robert E. Blum, the chairman of the committee preparing to celebrate the hundredth anniversary of the founding of Prospect Park in Brooklyn, wrote to Marianne Moore asking her for some verse to commemorate the occasion.[8] The assumption behind the request was presumably that some words from their illustrious fellow Brooklynite would lend a dimension of importance and durability to the moment they were celebrating. And the poet apparently agreed with them in her own way, for in obliging them with "The Camperdown Elm," Moore in turn called upon the work of some earlier American artists to preside over her own thoughts:

> I think, in connection with this weeping elm,
> of "Kindred Spirits" at the edge of a rockledge
>   overlooking a stream:
> Thanatopsis-invoking tree-loving Bryant
> conversing with Thomas Cole
> in Asher Durand's painting of them
> under the filigree of an elm overhead.

The importance of the Camperdown elm in Prospect Park is revealed and enhanced by setting that tree into the larger context of America's artistic heritage.

The elm in Asher Durand's painting overlooks the "spirits" of two nineteenth-century artists, the poet William Cullen Bryant and the landscape painter Thomas Cole. The elm is thus identified as part of an especially grand and deep moment of our cultural past. The written work of the "tree-loving Bryant" invests the scene with a certain poetic import for Moore, just as the Hudson River Valley paintings of Cole invested it for Durand, a painter painting a painter, the poet depicting a poet poetically. The whole of Durand's painting then endows Moore's poem with its sense of a glorious artistic past, of a general tradition of appreciation and preservation of natural beauty. This tradition becomes present as she turns to her specific contemporary subject, the Camperdown elm with its " 'intricate pattern' . . . hollowness . . . [and] six small cavities." Behind her conclusion, "We must save it," is the implicit message that we must save the whole context and import of this "mortal" tree, the elm—the grand, venerable scenery of America and the "kindred spirits" of our distinguished poets and painters of the past. The poem confers value by seeming merely to confirm it. The poet's lines make a difference between just a tree, a thing, and a tree as fully imbued with meaning. The poem changes the tree as a signified into a tree as a signifier. It makes the elm not just something referred to but more, something that refers to a greater whole from which the value of the single object is derived.

In a sense, this is what we expect our poets to do for us, to transform merely existing things and events into meaningful essences. The general reading public knows how to ask for this transformation of the more momentous, publicly shared occasions; the poet knows how to effect it on the usually unnoticed, difficult, or very private occasions. Any signified may become a signifier, for any thing or event will bear meaning to one who envisions it in a meaningful way. Thus the value or significance of the thing is both already there and not yet there in it when the artist arrives; the value is both human and non-human. The raw materials of art are raw until they go through the crucible, the artist's alchemical labor. This is the magic of art, its making something much more out of something that appears to be "mere" or not much at all. The poetry is the conferring and confirming of value where, without art, there seemed to be less or none. Durand revealed the "kindred spirits" of the poet and the painter, the "kindred spirits" of man and nature; now Moore reveals the deep fund of that heritage of art and nature in one aged weeping elm. Her oxymoron "our crowning curio" combines the subject before and after the artist's vision, the mere thing and its fullest resonance.

This conferring and confirming of value through art is an activity that appears in a wide range of cultures, and Moore has returned to the subject repeatedly in her poems. The carved scarab of "A Talisman," the "Egyptian Pulled Glass Bottle in the Shape of a Fish," the emblematic porcelain of "Nine Nectarines," the triskelion of "Walking-Sticks and Paper-Weights and Water Marks," Hans von Marées's painting of St. Hubert in "Saint Nicholas," the fifteenth-century tapestry depicting "Charity Overcoming Envy"—all of the many arts within Moore's art carry this ongoing sense of evinced or bestowed value, because such value—positive or negative, affirmed, cancelled, or questioned—is traditionally integral to Western art.

The 1967 piece "Tippoo's Tiger" shows in particularly graphic form the successive stages of artistic commemoration as a human conferral and confirming of value. As her notes indicate, Moore "derived" her poem from a Victoria and Albert Museum monograph by Mildred Archer, giving the history of a nearly six-foot-long wooden organ case carved to represent a huge tiger holding a prostrate man in his jaws.[9] This artifact is said to have been commissioned in India by the Sultan Tipu to commemorate the 1792 death of the son of his enemy Sir Hector Munro in the jaws of an enormous tiger. In fact, there are a number of different layers of the tiger piled up in this poem in a progressively memorial chain, each layer including a selective recognition of the ones preceding it. First, the tiger simply as an animal is barely visible in Moore's lines. It is like a thing-in-itself, mentioned as the poem's opening word and then subsumed immediately in the next layers, the tiger as name and as model. Moore notes in an early draft of the poem that " 'Tippoo' (or 'Tipu' in its more modern form) means 'tiger (conqueror of the woods):' / tiger or lion in Hindustani, the same thing."[10] The animal is made into a model or ideal that is attached to a person by means of the name. The naming may be considered a rudimentary form of verbal art, since the word as a name imaginatively constellates one element within another element, the qualities of the creature within the person. The emblematic depiction of the name is a form of pictorial art, the re-embodiment of the model creature in Tipu's royal artifacts: "The forefeet of this throne were tiger's feet," and "His weapons were engraved with tiger claws and teeth."

After these layers—the actual animal, the prototypical name, and the emblematic throne—another artifact appears, the central one. This is the "vast toy, a curious automaton," the huge organ case carved in the likeness of

> a man killed by a tiger; with organ pipes inside
> from which blood-curdling cries merged with inhuman
> > groans.
> The tiger moved its tail as the man moved his arm.

Mildred Archer suggests in her monograph that a century after the death of Sir Hector's son, one of his descendants, the author H. H. Munro pennamed "Saki," incorporated the family memory of this man-killing cat into one of his stories. "Sredni Vashtar" relates how a sickly ten-year-old boy's vicious polecat-ferret kills the boy's stern, hated aunt. At the center of her poem Moore has paraphrased Archer's quotation of Saki's account of how that creature

escaped through its unlatched hut-door along a plank
above a ditch; paused, drank, and disappeared.

We now have the beast, the name, the emblem, the organ case, and the
poet's paraphrase of the historian's quotation of fiction-writer's memory
of the man-killing cat. This new textual layer is a more specific and less
explicit art than the simple name was, but they have similar powers: in
Tipu's name and carved organ and in Saki's story, the animal acts as a
proxy for its owner. The tiger as prototype inspirits Tipu's actions; the
beast that ravaged Munro acted incidentally on Tipu's behalf by killing
his enemy; and the musical automaton fixes concretely in space an event
that its owner wishes memorialized, saved in his possession from the flux
of time. This memorial preserves the event in a form that is harmonious
with the values of its creator or with the norms of its society.

Likewise, the remaining layers of Tipu's tiger are all verbal ones.
Moore's poem quotes and paraphrases freely from Archer's monograph
on this history of Tipu and of the tiger-organ, which British troops captured and sent back to England's Victoria and Albert Museum. As in the
case of "Granite and Steel" and Alan Trachtenberg's book, the parent text
here gives the poet access to other sources, notably here Keats and Saki.
"Each subject kissed nine times / the carpet's velvet face of meadow
green" is an adaptation of lines from Keats's "The Cap and Bells" (stanza
xxxix). Archer quotes that passage from Keats's account of the "play-
thing of the Emperor's choice, / . . . a Man-Tiger-Organ, prettiest of his
toys." And finally Moore ends her verse by pointing to a text on Tipu
that is yet to be created: "This ballad still awaits a tiger-hearted bard."
She implies here that her own preceding lines are really just a sketch for a
future "real" telling of the story of Tipu's tiger. This projection into the
future comes full circle to the past by returning to the tiger as prototype,
this time not for the Sultan Tipu but for the poet, the "tiger-hearted
bard." The claim that the ballad still awaits its bard gives Moore's poem a
provisional quality, a self-consciousness. The poem recognizes that it is
but one stage in the ongoing transmission of this tale, in its progress toward the more satisfactory, nearly musical form of the bard's ballad.

The opening stanza of an early version of this poem has some of the narrative quality of a ballad: "In the Kingdom of Mysore / a saint had a devo-
tee who named his son, Tipu."[11] But Moore soon dropped this stanza,
and in her final version she traces mainly the spatial configurations of the
tale: the "four-square pyramid of silver stairs," the infantry jackets with
"little wooden stripes incurved like buttonholes," and the tiger claws and
teeth engraved on weapons "in spiral characters that said the conqueror is
God." She shows these still, lantern-slide images one after the other and

declines to undertake a narrative of the whole history of these shapes. The tiger-hearted Tipu recognized that on the occasion of the death of Munro, something was called for, some keepsake, a perpetuation of the event symbolizing his conquest. And Moore's poem recognizes that the story of the resulting keepsake and its tiger-hearted owner deserves a memorial, even if she is not prepared to write it. Her own interest appears to have been in Tipu's tiger as an emblem of the aphorism that she presents in the same early typescript,

> Great losses for the enemy
> can not make one's own loss less hard.

From the story of the double loss—Munro's loss of his son and Tipu's loss of his life and his "vast toy"—what Moore wanted was not the plot but the emblem for the moral.

This poem is an excellent illustration of the pervasively cultural nature of the world as Moore experienced it and an illustration of the ways in which culture is founded on value and value in turn on desire. Of the various layers of Tipu's tiger—the creature, the name, the emblems, the man-tiger organ case, the historic monograph, the derivative story and poem, and the ballad-to-be—all but the original creature are human constructs. These physical and verbal constructs are investments of physical materials and of texts with specific values, embodiments of desire, realities arranged by the light of an ideal. The cultural artifact is an arena of desire, expressing and curbing desire by reflecting and yet diverting it from its own impossible literalness. Tipu is a prototype of the artist, for he was able to turn an accident of the jungle into an embodiment of his own ferocious desire. He used the incidental materials of the real to represent an ideal.

The representational element—the "tiger's feet" of the throne, the "vast toy" on which "the tiger moved its tail as the man moved his arm"—connects the work of art with a recognizable reality. Imitation is the link between the found world and the fashioned work, since perception and memory of the world are as important raw materials of art as are words, paints, stone, and sounds. The element of desire enters the artistic construct, then, as a deliberate, if slight, distortion serving the form of gratification. Formalization itself involves distortion. If the form is conventional (the lines of the verse, the square bounds of the painting, the patterns of novels and symphonies), it is more easily and less consciously assimilated than if the form is unusual, like Tipu's music box emitting "blood-curdling cries merged with inhuman groans." The distortions here—a tiger shape with a pipe organ inside and a handle in its chest, the grotesque artifice of a musical instrument made to copy cries of anguish—are distortions honoring Tipu's desire for anguish and death to his enemy, the intruding British.

These opposites of imitation and formal distortion intermingle also in Moore's poem, since here too recognition of a certain reality is the basis for expression of an ideal or of desire. Moore's series of still images of Tipu's throne, regalia, weapons, and "vast toy" are all documentary: they draw the reader's imagination into what were more or less realities of the Sultan's reign. The formal distortions in this case are two that are quite characteristic of Moore's art: the emblematic vision and the ironic contrast between the prose of the body of the poem and the poetry of the coda.

The poet delivers Tipu and his tiger to us in a series of still images, punctuated in the middle briefly by the narrated escape of the polecat-ferret. As a refinement of the overall spatial axis in which her work is generally conceived, the emblematic form is desire's overcoming of time. What existed once may be kept, redeemed from time by the commemorative arts of memory and imagination. "If that which is at all were not forever," Moore asks in "The Pangolin," why would the artists of the cathedrals have labored the way they did? The spatial and emblematic vision sees the essential, the eternal, and it shapes its materials to reflect that dimension. Moore's poem is an inventory of emblems fashioned from the spatial imagination of the Sultan Tipu. The poem is a validation of her own method, a late portrait of the artist whose fulfillment of desire, embodied in the artifact, outlives his mortal self.

The prose-like body of the poem, its list of sentences quoting and paraphrasing Mildred Archer, Keats, and Saki, is closed by a rhymed triplet, a new formal note in the poem:

> This ballad still awaits a tiger-hearted bard.
>   Great losses for the enemy
> can't make the owner's loss less hard.

This traditional artifice of poetry, the closure of rhyme, is highlighted here by the absence of such closure in the preceding lines. The poem as a finite text, like the painting on a rectangular canvas, is a convention in itself, one which Moore chose to uphold while some of her contemporaries entered the unending lists of the long poem. Closure is a formal complement of the spatial imagination, in which the text itself becomes a configuration in sound and print, framed on the page in white—language bounded by wordlessness on all sides. All poems have duration, but the fiction of the short poem is like the fiction of the emblem, that paradox of the eternal instant, and like the fiction of rhyme, that enclosure of echoing sound. Tipu as an emblem of the artist belongs in this spatially conceived piece, while the history of the Sultan awaits its more appropriate narrative form elsewhere.

What then is the relation of the emblematic artist's work to the narrative that we usually have thought history to be? This question brings us to another revision of romanticism, for the notion of history as narrative is a romantic one, which imposes the ideas of linearity and thus of progress onto the events of the public world. But it is also possible to conceive of history as a momentary totality, as a series of contrasting whole situations, and to study its synchronic as opposed to its diachronic elements, the simultaneous components of a scene rather than a succession of events. Each of these whole situations may be viewed as a configuration, as "that past" or "this past" or "this present." Such a view replaces the illusion of linearity with the illusion of simultaneity; it replaces the metaphor of the plot, the conception that one event leads to the next on the way to a climax or denouement, with the metaphor of the photograph, the conception that all the pieces of the puzzle of a period fit together into a unified picture.

The enactment of this plotless, photographic view of history may be seen in the origin and technique of another of Moore's late poems, "Love in America." During the mid-sixties the new mores of counter-culture and the sexual revolution prompted a re-examination of the nature of love and its forms in contemporary society. The editors of the *Saturday Evening Post* evidently felt that poetry could play a role, alongside journalism and photography, in reflecting and interpreting a cultural situation, a varied but definable field. Thus in the fall of 1966, Thomas Congdon of the *Post* asked Moore for a poem for a special issue on the topic of "love in America," and she obliged him with her verse of that title.[12] This poem is a short version of her earlier definition poems like "The Mind is an Enchanting Thing," "Propriety," and "Style," in which something intangible is embodied in a catalogue of metaphors and similes: "It's fire in the dove-neck's / iridescence"; "It's / resistance with bent head, like foxtail / millet's"; and in this case, "it's a passion . . . It's a Midas of tenderness; / from the heart; / nothing else."

What is it that qualifies the poet, at least in some views, for this other public role beside commemoration—interpretation? What makes the poem a form of language from which we traditionally expect something in some sense true or important, something that will inspire or at least awaken us? Without necessarily subscribing to the view of the poet as an exceptional person, someone with keener insight into life than ordinary mortals, it is possible to see why poems are considered potent enough to be read ceremonially, inscribed, censored, reprinted, and learned "by heart." This power does not reside solely in the formal patterns, in the "special dance of the organs of speech," but it begins there. Even if the poet's experiences and insights are representative ones—and especially if they are so—it is the poet's craft, an exceptional way with words, that qualifies the poem to be taken seriously on a moral ground. Because words are both opaque and transparent, both self-contained and referential, the writer's sensibility cannot ultimately sever these two dimensions. The formalism and the referentiality of language, its poetic and practical qualities, cannot be easily isolated from one another. Sense is conveyed sensuously, and even the most sensuous word groups carry suggestions of meaning. And because the meaningful, even the ethical, force of language cannot be finally or completely dissociated from its aesthetic force, we assume that a work of exceptional artistry in the formal patterns of language will possess some related degree of excellence in sense and significance.

The sculptor's block of marble and the painter's paint belong more singularly to the individual sculptor and painter than words do to the poet. Everyone uses words, and the poet as bricoleur works with these old materials that are well-worn public property and often easily duplicated and re-used. But Moore's work encourages the view that the poet's use of this commonly owned medium carries a special force. An early typescript shows that she originally opened "Love in America" with a quotation from La Fontaine, suggesting that at least poets consider other poets worth listening to:

> La Fontaine hazarded this,
>   (about France):
> "Love is a curious fire. A god
> cursed by the loss he must bear
>   of his eyesight. . . ."
>
> It is at the inception of any
>   great work of art:
> Whatever it is, it's a passion . . . . [13]

Her notes identify Unamuno as her source for "nobility that is action" and Churchill for her paraphrase of his statement on modesty. The last line of the poem with its echoes of Molly Bloom is not explicitly linked to James Joyce as a source. But Molly's closing thoughts, the famous last words of *Ulysses* as she remembers consenting to her first lover, "yes I said yes I will Yes," [14] do seem relevant to Moore's closing lines on this "passion":

Whatever it is, let it be without
affectation.

Yes, yes, yes, *yes.*

The proprietary quotation marks are not present here, because the simply
affirmative "yes" belongs to the public domain. It is everyone's affirmative, a quotation of the contemporary scene as well as acceptance of it.

Words as discrete signs are not subject to ownership or possession, and
as we have seen all along, Moore's revisions of her sources do not consistently abide by a proprietary principle even for titles, phrases, and sentences. Her concern is for precision in wording, not exact copy in quotation or exhaustive documentation. In these late poems, "Tippoo's Tiger"
is the name of the museum artifact and also the title of Mildred Archer's
monograph, but Moore did not feel the need to put her use of it, or of
Keats's lines or of Saki's description or Archer's or Tipu's phrases, into
quotation marks. Nor did she place Lequeu's title "The Magician's Retreat" in quotation marks when she adopted it for her poem. As we have
already seen, the partial and often cryptic nature of Moore's notes makes
them less like academic acknowledgments and more like a selective sharing of a sense of each poem's genealogy, its communal authorship in the
public world of words.

The unique thing about verbal art is that its materials belong freely to
everyone and to many people at once. Words are thus imbued with conventional meanings and also with a certain private familiarity and history, which the writer counts on, plays on, and inexplicably enlarges.
Language, as much as action, is a medium by which the self opens its bor-
ders, metaphorically, on the public domain and overcomes the isolation
of speechlessness. Words can appear in countless texts and contexts at the
same time, can be passed through innumerable hands, and still have personal significance and revelatory power.

And so Moore was right to conceive of the poet as a "wizard" or magician, for the alchemy of art is the secret of making something valuable
out of the ordinary stuff of life. In this sense, art creates value for us,
while in another sense it is we who create art out of our sense of value.
This story of one body of work taking shape after shape is an individual
story, Marianne Moore's. At each point it is also a picture of what poetry
essentially is. But poetry as an art is always more varied than any one
body of work can reflect. And always the art of Marianne Moore's poetry, like the art of all fine poems, gives more than any one reader alone
can receive.

Biographical Sketch

1887   Marianne Craig Moore is born November 15th in Kirkwood, a suburb of St. Louis, Missouri. Lives with her mother Mary Warner Moore and brother Warner in the home of her grandfather, pastor of Kirkwood Presbyterian Church.

1894   Grandfather dies of pneumonia. Family moves briefly to cousins in Pittsburgh, then to Carlisle, Pennsylvania, where Mrs. Moore teaches at the Metzger Institute.

1896   Moore enters the Metzger Institute.

1905   Graduates from Metzger. Enters Bryn Mawr College, where she majors in "History, Economics and Politics" and minors in biology.

1907   First printed poems appear in the college magazine *Tipyn O'Bob*.

1909   Receives her A.B. degree from Bryn Mawr.

1910   Completes the business course at Carlisle Commercial College. Holds a clerical position at Melvil Dewey's Lake Placid Club.

1911   Marianne and Mrs. Moore spend the summer traveling in England and France. Begins four years of teaching commercial subjects at the United States Indian School in Carlisle.

1915   Poems appear in *The Egoist, Poetry,* and *Others*. Visit to New York where she meets Alfred Kreymborg.

1916   Move to Warner's new parsonage at Ogden Memorial Church in Chatham, New Jersey.

1918   Move to 14 St. Luke's Place, Greenwich Village. Brief employment as secretary and as private tutor.

1920 Poems appear in *The Dial,* published by Scofield Thayer and Dr. James Sibley Watson.

1921 Bryher and Hilda Doolittle publish Moore's first collection, *Poems,* in London. Begins four years of part-time work at Hudson Park Branch of the New York Public Library.

1924 *Observations* published by The Dial Press; receives the Dial Award for 1924.

1925 Becomes acting editor, and in 1926 editor, of *The Dial.*

1927 Visit to England with her mother.

1929 *The Dial* closes. Marianne and Mrs. Moore move to 280 Cumberland Street in Brooklyn near the Navy Yard.

1932 Wins the Helen Haire Levinson Prize from *Poetry* for "Part of a Novel, Part of a Poem, Part of a Play."

1935 *Selected Poems* published by Faber & Faber in London and Macmillan in New York. Moore awarded the Ernest Hartsock Memorial Prize.

1936 *The Pangolin and Other Verse* published by The Brendin Publishing Company in London.

1940 Receives the Shelley Memorial Award.

1941 *What Are Years* published by Macmillan, New York.

1944 *Nevertheless* published by Macmillan. Moore receives the Harriet Monroe Poetry Award.

1945 Awarded a Guggenheim Fellowship. With Elizabeth Mayer translates Adalbert Stifter's *Rock Crystal, A Christmas Tale.* Begins translation of La Fontaine's fables.

1946 Joint grant from American Academy of Arts and Letters and the National Institute of Arts and Letters.

1947 Mary Warner Moore dies. Marianne elected to membership in the National Institute of Arts and Letters.

1951 *Collected Poems* published by Macmillan. Moore receives the Pulitzer Prize for Poetry and the National Book Award.

1953 Visiting lecturer at Bryn Mawr. Receives the M. Carey Thomas Award from the College, the Bollingen Prize, and the Gold Medal of the National Institute of Arts and Letters.

1954   Translation, *The Fables of La Fontaine,* published by Viking, New York. Writes *The Absentee,* a play based on Maria Edgeworth's novel.

1955   *Predilections,* a selection of her essays, published by Viking. Election to the American Academy of Arts and Letters.

1956   *Like a Bulwark* published by Viking.

1959   *O to Be a Dragon* and *The Marianne Moore Reader* published by Viking.

1962   Visit to Italy and Greece with friends.

1963   Translation of three Charles Perrault tales, *Puss in Boots, the Sleeping Beauty, and Cinderella,* published by Macmillan.

1964   *The Arctic Ox* published by Faber & Faber, London. Visits England and Ireland with friends.

1966   *Tell Me, Tell Me: Granite, Steel, and Other Topics* published by Viking. Moves from Brooklyn to 35 West Ninth Street in Manhattan.

1967   *The Complete Poems of Marianne Moore* published jointly by Macmillan and Viking. Receives the Poetry Society of America's Gold Medal for Distinguished Achievement and the Edward MacDowell Medal. Named Chevalier de l'Ordre des Arts et des Lettres in France.

1968   Awarded America's highest literary honor, the National Medal for Literature. Throws the first baseball of the season in Yankee Stadium.

1969   Honorary doctorate from Harvard University, her sixteenth honorary degree.

1972   Marianne Moore dies on February 5th at the age of eighty-four.

Chronology of Moore's Published Poems

Revised titles are in parentheses.

1907–13
The Bryn Mawr Poems

"Under a Patched Sail," *Tipyn O'Bob,* 4 (February 1907), 12.
"To Come After a Sonnet," *Tipyn O'Bob,* 4 (February 1907), 25.
"To My Cup-Bearer," *Tipyn O'Bob,* 5 (April 1908), 21.
"The Sentimentalist," *Tipyn O'Bob,* 5 (April 1908), 26.
"To a Screen-Maker," *Tipyn O'Bob,* 6 (January 1909), 2–3.
"Ennui," *Tipyn O'Bob,* 6 (March 1909), 7.
"A Red Flower," *Tipyn O'Bob,* 6 (May 1909), 14.
"Progress" ("I May, I Might, I Must"), *Tipyn O'Bob,* 6 (June 1909), 110.
"A Jelly-Fish," *The Lantern,* 17 (Spring 1909), 110.
"My Lantern," *The Lantern,* 18 (Spring 1910), 28.
"Tunica Pallio Proprior," *The Lantern,* 18 (Spring 1910), 102.
"My Senses Do Not Deceive Me," *The Lantern,* 18 (Spring 1910), 103.
"Qui S'Excuse, S'Accuse," *The Lantern,* 18 (Spring 1910), 13.
"A Talisman," *The Lantern,* 20 (Spring 1912), 61.
"Leaves of a Magazine," *The Lantern,* 20 (Spring 1912), 10.
"The Beast of Burden," *The Lantern,* 21 (Spring 1913), 57.
"Councell to a Bachelor," *The Lantern,* 21 (Spring 1913), 106.
"Things Are What They Seem," *The Lantern,* 21 (Spring 1913), 109.

1915–17
The Carlisle Poems

"To a Man Working His Way Through the Crowd," *The Egoist,* 2 (April 1, 1915), 62.
"To the Soul of 'Progress,' " *The Egoist,* 2 (April 1, 1915), 62.
"That Harp You Play So Well," *Poetry,* 6 (May 1915), 70.
"Appellate Jurisdiction," *Poetry,* 6 (May 1915), 71.

"To an Intra-Mural Rat," *Poetry,* 6 (May 1915), 71.

"The Wizard in Words," *Poetry,* 6 (May 1915), 72.

"To William Butler Yeats on Tagore," *The Egoist,* 2 (May 1, 1915), 77.

"The North Wind to a Dutiful Beast Midway Between the Dial and the Foot of a Garden Clock," *The Lantern,* 23 (Spring 1915), 17.

"Isaiah, Jeremiah, Ezekiel, Daniel," *The Lantern,* 23 (Spring 1915), 60.

"To Disraeli on Conservatism" ("To a Strategist") *The Lantern,* 23 (Spring 1915), 60.

"To Browning" ("Injudicious Gardening"), *The Egoist,* 2 (August 2, 1915), 126.

"To Bernard Shaw: A Prize Bird" ("To a Prize Bird"), *The Egoist,* 2 (August 2, 1915), 126.

"Diligence Is To Magic As Progress Is To Flight," *The Egoist,* 2 (October 1, 1915), 158.

"To a Steam Roller," *The Egoist,* 2 (October 1, 1915), 81.

"To Statecraft Embalmed," *Others,* 1, No. 6 (December 1915), 104.

"To a Friend in the Making," *Others,* 1, No. 6 (December 1915), 105.

"Blake," *Others,* 1, No. 6 (December 1915), 105.

"George Moore," *Others,* 1, No. 6 (December 1915), 106.

"*So far as the future is concerned . . .*" ("The Past is the Present"), *Others,* 1, No. 6 (December 1915), 106.

"Diogenes," *Contemporary Verse,* 1 (January 1916), 6.

"Masks" ("A Fool, A Foul Thing, A Distressful Lunatic") *Contemporary Verse,* 1 (January 1916), 6.

" 'Sun!' " ("Fear is Hope," " 'Sun,' " "Sun"), *Contemporary Verse,* 1 (January 1916), 7.

" 'He Wrote the History Book,' " *The Egoist,* 3 (May 1, 1916), 71.

"You are Like the Realistic Product of an Idealistic Search for Gold at the Foot of the Rainbow," ("To a Chameleon") *The Egoist,* 3 (May 1, 1916), 71.

"Is Your Town Nineveh?", *The Lantern,* 24 (Spring 1916), 19.

"You Are Fire-Eaters," *The Lantern,* 24 (Spring 1916), 59.

"Pedantic Literalist," *The Egoist,* 3 (June 1, 1916), 96.

"Critics and Connoisseurs," *Others,* 3 (July 1916), 4.

"In This Age of Hard Trying Nonchalance Is Good And," *The Chimaera,* 1, No. 2 (July 1916), 56.

"To Be Liked by You Would Be a Calamity," *The Chimaera,* 1, No. 2 (July 1916), 56.

"Feed Me, Also, River God," *The Egoist,* 3 (August 1916), 118.

"Apropos of Mice," *Bruno's Weekly,* 3 (October 7, 1916), 1137.

"Holes Bored in a Workbag by the Scissors," *Bruno's Weekly,* 3 (October 7, 1916), 1137.

"In 'Designing a Cloak to Cloak his Designs,' you Wrested From Oblivion, a Coat of Immortality for your own Use," *Bruno's Weekly*, 3 (December 30, 1916), 1233.

"The Just Man And," *Bruno's Weekly*, 3 (December 30, 1916), 1233.

"Those Various Scalpels," *The Lantern*, 25 (Spring 1917), 50–1.

"The Past is the Present" (not reprinted; title transferred to "*So far as the future is concerned . . .* "), *Others: An Anthology of New Verse*, ed., Alfred Kreymborg (New York: Alfred A. Knopf, 1917), pp. 74–5.

"Like a Bulrush," *Others*, p. 76.

"My Apish Cousins" ("The Monkeys"), *Others*, p. 76.

"French Peacock" ("To the Peacock of France"), *Others*, p. 77.

"Sojourn in the Whale," *Others*, p. 78.

"Roses Only," *Others*, pp. 80–1.

1918–25
The Later "Observations"

"An Ardent Platonist," *The Lantern*, 26 (Spring 1918), 22.

"Melancthon" ("Black Earth"), *The Egoist*, 4 (April 1918), 55–6.

"Reinforcements," *The Egoist*, 5 (June–July 1918), 83.

"The Fish," *The Egoist*, 5 (August 1918), 95.

"You Say You Said," *The Little Review*, 5, No. 8 (December 1918), 21.

"Radical," *Others*, 5 (March 1919), 15.

"Poetry," *Others*, 5 (July 1919), 5.

"In the Days of Prismatic Color," *The Lantern*, 27 (1919), 35.

"Picking and Choosing," *The Dial*, 68 (April 1920), 421–2.

"England," *The Dial*, 68 (April 1920), 422–3.

"Dock Rats," *Others for 1919*, ed., Alfred Kreymborg (New York: Nicholas I. Brown, 1920), pp. 127–8.

"When I Buy Pictures," *The Dial*, 71 (July 1921), 33.

"A Graveyard" ("A Grave"), *The Dial*, 71 (July 1921), 34.

"New York," *The Dial*, 71 (December 1921), 637.

"Labours of Hercules," *The Dial*, 71 (December 1921), 637–8.

"Snakes, Mongooses, Snake-Charmers, and the Like," *Broom*, 1 (January 1922), 193.

"People's Surroundings," *The Dial*, 72 (June 1922), 588–90.

"Novices," *The Dial*, 74 (February 1923), 183–4.

"Bowls," *Secession*, 5 (July 1923), 12.

"Marriage," *Manikin, Number Three* (New York City: Monroe Wheeler, 1923).

"Silence," *The Dial*, 77 (October 1924), 290.

"Sea Unicorns and Land Unicorns," *The Dial,* 77 (November 1924), 411–13.

"An Octopus," *The Dial,* 77 (December 1924), 475–81.

"An Egyptian Pulled Glass Bottle in the Shape of a Fish," *Observations* (New York: The Dial Press, 1924), p. 20.

"To a Snail," *Observations,* p. 23.

" 'The Bricks Are Fallen Down, We Will Build With Hewn Stones. The Sycamores Are Cut Down, We Will Change to Cedars,' " *Observations,* p. 24.

" 'Nothing Will Cure the Sick Lion But To Eat An Ape,' " *Observations,* p. 26.

"Peter," *Observations,* p. 51.

"The Monkey Puzzle," *The Dial,* 78 (January 1925), 8.

1932–36
The Animiles

"The Steeple-Jack," *Poetry,* 40 (June 1932), 119–22. (This and the next two poems were printed together under the title "Part of a Novel, Part of a Poem, Part of a Play.")

"The Student," *Poetry,* 40 (June 1932), 122–6.

"The Hero," *Poetry,* 40 (June 1932), 126–8.

"No Swan So Fine," *Poetry,* 41 (October 1932), 7.

"The Jerboa," *Hound and Horn,* 7 (October–December 1932), 108–13.

"Old Tiger," *Profile, An Anthology Collected in MCMXXXI,* ed., Ezra Pound (Milan: John Scheiwiller, 1932), pp. 61–4.

"The Plumet Basilisk," *Hound and Horn,* 7 (October–December 1932), 29–34.

"Camellia Sabina," *Active Anthology,* ed., Ezra Pound (London: Faber & Faber, 1932), pp. 189–91.

"The Frigate Pelican," *Criterion,* 12 (July 1934), 557–60.

"The Buffalo," *Poetry,* 45 (November 1934), 61–4. (This and the following poem were printed together under the title "Imperial Ox, Imperial Dish.")

"Nine Nectarines and Other Porcelain," *Poetry,* 45 (November 1934), 64–7.

"Half Deity," *Direction,* 1 (January–March 1935), 74–5.

"Smooth Gnarled Crape Myrtle," *New English Weekly,* 8 (October 17, 1935), 13.

"Pigeons," *Poetry,* 47 (November 1935), 61–5.

"Virginia Brittania," *Life and Letters Today,* 13 (December 1935), 66–70.

"Bird-Witted," *The New Republic,* 85 (January 22, 1936), 311.

"Walking-Sticks and Paper-Weights and Water Marks," *Poetry,* 49 (November 1936), 59–64.

"See in the Midst of Fair Leaves," *New Directions in Prose and Poetry,* I, ed., James Laughlin IV (Norfolk, Conn.: New Directions, 1936), pages unnumbered.

"The Pangolin," *The Pangolin and Other Verse* (London: The Brendin Publishing Co., 1936).

1940–44
The Lyrics of the War Years

"Four Quartz Crystal Clocks," *The Kenyon Review,* 2 (Summer 1940), 284–5.

"What Are Years?", *The Kenyon Review,* 2 (Summer 1940), 286.

"A Glass-Ribbed Nest" ("The Paper Nautilus"), *The Kenyon Review,* 2 (Summer 1940), 287–8.

"Rigorists," *Life and Letters Today,* 26 (September 1940), 243–4.

"Light is Speech," *Decision,* 1 (March 1941), 26.

"He 'Digesteth Harde Yron,' " *Partisan Review,* 8 (July–August 1941), 312.

"Spenser's Ireland," *Furioso,* 1 (Summer 1941), 24–5.

"The Wood-Weasel," *The Harvard Advocate,* 128 (April 1942), 11.

"In Distrust of Merits," *The Nation,* 156 (May 1, 1943), 363.

"It is Late, I Can Wait" ("Nevertheless"), *Contemporary Poetry,* 3, No. 2 (Summer 1943), 5.

"Elephants," *The New Republic,* 109 (August 23, 1943), 250–1.

"The Mind Is an Enchanting Thing," *The Nation,* 157 (December 18, 1943), 735.

"A Carriage from Sweden," *The Nation,* 158 (March 11, 1944), 311.

" 'Keeping Their World Large,' " *Contemporary Poetry,* 4 (Autumn 1944), 5–6.

"His Shield," *Title,* Bryn Mawr College (November 1944), 4.

"Propriety," *The Nation,* 159 (November 25, 1944), 656.

1946–56
The Poems of the Fable Years

"Advent," *The Lafayette Record* (January 1946), 11.

"A Face," *Horizon,* 16 (October 1947), 58.

"Voracities and Verities Sometimes Are Interacting," *Spearhead: Ten Years' Experimental Writing in America,* (New York, 1947), p. 190.

"Efforts of Affection," *The Nation,* 167 (October 16, 1948), 430.

"At Rest in the Blast" ("Bulwarked Against Fate," "Like a Bulwark"), *Botteghe Oscure,* 2 (1948), 287.

"By Disposition of Angels," *Quarterly Review of Literature,* 4, No. 2 (1948), 121.

"Armor's Undermining Modesty," *The Nation,* 170 (February 25, 1950), 181.

"The Icosasphere," *Imagi,* 5, No. 5 (1950), 2.

"Pretiolae," *Wake,* No. 9 (1950), 4.

"Quoting an also Private Thought," *University of Kansas City Review,* 16, No. 3 (Spring 1950), 163.

"We Call Them the Brave," *The Nation,* 170 (May 5, 1950), 423.

"Apparition of Splendor," *The Nation,* 175 (October 25, 1952), 383.

"Then the Ermine," *Poetry,* 81 (October 1952), 55–6.

"Tom Fool at Jamaica," *The New Yorker,* 29 (June 13, 1953), 32.

"The Web One Weaves of Italy," *The Times Literary Supplement,* (September 17, 1954), xlviii.

"Rosemary," *Vogue,* 124 (December 1954), 101.

"The Staff of Aesculapius," *What's New,* Abbott Laboratories, Chicago, 186 (December 1954), 9.

"The Sycamore," *Art News Annual* (1955), p. 94.

"Lines on a Visit of Anne Carroll Moore to Hudson Park Branch," *The Villager,* XXIII, 42 (January 19, 1956), 16.

"Style," *The Listener,* 55 (April 12, 1956), 423.

"Logic and 'The Magic Flute,' " *Shenandoah,* 7 (Summer 1956), 18–19.

"Blessed Is the Man," *The Ladies' Home Journal,* 73 (August 1956), 101.

1956–66
The Late Poems

"Values in Use," *The Partisan Review,* 23 (Fall 1956), 506.

"Hometown Piece for Messrs. Alston and Reese," *The New York Herald Tribune,* October 3, 1956, p. 1.

"O to Be a Dragon," *Sequoia,* 3, No. 1 (Autumn 1957), 20.

"Enough: Jamestown, 1607–1957," *The Virginia Quarterly Review,* 33 (Fall 1957), 500–2.

"Melchior Vulpius," *The Atlantic,* 201 (January 1958), 59.

"In the Public Garden," *The Boston Globe,* June 15, 1958, p. 6.

"The Arctic Ox (or Goat)," *The New Yorker,* 34 (September 13, 1958), 40.

"Saint Nicholas," *The New Yorker,* 34 (December 27, 1958), 28.

"For February 14th," *The New York Herald Tribune*, February 13, 1959, p. 1.

"No Better Than 'a Withered Daffodil,' " *Art News*, 58 (March 1959), p. 44.

"Combat Cultural," *The New Yorker*, 35 (June 9, 1959), 40.

"Leonardo da Vinci's," *The New Yorker*, 35 (July 18, 1959), 22.

"Saint Valentine," *The New Yorker*, 35 (February 13, 1960), 30.

"Tell Me, Tell Me," *The New Yorker*, 36 (April 30, 1960), 44.

"Glory" ("Carnegie Hall: Rescued"), *The New Yorker*, 36 (August 13, 1960), 37.

"Rescue with Yul Brynner," *The New Yorker*, 37 (May 20, 1961), 40.

"To Victor Hugo of My Crow Pluto," *Harper's Bazaar*, 95 (October 1, 1961), 120.

"To Yvor Winters," *Sequoia*, 6 (Winter 1961), facing p. 1.

"Baseball and Writing," *The New Yorker*, 37 (December 9, 1961), 48.

"Arthur Mitchell," *City Center Music and Drama Souvenir Program*, January 1962.

"Blue Bug," *The New Yorker*, 38 (May 26, 1962), 40.

"To a Giraffe," *Poetry in Crystal* (Steuben Glass, Inc., 1963), p. 44.

"Charity Overcoming Envy," *The New Yorker*, 39 (March 30, 1963), 44.

"I've Been Thinking" ("Occasionem Cognosce," " 'Avec Ardeur' "), *Occasionem Cognosce: A Poem* (Lunenberg, Ver.: Stinehour Press, 1963).

"W.S. Landor," *The New Yorker*, 40 (February 22, 1964), 26.

"The Master Tailor," *The New York Herald Tribune*, June 6, 1963, p. 19.

"An Expedient—Leonardo da Vinci's—and a Query," *The New Yorker*, 40 (August 29, 1964), 52.

"Old Amusement Park," *The New Yorker*, 40 (August 29, 1964), 34.

"Dream," *The New Yorker*, 41 (October 16, 1965), 52.

"In Lieu of the Lyre," *The Harvard Advocate*, 100 (November 1965), 5.

"The Mind, Intractable Thing," *The New Yorker*, 41 (November 27, 1965), 60.

"Granite and Steel," *The New Yorker*, 42 (July 9, 1966), 32.

1966–70
The Final Poems

"Love in America?", *The Saturday Evening Post*, 239 (December 31, 1966), 78.

"Velvet Mat," *The New York Post*, February 18, 1967, p. 31.

"For Katharine Elizabeth McBride," Menu insert, Bryn Mawr College, March 1, 1967.

"Camperdown Elm," *The New Yorker,* 43 (September 23, 1967), 48.

"Tippoo's Tiger," *Tippoo's Tiger* (New York: The Phoenix Book Shop, September 25, 1967).

"Assistance," *Tambourine,* Washington University (1967–68), 1.

"Mercifully," *The New Yorker,* 44 (July 20, 1968), 34.

"Like a Wave at the Curl," *The New Yorker,* 45 (November 29, 1969), 44.

"Santa Claus," *The New York Times Magazine,* December 21, 1969, p. 5.

"Enough," *The New Yorker,* 46 (January 17, 1970), 28.

"The Magician's Retreat," *The New Yorker,* 46 (February 21, 1970), 40.

"Prevalent at one time," Philadelphia, privately printed, 1970.

Notes

1. Art as Exact Perception

1 Donald Hall, "An Interview with Marianne Moore," *McCall's*, XCIII, 3 (December 1965), 182.
2 Mary Seth, "An Instinctive Wish to Share," *Presbyterian Life*, VIII, 8 (April 16, 1955), 16.
3 This and the following passage are from Marianne Moore, "Education of a Poet," *Writer's Digest*, 43, No. 10 (October 1963), 35; reprinted in *The Complete Prose of Marianne Moore*, ed. Patricia C. Willis (New York: Viking, 1986), pp. 571–2.
4 Elizabeth Bishop, "Efforts of Affection," *Vanity Fair*, 46, No. 4 (June 1983), 45.
5 Reminiscence of Peggy Kellogg-Smith, Class of 1910, Marianne Moore Collection, Bryn Mawr College Archive.
6 Marianne Moore, M. Carey Thomas Award Acceptance Speech, transcript in the Marianne Moore Collection, Bryn Mawr College Archive.
7 This passage, continued in the next paragraph, is from Moore's letter to Bryher of August 31, 1921, Rosenbach Museum and Library.
8 Marianne Moore to Mary Warner Moore, February 10, 1907, Rosenbach; also in *Marianne Moore Newsletter*, V, No. 1 (Spring 1981), 5.
9 Imitative Writing Notes, Rosenbach 1251/27, p. 42.
10 This and the following phrase appear in Ezra Pound, *Literary Essays of Ezra Pound*, ed. T. S. Eliot (New York: New Directions, 1968), p. 3.
11 *Tipyn O'Bob*, 4 (February 1907), 12.
12 Laurence Stapleton [*Marianne Moore, The Poet's Advance* (Princeton: Princeton University Press, 1978)] has confirmed in conversation the nickname with which Moore signed one of her poems, "You Say You Said" of 1918.
13 Elizabeth Bishop, "Efforts of Affection," 55.
14 Moore composed these newsletters, mainly *The File* and *The Scale*, from about 1912 till about 1916. Her own news, stories, doggerel, and glued-up

clippings from newspaper headlines and advertisements ("Rat Suits Half Price") may be seen in the Rosenbach.

15 Imitative Writing Notes, p. 39.

16 W. H. Auden, *Making, Knowing and Judging* (Oxford: The Clarendon Press, 1956), p. 7, and Bryn Mawr alumna Peggy Kellogg-Smith's adjectives for Moore's early poems, Bryn Mawr College Archive.

17 A discussion of "spatial form" in modernism, based on different premises from mine about the nature of language and poetry, may be found in Joseph Frank's *The Widening Gyre* (New Brunswick, N.J.: Rutgers University Press, 1963), pp. 3–62.

18 Marianne Moore, "The Plums of Curiosity," *Vogue*, 136, No. 2 (August 1960), 83; rpt. *Complete Prose*, p. 543.

19 Edward Said wrote this of John Berger's work in "Bursts of Meaning," a discussion of photographic versus narrative-historical approaches to meaning in *The Nation*, 235, No. 19 (December 4, 1982), 596.

20 D. H. Lawrence, *The Complete Poems*, ed. Vivian de Sola Pinto and Warren Roberts (New York: Penguin Books, 1977), pp. 386–92.

21 William Carlos Williams, "Marianne Moore (1925)," collected in *Marianne Moore, A Collection of Critical Essays*, ed. Charles Tomlinson (Englewood Cliffs, N.J.: Prentice-Hall, Inc., 1969), p. 54.

22 Marie Boroff, *Language and the Poet* (Chicago: University of Chicago Press, 1979), p. 101.

23 Bonnie Costello, *Marianne Moore, Imaginary Possessions* (Cambridge: Harvard University Press, 1981), p. 202.

24 Rosemary Freeman, *English Emblem Books* (London: Chatto and Windus, 1948), p. 33.

25 Freeman, pp. 24 and 29.

26 Freeman, p. 153.

27 Pound, *Literary Essays*, p. 4.

28 See the article on "Councell to a Bachelor," *Marianne Moore Newsletter*, IV, 2 (Fall 1980), 9–10, which includes a photograph of this particular trencher with its painted verse.

29 Randall Jarrell, "Her Shield," Tomlinson, p. 117.

30 Marianne Moore to John Warner Moore, February 26, 1915, Rosenbach.

2. Diligence, Magic

1 This and the passages in the following paragraph appear in Harry Gilroy, "Marianne Moore Steps Out," *The New York Times*, Wednesday, November 15, 1967, p. 42.

2 Moore to P. Casper Harvey, January 27, 1925, quoted in *Marianne Moore Newsletter*, IV, No. 1 (Spring 1980), 15.

3 Hilda Doolittle to Marianne Moore, August 21, 1915, Rosenbach Museum and Library.

4   Marianne Moore to John Warner Moore, December 19, 1915, Rosenbach.
5   William Carlos Williams to Marianne Moore, May 18, 1916, and May 25, 1917, Rosenbach. The first letter appears in *The Selected Letters of William Carlos Williams,* ed. John C. Thirlwall (New York: McDowell, Obolensky, 1957), p. 35.
6   Rosenbach 1250.
7   T. S. Eliot, "Introduction" to Moore's *Selected Poems* (New York: The Macmillan Co., 1935), p. xiii.
8   Moore, "Some Answers to Questions Posed by Howard Nemerov," in *Poets on Poetry,* ed. Howard Nemerov (New York: Basic Books, Inc., 1966), p. 9; reprinted in *The Complete Prose of Marianne Moore,* ed. Patricia C. Willis (New York: Viking, 1986), pp. 588–9.
9   Moore, *The Accented Syllable* (New York: The Albondocani Press, 1969), no page numbers. First published in *The Egoist* in October of 1916; rpt. *Complete Prose,* p. 34.
10 Moore, "Some Answers," Nemerov, p. 8; *Complete Prose,* p. 588.
11 Published versions of " 'Sun!' " include *Contemporary Verse,* 1 (January 1916), 7; *The New Poetry,* ed. Harriet Monroe and Alice Corbin Henderson (New York: Macmillan, 1923), p. 367; "Fear is Hope," in *Observations* (New York: The Dial Press, 1924), p. 15; *The Mentor Book of Religious Verse,* ed. Horace Gregory and Marya Zaturenska (New York: New American Library, 1957), p. 31; *A Marianne Moore Reader* (New York: The Viking Press, 1961), p. 88; *The Arctic Ox* (London: Faber and Faber, 1964), p. 47; *Tell Me, Tell Me* (New York: The Viking Press, 1966), p. 49.
12 Moore, Nemerov, p. 9; *Complete Prose,* p. 588.
13 Moore to Joseph X. McGovern, November 2, 1935, copy in the James Sibley Watson Collection, Bryn Mawr College Library.
14 Elder Olson, "A Dialogue on Symbolism," in *Critics and Criticism, Ancient and Modern* (Chicago: University of Chicago Press, 1952), p. 590.
15 This and the following passage are from Paul Fussell, *The Great War and Modern Memory* (New York: Oxford University Press, 1975), pp. 23 and 21.
16 Moore to Joseph X. McGovern, note 13 above.
17 T. E. Hulme, *Speculations: essays on humanism and the philosophy of art,* ed. Herbert Read (New York: Harcourt Brace & Co., Inc., 1924), p. 116. The quoted passages that follow in this and the next paragraph are from pp. 120, 126, and 127 of this work.
18 Samuel Taylor Coleridge, "Biographia Literaria," in *The Portable Coleridge,* ed. I. A. Richards from the Shawcross edition (New York: The Viking Press, 1950), p. 516.
19 Bernard Engel, *Marianne Moore* (New York: Twayne Publishers, 1964), p. 62.
20 T. S. Eliot, *The Complete Poems and Plays 1909–1950* (New York: Harcourt, Brace & World, Inc., 1958), p. 9.
21 William Carlos Williams, *Selected Poems* (New York: New Directions, 1968), p. 35.

22 Ezra Pound, *Selected Poems,* ed. T. S. Eliot (London: Faber and Faber Ltd., 1928), p. 48.
23 *The Thousand Nights and a Night,* trans. Richard F. Burton (Aden Edition, undated), VI, 67.
24 Robert Silverberg, *The Realm of Prester John* (Garden City, N.Y.: Doubleday & Co., Inc., 1972), p. 7.
25 Eliot, "Introduction" to Moore's *Selected Poems,* p. x.
26 Elizabeth Bishop, "As We Like It, Miss Moore and Edgar Allen Poe," *Quarterly Review of Literature,* IV, 2 (1948), 132.
27 Moore on Stevens, "Conjuries That Endure," in *Predilections* (New York: The Viking Press, 1955), p. 34. First printed in *Poetry,* February 1937; rpt. *Complete Prose,* p. 348.
28 Paul Klee, *Handzeichnungen* (Wiesbaden: Insel-Verlag, undated), no page numbers; this statement (my translation) is the epigraph.
29 Moore, *Reader,* p. xv; rpt. *Complete Prose,* p. 551.
30 Robert Pinsky, *The Situation of Poetry* (Princeton: Princeton University Press, 1976), p. 59.
31 Rosenbach 1250/24, p. 32.
32 Claude Lévi-Strauss, *The Savage Mind* (London: Weidenfeld and Nicolson, 1962), pp. 16 and 35.
33 Lévi-Strauss, pp. 21–2.
34 Rosenbach 1250/1, p. 111.
35 Rosenbach 1250/1, p. 11.

3. The Romance of the Text

1 *The File End,* August 20, 1916, Rosenbach Museum and Library.
2 Donald Hall, "An Interview with Marianne Moore," *McCall's,* XCIII, 3 (December 1965), 184.
3 Moore, "Crossing Brooklyn Bridge at Twilight," *The New York Times,* Saturday, August 5, 1967, p. 22; reprinted in *The Complete Prose of Marianne Moore,* ed. Patricia C. Willis (New York: Viking, 1986), p. 611.
4 Moore to Hildegarde Watson, May 23, 1934, Bryn Mawr College Library.
5 Alfred Kreymborg, *Troubadour* (New York: Sagamore Press Inc., 1957), pp. 186–7 and 190.
6 Stanley Lordeaux suggests this in "Toads in Gardens," *Modern Philology,* 80 (November 1982), pp. 166–7.
7 Williams to Moore, December 23, 1919, Rosenbach.
8 *A Marianne Moore Reader,* (New York: The Viking Press, 1961), p. 258.
9 This and the following passage are from McAlmon's letter to Moore of April 12, 1921, in the Rosenbach.
10 Hall, *McCall's,* p. 182.
11 Eliot, "Introduction" to Moore's *Selected Poems* (New York: The Macmillan Co., 1935), p. x.
12 Moore quotes Robert Herring of *Life and Letters Today* in her essay "*The*

Dial: A Retrospect," in *Predilections,* (New York: The Viking Press, 1955), p. 106; rpt. *Complete Prose,* p. 359.

13   Typescript of "A Graveyard in the Middle of the Sea" in the Rosenbach.

14   Ezra Loomis Pound, *The Selected Letters, 1907–1941,* ed. D. D. Paige (London: Faber and Faber, 1950), p. 142. The letter is dated December 16, 1918.

15   *Profile, An Anthology Collected in MCMXXXI,* ed. Ezra Pound (Milan: John Scheiwiller, 1932), pp. 59–60.

16   In her Reading Diary, Rosenbach 1250/4, p. 47, Moore notes her source as "Graphic August 25 1923 / The Octopus in the Channel Islands MC Carey."

17   Rosenbach 1250/1, p. 121.

18   Typescript of "In the Days of Prismatic Color," Rosenbach.

19   Rosenbach 1250/24, p. 33.

20   Laurence Stapleton, *Marianne Moore, The Poet's Advance* (Princeton: Princeton University Press, 1978), p. 37.

21   Rosenbach 1251/17, pp. 5 and 21.

22   Rosenbach 1250/4, p. 11.

23   Typescript of "The Fish" marked "Chatham, New Jersey, U.S.A.," Rosenbach.

24   "The Art of Poetry: Marianne Moore, An Interview with Donald Hall," in Charles Tomlinson, ed., *Marianne Moore, A Collection of Critical Essays* (Englewood Cliffs, N.J.: 1969), p. 27.

25   Moore's loss of her source is reported by Laurence Stapleton from the transcript of a telephone conversation with Hildegarde Watson, Bryn Mawr College Library. The relevance of the line (IV, 800) from *Paradise Lost* (London: Longmans, Green & Co., Ltd., 1968), p. 661, was suggested to me in conversation. See note 6 in this chapter for the first suggestion.

26   Robert Cross, *Raphael's Horary Astrology,* 12th edition (London: W. Foulsham & Co., Ltd., 1927), pp. 18–24.

27   Helen Gardner, *In Defence of the Imagination* (Cambridge: Harvard University Press, 1982), p. 118.

28   Moore, *Reader,* "Foreword," p. xv; rpt. *Complete Prose,* p. 551.

29   *Rules and Regulations, Mount Rainier National Park,* Department of the Interior, 1922. Moore's annotated copy belongs to the Rosenbach.

30   Stapleton, pp. 36–7.

31   Rosenbach 1250/4, pp. 29–30.

32   This and the next two passages appear in Moore's *Predilections* pp. 103, 105, and 107; rpt. *Complete Prose,* pp. 357–9.

33   Moore, *Reader,* p. 267, and Patricia C. Willis, "William Carlos Williams, Marianne Moore, and *The Dial,*" *Sagetrieb,* 3, No. 2 (Fall 1984), 59.

34   Moore to Lola Ridge, January 1, 1927, copy in Bryn Mawr College Library.

4. Poetic Fact, Poetic Value

1   Moore to Lola Ridge, September 19, 1929, copy in Bryn Mawr College Library.

2   Hildegarde Lasell Watson, *The Edge of the Woods* (Lunenburg, Vt.: The Stinehour Press, 1979), p. 102.

3   The passages quoted in this paragraph appear in Moore's "Brooklyn from Clinton Hill," in *A Marianne Moore Reader* (New York: The Viking Press, 1961), pp. 182, 185–6, and 192; reprinted in *The Complete Prose of Marianne Moore,* ed. Patricia C. Willis (New York: Viking, 1986), pp. 540, 542–3, and 547.

4   Donald Hall, "An Interview with Marianne Moore," *McCall's,* XCIII, 3 (December 1965), 185.

5   Moore, "Education of a Poet," *Writer's Digest,* 43, No. 10 (October 1963), 72; rpt. *Complete Prose,* p. 572.

6   Rosenbach 1250/23, p. 17.

7   Williams to Moore, February 21, 1917, Rosenbach Museum and Library; also included in *The Selected Letters of William Carlos Williams,* ed. John C. Thirlwall (New York: McDowell, Obolensky, 1957), p. 40.

8   Moore to Williams, Draft of February 23, 1917, Rosenbach.

9   Mary Warner Moore to Lola Ridge, February 29, 1928, copy in Bryn Mawr College Library.

10   Elizabeth Bishop, "Efforts of Affection," *Vanity Fair,* 46, No. 4 (June 1983), 49.

11   Laurence Stapleton, *Marianne Moore, The Poet's Advance* (Princeton: Princeton University Press, 1978), pp. 130–40.

12   Grace Schulman, ed., "Conversation with Marianne Moore," *Quarterly Review of Literature,* 16, Nos. 1–2 (1969), 164.

13   Moore, "Education of a Poet," p. 72; rpt. *Complete Prose,* pp. 572–3.

14   Moore to Hildegarde Watson, November 30, 1941, Bryn Mawr College Library.

15   T. S. Eliot to Marianne Moore, June 20, 1934, and Moore to Eliot, July 2, 1934, Rosenbach.

16   The percentages by my count are that the first person form appears in 31% of the later "observations" (1918–24), in 52% of the animiles of 1932–36, and in 66% of the lyrics of 1940–44.

17   "Old Tiger" is discussed by Ezra Pound in a letter to Moore of January 9, 1919, in Charles Tomlinson, ed., *Marianne Moore, A Collection of Critical Essays* (Englewood Cliffs, N. J.: Prentice-Hall, Inc., 1969), pp, 18–19. The poem was published in Pound's *Profile, An Anthology,* pp. 61–4.

18   "A Defence of Poetry," in *Selected Prose Works of Shelley* (London: Watts & Co., 1922), p. 87.

19   T. E. Hulme, *Speculations: essays on humanism and the philosophy of art,* ed. Herbert Read (New York: Harcourt Brace & Co., Inc., 1924), p. 120.

20   Charles Olson, "Projective Verse," *The Poetics of the New American Poetry,* ed. Donald Allen and Warren Tallman (New York: Grove Press, Inc., 1973), p. 147.

21   Paul Fussell, *Poetic Meter and Poetic Form,* revised edition (New York: Random House, 1979), pp. 13–14.

22 Marianne Moore, *Tell Me, Tell Me* (New York: The Viking Press, 1966), p. 46; rpt. *Complete Prose*, p. 504.

23 Hugh Kenner, "Disliking It," in *A Homemade World, The American Modernist Writers* (New York: Alfred A. Knopf, 1975), pp. 99–100.

24 Kenner, "Disliking It," pp. 98–99.

25 Moore, *Tell Me, Tell Me*, p. 47; rpt. *Complete Prose*, p. 505.

26 Moore, *Tell Me, Tell Me*, p. 46; rpt. *Complete Prose*, p. 504.

27 Moore, "Interview with Donald Hall," Tomlinson, p. 27.

28 Kenner, "Disliking It," p. 100.

29 Kenner, "Disliking It," p. 99.

30 Moore, "A Letter to Ezra Pound," Tomlinson, p. 17.

31 Moore, "Interview with Donald Hall," Tomlinson, p. 34.

32 Kenner, "Disliking It," p. 99.

33 Report of a private conversation.

34 Max Black, "Metaphor," in *Philosophical Perspectives on Metaphor*, ed. Mark Johnson (Minneapolis: University of Minnesota Press, 1981), pp. 73 and 75.

35 Rosenbach 1251/19, p. 7.

36 A. J. Ayer, *Language, Truth and Logic* (New York: Dover Publications, Inc., 1946), pp. 31 and 45, and the first edition (London: Victor Gollancz, 1936), pp. 37–9.

37 Ludwig Wittgenstein, *Tractatus Logico-Philosophicus* (London: Kegan Paul, French, Trubner & Co., Ltd., 1922), p. 183. The section is Par. 6.41.

38 Wittgenstein, p. 21.

39 Ray Lepley, ed., *The Language of Value* (New York: Columbia University Press, 1957), p. 238.

40 I. A. Richards, *Science and Poetry* (London: Kegan Paul, French, Trubner & Co., Ltd., 1935), p. 29.

41 Paul Ricoeur, *The Rule of Metaphor*, trans. Czerny, McLaughlin, and Costello (Toronto: University of Toronto Press, 1977), pp. 139–40.

42 Ricoeur, p. 138.

43 Barthes's phrase is quoted by Peggy Rosenthal, "Deciphering S/Z," *College English*, XXXVII, 2 (October 1975), 134, and Derrida's by Frank Lentricchia, *After the New Criticism* (Chicago: University of Chicago Press, 1980), p. 170.

44 "No Swan So Fine," *Marianne Moore Newsletter*, II, 2 (Spring 1978), 2.

45 Marianne Moore to T. S. Eliot, July 2, 1934, Rosenbach.

46 Bernard F. Engel may have started this trend by titling his chapter on *Selected Poems* "The Armored Self," even though the word never appeared in any of those poems; *Marianne Moore* (New York: Twayne Publishers, Inc., 1964). Randall Jarrell has extended the motif to her techniques with his phrases "exactness as armour . . . quotation is armour" in "Her Shield," Tomlinson, p. 120. And Suzanne Juhasz has claimed that "themes of defense, of 'armor,' dominate her poetry throughout her career" and that for Moore "effacing is preferable to facing, especially if one is unsure whether the armor is perfect." *Naked and Fiery Forms* (New York: Harper & Row, 1976), pp. 42 and 49.

47 Engel, p. 17.
48 Engel, p. 97.
49 Moore, "Sir Francis Bacon," in *Predilections* (New York: The Viking Press, 1955), p. 118; rpt. *Complete Prose,* p. 100.
50 Rosenbach 1251/19, p. 5.

5. The Sense of a Voice

1 Elizabeth Bishop, "Efforts of Affection," *Vanity Fair,* 46, No. 4 (June 1983), 45.
2 Moore to Hildegarde Watson, March 18, 1934, Bryn Mawr College Library.
3 Moore to Bishop, October 16, 1940, and Bishop to Moore, October 17, 1940, Rosenbach Museum and Library.
4 Typescript of notes for "Lectures given at Bryn Mawr College," February 17, 1953, Bryn Mawr College Archive.
5 Stephen Fender, *The American Long Poem* (London: Edward Arnold Ltd., 1977), p. 8.
6 Marianne Moore to Lewis Turco, October 19, 1968, Bryn Mawr College Library.
7 Marianne Moore to Joseph X. McGovern, November 2, 1935, Bryn Mawr College Library.
8 Rosemond Tuve, *Elizabethan and Metaphysical Imagery, Renaissance and Twentieth Century Critics* (Chicago: University of Chicago Press, 1947), p. 21.
9 Laurence Stapleton, *Marianne Moore, The Poet's Advance* (Princeton: Princeton University Press, 1978), pp. 134 and 249, n. 5.
10 Moore, *Reader,* p. 261. This passage is omitted in Charles Tomlinson's reprint of the "Interview with Donald Hall," in *Marianne Moore, A Collection of Critical Essays* (Englewood Cliffs, N.J.: Prentice-Hall, Inc., 1969), p. 31.
11 The 1937 Year Book, Rosenbach 1251/12, entry dated by Moore as May 12, 1944, on the page printed February 24, 1937.
12 "Signs, Symbols and Emblems," program for an exhibit of rare books and objects, Spring 1983, Bryn Mawr College Library.
13 Rosemary Freeman, *English Emblem Books* (London: Chatto and Windus, 1948), p. 29.
14 Philip Wheelright, *Metaphor and Reality* (Bloomington: Indiana University Press, 1962), p. 92.
15 Wheelright, p. 93.
16 Mary Seth, "An Instinctive Wish to Share," *Presbyterian Life,* VIII, 8 (April 16, 1955), 16.

6. Nonchalances of the Mind

1 Moore to Hildegarde Watson, August 13, 1946, Bryn Mawr College Library.
2 Moore to Hildegarde Watson, May 8, 1947, Bryn Mawr College Library.
3 Moore to Hildegarde Watson, June 29, 1947, Bryn Mawr College Library.

4   Moore to Hildegarde Watson, July 16, 1947, Bryn Mawr College Library.

5   Lewis Nichols, "Talk with Marianne Moore," *New York Times Book Review,* May 16, 1954, p. 30.

6   Moore to Hildegarde Watson, May 21, 1954, Bryn Mawr College Library.

7   Moore to Hildegarde Watson, November 11, 1948, Bryn Mawr College Library.

8   *The Thomas Years,* ed. Caroline Smith Rittenhouse, bound typescript, Oral History Collection, Bryn Mawr College Archive, 1986, p. 25.

9   Hilton Kramer, "Freezing the Blood and Making One Laugh," *New York Times Book Review,* March 15, 1981, p. 7.

10 Eileen Foley, "Genius at Work," *The Evening Bulletin* (Philadelphia), Tuesday, October 26, 1965, p. 58B.

11 *The Evening Bulletin* (Philadelphia), Friday, November 17, 1972, p. 8B.

12 W. K. Wimsatt, *The Verbal Icon* (The University Press of Kentucky, 1954), p. 154.

13 This and the immediately following quotation are also from Wimsatt, p. 154.

14 Wimsatt, pp. 165–6.

15 Quoted from Viktor Shklovsky, "On Poetry and Transrational Language," in Boris Ejxenbaum's "The Theory of the Formal Method" in *Readings in Russian Poetics: Formalist and Structuralist Views,* ed. Ladislav Matejka and Krystyna Pomorska (Ann Arbor: Michigan Slavic Publications, 1978), p. 10.

16 Wimsatt, p. 159.

17 *The Fables of La Fontaine,* trans. Marianne Moore (New York: The Viking Press, 1954), p. 211. The passage is from Book IV, fable iii.

18 Moore to Sidney Salt, September 26, 1936, copy in the Watson Collection, Bryn Mawr College Library.

19 S. V. Baum, "Moore, Marianne Craig," in *Notable American Women, The Modern Period,* ed. Barbara Sicherman and Carol Hurd Green (Cambridge: The Belknap Press of Harvard University Press, 1980), p. 491.

20 "Marianne Moore on Ezra Pound, 1909–1915," *Marianne Moore Newsletter,* III, 2 (Fall 1979), p. 5.

21 T. S. Eliot, "Introduction" to Moore's *Selected Poems* (New York: The Macmillan Co., 1935), p. xi.

22 Typescript of "Then the Ermine," poem file, Rosenbach Museum and Library.

23 Laurence Stapleton, *Marianne Moore, The Poet's Advance* (Princeton: Princeton University Press, 1978), p. 166.

24 Moore to Walter Pistole, "4–7–45," quoted by Rosalee Sprout in *Marianne Moore: The Poet as Translator* (Ph.D. Diss., Ann Arbor: University Microfilms, 1980), p. 22.

25 This and the two subsequent quotations are from Sprout, pp. 265–6.

26 Sprout quotes Moore's notes for a 1954 talk at Vassar College on p. 91 of her useful Chapter III, "La Fontaine and His Translators into English," pp. 86–144.

27 Sprout quotes the French and English versions of this stanza on p. 99. I have taken the text from *Fables of La Fontaine,* ed. M. Félix Lemaistre (Paris: Garnier Frères, 1923), p. 97, and Moore's *Fables,* p. 88.

28 Wimsatt, pp. 165–6.

29 Wimsatt, p. 165.

30 This and the following phrase are from Ejxenbaum, p. 8.

31 Shklovsky is quoted by Ejxenbaum, p. 10.

32 Shklovsky quoted by Ejxenbaum, p. 14.

33 W. H. Auden, "New Poems," a review of *Nevertheless* in *The New York Times Book Review,* October 15, 1944, p. 20. The article begins on p. 7.

34 Edward W. Said, "The Text, the World, the Critic," in *Textual Strategies, Perspectives in Post-Structuralist Criticism,* ed. Josué V. Harari (Ithaca: Cornell University Press, 1979), p. 165.

35 Fredric Jameson, *The Political Unconscious, Narrative as a Socially Symbolic Act* (Ithaca: Cornell University Press, 1981), p. 82.

36 Winfield Townley Scott, "A Place for the Genuine," *The Saturday Review,* XL, No. 5 (February 2, 1957), 17–18.

37 Stapleton, pp. 189–90.

7. The Celebrative Air

1 Moore to Hildegarde Watson, August 14, 1956, Bryn Mawr College Library.

2 *A Marianne Moore Reader* (New York: The Viking Press, 1961), p. 262.

3 Moore to Hildegarde Watson, August 29, 1957, and August 14, 1957, Bryn Mawr College Library; Rosenbach Museum and Library 1251/8, p. 69.

4 Moore to Hildegarde Watson, April 11, 1959, Bryn Mawr College Library.

5 Moore to Hildegarde Watson, March 6, 1954, Bryn Mawr College Library.

6 Mary Seth, "An Instinctive Wish to Share," *Presbyterian Life,* VIII, 8 (April 16, 1955), 17.

7 Jane Howard, "Leading Lady of U.S. Verse," *Life,* January 13, 1967, p. 40.

8 Alyse Gregory to Hildegarde Watson, September 15, 1964, transcript in the Watson Collection, Bryn Mawr College Library.

9 Moore to Hildegarde Watson, June 6, 1964, Bryn Mawr College Library, and Howard, p. 37.

10 "Enquiry," *Twentieth Century Verse,* 12/13 (October 1938), pp. 107 and 114; rpt. *The Complete Prose of Marianne Moore,* ed. Patricia C. Willis (New York: Viking, 1986), p. 675.

11 W. H. Auden, *Making, Knowing and Judging* (Oxford: The Clarendon Press, 1956), p. 32.

12 Quoted by Rosalee Sprout, *Marianne Moore: The Poet as Translator* (Ph.D. Diss., Ann Arbor: University Microfilms, 1980), p. 56.

13 "Lecture Notes," typescript, Rosenbach.

14 The 1937 Year Book, Rosenbach 1251/8, p. 160.

15 Boris Ejxenbaum, "The Theory of the Formal Method," in *Readings in Rus-*

sian Poetics: Formalist and Structuralist Views, ed. Ladislav Matejka and Krystyna Pomorska (Ann Arbor: Michigan Slavic Publications, 1978), p. 10.

16 The 1937 Year Book, Rosenbach 1251/8, page for Sunday, December 12, 1937.

17 Moore to Sister Mary James, September 18, 1933, Bryn Mawr College Library.

18 A relation between Moore's sound patterns and the Welsh *cynghanedd* is suggested by Laurence Stapleton, *Marianne Moore, The Poet's Advance* (Princeton: Princeton University Press, 1978), p. 152.

19 Moore to Katharine Sargeant White, October 4, 1961, Bryn Mawr College Library.

20 Ibid.

21 Moore, *Reader,* p. 269.

22 Alan Trachtenberg, *Brooklyn Bridge, Fact and Symbol* (New York: Oxford University Press, 1965), p. 158; hereafter cited in the text as BB.

23 These two and the following passage are from *The Complete Poems of Marianne Moore* (New York: The Macmillan Company/The Viking Press, 1981), p. 262, "A Note on the Notes"; and Moore's *Reader,* p. xv, rpt. *Complete Prose,* p. 551.

24 Edward W. Said, "The Text, the World, the Critic," in *Textual Strategies, Perspectives in Post-Structuralist Criticism,* ed. Josué V. Harari (Ithaca: Cornell University Press, 1979), p. 165.

8. A Magician's Retreat

1 *A Marianne Moore Reader* (New York: The Viking Press, 1961), p. 182; rpt. *The Complete Prose of Marianne Moore,* ed. Patricia C. Willis (New York: Viking, 1986), p. 539.

2 Moore to Hildegarde Watson, May 17, 1967, Bryn Mawr College Library.

3 Carbon typescript, Bryn Mawr College Archive.

4 Kenneth Burke, untitled carbon typescript of February 6, 1972, Bryn Mawr College Library.

5 Elizabeth Bishop, "Efforts of Affection," *Vanity Fair,* 46, No. 4 (June 1983), 54.

6 "Discoveries: 'The Magician's Retreat,' " *Marianne Moore Newsletter,* I, No. 2 (Fall 1977), 2–5.

7 The tidbit "Velvet Mat" was commissioned by the Lead Pencil Manufacturers' Association for Pencil Week, announced in *The New York Post,* February 18, 1967, p. 31.

8 Robert E. Blum to Marianne Moore, March 4, 1966, Rosenbach Museum and Library.

9 Mildred Archer, *Tippoo's Tiger* (London: Victoria and Albert Museum, 1959), Rosenbach.

10 Early typed draft of "Tippoo's Tiger," poem file, Rosenbach.

11 Ibid.

12   Moore to Thomas Congdon, November 16, 1966, and Thomas Congdon to Moore, December 16, 1966, Rosenbach.
13   Early typed draft of "Love in America?", Rosenbach.
14   James Joyce, *Ulysses* (New York: Random House, 1946), p. 768.

Bibliography

I. Works by Marianne Moore

Moore, Marianne. "The Accented Syllable." *The Egoist,* 3 (October 1916), 151–2. Rpt. under that title in New York: The Albondocani Press, 1969.

Poems. London: The Egoist Press, 1921.

Observations. New York: The Dial Press, 1924.

Selected Poems. New York: The Macmillan Company, 1935.

The Pangolin and Other Verse. London: The Brendin Publishing Company, 1936.

Answer to an "Enquiry." *Twentieth Century Verse,* 12/13 (October 1938), 114.

What Are Years. New York: The Macmillan Company, 1941.

Nevertheless. New York: The Macmillan Company, 1944.

Collected Poems. New York: The Macmillan Company, 1951.

tr. *The Fables of La Fontaine.* New York: The Viking Press, 1954.

Predilections. New York: The Viking Press, 1955.

Like a Bulwark. New York: The Viking Press, 1956.

O to Be a Dragon. New York: The Viking Press, 1959.

A Marianne Moore Reader. New York: The Viking Press, 1959.

"Education of a Poet." *Writer's Digest,* 43, 10 (October 1963), 35, 72.

The Arctic Ox. London: Faber and Faber, 1964.

Omaggio a Marianne Moore. Prepared by Vanni Scheiwiller. Milan: All'insegna del Pesce d'Oro, 1964.

Tell Me, Tell Me: Granite, Steel, and Other Topics. New York: The Viking Press, 1966.

The Complete Poems of Marianne Moore. New York: The Macmillan Company and The Viking Press, 1967. Rpt. New York: The Viking Press, 1981, with revisions.

Unfinished Poems by Marianne Moore. Philadelphia: The Philip H. and A. S. W. Rosenbach Foundation, 1972.

The Complete Prose of Marianne Moore. Ed. Patricia C. Willis. New York: Viking, 1986.

II. Contributory Studies

Alciati, Andrea. *Emblemata cum Commentaris amplissimis*. Patavij: Typis Pauli Framboti, 1661.

Archer, Mildred. *Tippoo's Tiger*. London: Victoria and Albert Museum, 1959.

Auden, W. H. *Making, Knowing and Judging*. Oxford: The Clarendon Press, 1956.

"*Nevertheless*" (a review). *The New York Times Book Review*, October 15, 1944, pp. 17 and 20.

Ayer, A. J. *Language, Truth and Logic*. London: Victor Gollancz, 1936, and New York: Dover Publications, Inc., 1946.

Bishop, Elizabeth. "As We Like It, Miss Moore and Edgar Allen Poe." *Quarterly Review of Literature*, IV, 2 (1948), 132–34.

"Efforts of Affection, A Memoir of Marianne Moore." *Vanity Fair*, 46, No. 4 (June 1983), 46–61.

Bloom, Harold, et al. *Deconstruction and Criticism*. New York: Continuum, 1979.

Borroff, Marie. *Language and the Poet*. Chicago: University of Chicago Press, 1979.

Bromwich, David. "Marianne Moore's Poems." *Poetry*, 139, No. 6 (March 1982), 340–52.

Brooke-Rose, Christine. *A Grammar of Metaphor*. London: Secker and Warburg, 1958.

Casey, John. *The Language of Criticism*. London: Methuen and Co., Ltd., 1966.

Coleridge, Samuel Taylor. "Biographia Literaria." *The Portable Coleridge*. Ed. I. A. Richards from the Shawcross Edition. New York: The Viking Press, 1950.

Costello, Bonnie. *Marianne Moore, Imaginary Possessions*. Cambridge: Harvard University Press, 1981.

Crane, R. S., ed. *Critics and Criticism, Ancient and Modern*. Chicago: University of Chicago Press, 1952.

Cross, Robert. *Raphael's Horary Astrology*. 12th Edition. London: W. Foulsham & Co., Ltd., 1927.

Culler, Jonathan. *Ferdinand de Saussure*. New York: Penguin Books, 1976.

de Man, Paul. "Semiology and Rhetoric." *Textual Strategies, Perspectives in Post-Structuralist Criticism*. Ed. Josué V. Harari. Ithaca: Cornell University Press, 1979, 121–40.

Derrida, Jacques. *Positions*. Tr. Alan Bass. Chicago: University of Chicago Press, 1981.

Donoghue, Denis. *Ferocious Alphabets*. Boston: Little, Brown and Company, 1981.

Ejxenbaum, Boris. "The Theory of the Formal Method." *Readings in Russian Poetics: Formalist and Structuralist Views*. Ed. Ladislav Matejka and Krystyna Pomorska. Ann Arbor: Michigan Slavic Publications, 1978.

Engel, Bernard F. *Marianne Moore*. New York: Twayne Publishers, 1964.

Fender, Stephen. *The American Long Poem*. London: Edward Arnold, Ltd., 1977.

Foley, Eileen. "Genius at Work." *The Evening Bulletin* (Philadelphia), Tuesday, October 26, 1965, 58B.

Foucault, Michel. "What Is an Author?" *Textual Strategies, Perspectives in Post-Structuralist Criticism.* Ed. Josué V. Harari. Ithaca: Cornell University Press, 1979, 141–60.

Frank, Joseph. *The Widening Gyre, Crisis and Mastery in Modern Literature.* New Brunswick: Rutgers University Press, 1963.

Freeman, Rosemary. *English Emblem Books.* London: Chatto and Windus, 1948.

Fussell, Paul. *The Great War and Modern Memory.* New York: Oxford University Press, 1975.

    Poetic Meter and Poetic Form. Revised Edition. New York: Random House, 1979.

Gallagher, Tess. "Throwing the Scarecrows from the Garden." *Parnassus, Poetry in Review,* XII, 2 and XIII, 1 (1985), 45–60.

Gardner, Helen. *In Defence of Imagination.* Cambridge: Harvard University Press, 1982.

Garrigue, Jean. *Marianne Moore.* Minneapolis: University of Minnesota Press, 1965.

Gelpi, Albert, ed. *Wallace Stevens: The Poetics of Modernism.* New York: Cambridge University Press, 1985.

Gilbert, Sandra M. and Susan Gubar. *Shakespeare's Sisters, Feminist Essays on Women Poets.* Bloomington: Indiana University Press, 1979.

Gilroy, Harry. "Marianne Moore Steps Out." *The New York Times,* Wednesday, November 15, 1967, 42.

Hall, Donald. "An Interview with Marianne Moore." *McCall's,* XCIII, 3 (December 1965), 182.

    Marianne Moore, The Cage and the Animal. New York: Pegasus, Western Publishing Company, Inc., 1970.

Hawkes, Terence. *Metaphor.* New York: Methuen and Co., Ltd., 1972.

Howard, Jane. "Leading Lady of U.S. Verse." *Life,* LXII, January 13, 1967, 37ff.

Hulme, T. E. *Speculations: essays on humanism and the philosophy of art.* Ed. Herbert Read. New York: Harcourt, Brace and Co., Ltd., 1924.

Jaffé, Aniela. *The Myth of Meaning.* Tr. R.F.C. Hull. New York: G. P. Putnam's Sons, 1971.

Jameson, Frederic. *The Political Unconscious, Narrative as a Socially Symbolic Act.* Ithaca: Cornell University Press, 1981.

Johnson, Mark, ed. *Philosophical Perspectives on Metaphor.* Minneapolis: University of Minnesota Press, 1981.

Juhasz, Suzanne. *Naked and Fiery Forms: Modern American Poetry by Women, A New Tradition.* New York: Harper Colophon, 1976.

Kenner, Hugh. *A Homemade World, The American Modernist Writers.* New York: Alfred A. Knopf, 1975.

Kermode, Frank. *Romantic Image.* London: Routledge and Kegan Paul, 1957.

Kohler, Wolfgang. *The Place of Value in a World of Facts.* New York: Liveright Publishing Corp., 1938.

Kramer, Hilton. "Freezing the Blood and Making One Laugh." *The New York Times Book Review,* March 15, 1981, 7.

Kreymborg, Alfred. *Troubadour, An American Autobiography*. New York: Saga-more Press Inc., 1957.

Langbaum, Robert. *The Modern Spirit, Essays on the Continuity of Nineteenth- and Twentieth-Century Literature*. New York: Oxford University Press, 1970.

Lentricchia, Frank. *After the New Criticism*. Chicago: University of Chicago Press, 1980.

Lepley, Ray, ed. *The Language of Value*. New York: Columbia University Press, 1957.

Lévi-Strauss, Claude. *The Savage Mind*. London: Weidenfeld and Nicolson, 1962.

Lordeaux, Stanley. "Toads in Gardens." *Modern Philology,* 80 (November 1982), 166–7.

Moran, Eileen. *Selected Letters of Marianne Moore to Hildegarde Watson, Edited, with a Critical Introduction*. Diss. Bryn Mawr College, 1985. Ann Arbor: University Microfilms International, 1985. 8522601.

Nemerov, Howard, ed. *Poets on Poetry*. New York: Basic Books, 1966.

Nichols, Lewis. "Talk with Marianne Moore." *New York Times Book Review,* May 16, 1954, 30.

Nitchie, George W. *Marianne Moore, An Introduction to the Poetry*. New York: Columbia University Press, 1969.

Olson, Charles. "Projective Verse." *The Poetics of the New American Poetry*. Ed. Donald Allen and Warren Tallman. New York: Grove Press, Inc., 1973, 147–58.

Pearce, Roy Harvey. *The Continuity of American Poetry*. Princeton: Princeton University Press, 1961.

Pinsky, Robert. *The Situation of Poetry, Contemporary Poetry and Its Traditions*. Princeton: Princeton University Press, 1976.

Pound, Ezra Loomis. *Literary Essays of Ezra Pound*. Ed. T. S. Eliot. New York: New Directions, 1968.

ed. *Profile, An Anthology Collected in MCMXXXI*. Milan: John Scheiwiller, 1932.

The Selected Letters, 1907–1941. Ed. D. D. Paige. London: Faber and Faber, 1950.

Richards, I. A. *Science and Poetry*. London: Kegan Paul, French, Trubner and Co., Ltd., 1935.

Ricoeur, Paul. *The Rule of Metaphor, Multi-disciplinary studies of the creation of meaning in language*. Tr. Robert Czerny with Kathleen McLaughlin and John Costello, SJ. Toronto: University of Toronto Press, 1977.

Rittenhouse, Caroline Smith, ed. *The Thomas Years, Recollections of Bryn Mawr College during the Presidency of M. Carey Thomas, 1894–1922*. Typescript, 1986. Oral History Collection, Bryn Mawr College Archive.

Rosenthal, Peggy. "Deciphering S/Z." *College English,* 37, No. 2 (October 1975), 125–44.

Rules and Regulations, Mount Rainier National Park. Department of the Interior, 1922.

Said, Edward W. "The Text, the World, the Critic." *Textual Strategies, Perspec-*

tives in Post-Structuralist Criticism. Ed. Josué V. Harari. Ithaca: Cornell University Press, 1979, 161–88.

Schulman, Grace Jan, ed. "Conversation with Marianne Moore." *Quarterly Review of Literature,* 16, Nos. 1–2 (1969), 154–71.

Marianne Moore, The Poetry of Engagement. Diss. New York University, 1971. Ann Arbor: University Microfilms International, 1971.

Scully, James, ed. *Modern Poets on Modern Poetry.* London: Collins, Fontana, 1966.

Seth, Mary. "An Instinctive Wish to Share." *Presbyterian Life,* VIII, 8 (April 16, 1955), 16–17.

Shelley, Percy Bysshe. *Selected Prose Works of Shelley.* London: Watts and Company, 1922.

Silverberg, Robert. *The Realm of Prester John.* Garden City: Doubleday and Co., Inc., 1972.

Sitwell, Edith. "Some Notes on My Own Poetry." *Selected Poems.* Middlesex: Penguin Books, 1952, ix–xxxix.

Sontag, Susan. *Against Interpretation and Other Essays.* New York: Farrar, Strauss and Giroux, 1961.

Sorley, Charles Hamilton. *Marlborough and other poems.* Cambridge at the University Press, 1916.

Sprout, Rosalee. *Marianne Moore: The Poet as Translator.* Diss. Ann Arbor: University Microfilms, 1980.

Stapleton, Laurence. *Marianne Moore, The Poet's Advance.* Princeton: Princeton University Press, 1978.

Taylor, Harold. *Art and the Intellect, Moral Values and the Experience of Art.* New York: Doubleday, The Museum of Modern Art, 1960.

Tomlinson, Charles. *Marianne Moore, A Collection of Critical Essays.* Englewood Cliffs: Prentice-Hall, Inc., 1969.

Trachtenberg, Alan. *Brooklyn Bridge, Fact and Symbol.* New York: Oxford University Press, 1965.

Tuve, Rosemond. *Elizabethan and Metaphysical Imagery: Renaissance and Twentieth-Century Critics.* Chicago: University of Chicago Press, 1947.

Vendler, Helen. *Part of Nature, Part of Us.* Cambridge: Harvard University Press, 1980.

Villa, José Garcia, ed. "Marianne Moore Issue." *Quarterly Review of Literature,* 4, No. 2 (1948).

Waggoner, Hyatt H. "Visionary Poetry, Learning to See." *The Sewanee Review,* 84, No. 2 (Spring 1981), 228–47.

Wasserstrom, William. *The Time of the Dial.* Syracuse: Syracuse University Press, 1963.

Watson, Hildegarde Lasell. *The Edge of the Woods.* Lunenburg, Ver.: The Stinehour Press, 1979.

Weatherhead, A. Kingsley. *The Edge of the Image, Marianne Moore, William Carlos Williams, and Some Other Poets.* Seattle: University of Washington Press, 1967.

Wieskel, Thomas. *The Romantic Sublime, Studies in the Structure and Psychology of Transcendence*. Baltimore: The Johns Hopkins University Press, 1976.

Wescott, Glenway. "Concerning Miss Moore's 'Observations.' " *The Dial,* 78 (1925), 1–4.

Wheelright, Philip. *Metaphor and Reality*. Bloomington: Indiana University Press, 1962.

Whitehead, Alfred North. *Symbolism, Its Meaning and Effect*. New York: G. P. Putnam's Sons, 1959.

Williams, William Carlos. *The Selected Letters of William Carlos Williams*. Ed. John C. Thirlwall. New York: McDowell, Obolensky, 1957.

Willis, Patricia C., ed. *Marianne Moore Newsletter,* passim.

"William Carlos Williams, Marianne Moore, and *The Dial.*" *Sagetrieb,* 3, No. 2 (Fall 1984), 59.

Wimsatt, W. K. *The Verbal Icon, Studies in the Meaning of Poetry*. The University of Kentucky Press, 1954.

Winters, Yvor. *In Defense of Reason*. Denver: University of Denver Press, 1947.

"Holiday and Day of Wrath." *Poetry,* 26 (April 1925), 39–44.

Wittgenstein, Ludwig. *Tractatus Logico-Philosophicus*. London: Kegan Paul, French, Trubner and Co., Ltd., 1922.

Index